A PLUME BOOK

THE BIG BOOK OF RULES

STEPHANIE SPADACCINI is a world-renowned puzzle constructor and former managing editor of *GAMES* magazine. She has written for game shows such as *Jeopardy!*, *Who Wants to Be a Millionaire*, and *High Rollers*, and is a contributor to and project editor of the bestselling *Uncle John's Bathroom Reader* series.

—THE—
BIG
BOOK
OF RULES

BOARD GAMES,
KIDS' GAMES,
CARD GAMES,
FROM BACKGAMMON AND BOCCE TO
TIDDLYWINKS AND STICKBALL

·········

STEPHANIE SPADACCINI

ILLUSTRATIONS BY JOHN FARNSWORTH

A PLUME BOOK

PLUME
Published by Penguin Group
Penguin Group (USA) Inc., 375 Hudson Street, New York, New York 10014, U.S.A.
Penguin Group (Canada), 90 Eglinton Avenue East, Suite 700,
Toronto, Ontario, Canada M4P 2Y3 (a division of Pearson Penguin Canada Inc.)
Penguin Books Ltd., 80 Strand, London WC2R 0RL, England
Penguin Ireland, 25 St. Stephen's Green, Dublin 2, Ireland (a division of Penguin Books Ltd.)
Penguin Group (Australia), 250 Camberwell Road, Camberwell, Victoria 3124, Australia
(a division of Pearson Australia Group Pty. Ltd.)
Penguin Books India Pvt. Ltd., 11 Community Centre, Panchsheel Park,
New Delhi – 110 017, India
Penguin Books (NZ), cnr Airborne and Rosedale Roads, Albany, Auckland 1310, New Zealand
(a division of Pearson New Zealand Ltd.)
Penguin Books (South Africa) (Pty.) Ltd., 24 Sturdee Avenue, Rosebank,
Johannesburg 2196, South Africa

Penguin Books Ltd., Registered Offices: 80 Strand, London WC2R 0RL, England

First published by Plume, a member of Penguin Group (USA) Inc.

First Printing, October 2005
3 5 7 9 10 8 6 4 2

 REGISTERED TRADEMARK—MARCA REGISTRADA

LIBRARY OF CONGRESS CATALOGING-IN-PUBLICATION DATA

Spadaccini, Stephanie.
    The big book of rules / by Stephanie Spadaccini ; illustrated by John Farnsworth.
        p. cm.
    ISBN 0-452-28644-1 (pbk.)
    1. Games—Rules.   I. Title.
GV1201.42.S62 2005
790.1—dc22

                                                        2005014679

Printed in the United States of America
Set in Berkeley Old Style
Designed by Joseph Rutt

CONTENTS

BRAINY GAMES

FAMILY GAMES

PARTY GAMES
BABY SHOWER GAMES

WEDDING SHOWER GAMES

PARLOR GAMES

MURDER GAMES

PARTY GAMES FOR KIDS

CHILDHOOD GAMES

KIDS' OUTDOOR GAMES

TRAVEL GAMES

SPORTY GAMES

CARD GAMES

GAMES FOR GROWN-UPS

THE BIG BOOK OF RULES

·········

INTRODUCTION

When I first got deep into the research for this book—at a point when my mind was awash in Frisbees and pinochle decks and pieces of paper marked X—someone asked me what my "vision" for the book was. The first thing that popped into my mind was that I wanted the book to be as much fun to read as the games were to play. But more than that, I wanted to write a book of rules that was easy to understand, so that anyone could pick up this book and, without too much hesitation, start to play.

As I got further into the research, I found out a lot more about games in general. Like the fact that rules differ from country to country, region to region, and even neighborhood to neighborhood. So I've relied as much on personal experiences (both mine and those of friends and relatives) as the official rulebooks.

The next thing I discovered was that I wouldn't be able to include all the games on earth—if I wanted to see the book published before the next Ice Age. But I did want to include as wide a variety as possible, to introduce readers to game categories they might not have previously been exposed to. That's why you'll find offbeat games like Bunco and Mafia and Jelly Bean Taste Test alongside the classics.

I also found out that the only games that have hard-and-fast rules are played in tournaments or professionally or at gaming tables. At-home games are a different story: What do you do when the whole family's playing Charades and the player whose turn it is accidentally *says out loud* the word she's been trying to convey? She's broken the most important rule in Charades. *Should we tell her she's lost her turn?* Well, yes, but what if she's eight years old and this is the first time she's ever played the game and losing her turn would make her cry? That's why you won't find many penalties for breaking the rules in this book: so that Little Miss Blooper and her ilk can have their do-overs if they need them.

I couldn't have written this book without the help of the world's leading authorities (at least in *my* world): Helen Strodl, able assistant, cardsharp, and Backgammon fiend; Michelle Acosta, as adept at Canasta as she is at Bocce; and my sports authorities: Mike Walbridge, Xander Walbridge, and Peter Walbridge. Thanks to Jim Spadaccini for reminding me about Table Football, and to both Jim and Michael Spadaccini for their encouragement.

CLASSIC BOARD AND TABLE GAMES

BACKGAMMON

CHECKERS
Giveaway Checkers
Diagonal Checkers
Italian Checkers
Spanish Checkers
International Checkers
Canadian Checkers
Spanish Pool
Turkish Checkers

CHESS
The Pawn's Game
The Queen and Pawn Game
The King and Pawn Game
Giveaway Chess
Random Chess
Two-Move Chess
Progressive Chess

CHINESE CHECKERS

DOMINOES
Black Dominoes
Cross Dominoes
Double Cross
Maltese Cross
Blind Hughie
Matador
Bergen
Muggins
All Threes
Fives and Threes
Domino Solitaire
Count Them Out
Grace's Patience
Five Piles
Concentration

GO

TIDDLYWINKS

WARI
Grand Slam

BACKGAMMON

Backgammon is the oldest known recorded game. Its closest ancient relative, some five thousand years old, was unearthed by archeologists in what is now present-day Iraq. The game was probably brought to Europe by returning Crusaders.

EQUIPMENT

- A backgammon board

- 30 playing pieces (15 dark and 15 light). No matter what color the dark pieces are, they're called Black. The light pieces are always called White.

- A pair of dice

PLAYERS

2

OBJECT

To be the first player to get all of his pieces "home" and then off the board.

SETUP

The board should be set up as shown.

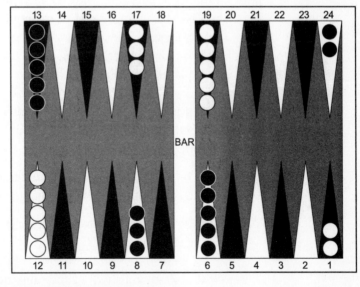

The numbers are for reference only. They illustrate White's journey—from 1 to 24. White will have to move all her pieces into her home board (19–24) before she can begin to bear them off. Black will move in the opposite direction—from 24 to 1.

So, to get all their pieces home:

- White moves to the left, up and across and to the right: 19 to 24 are her "home field."

- Black moves to the left, down and across, and to the right: 6 to 1 on this diagram are his "home field," though if we were counting from Black's side of the board, the numbers would appear reversed.

Each side of the board has a track of twelve adjacent points. The tracks make a continuous chain of twenty-four points, numbered from 1 to 24 in this case. Black's pieces will move from higher-numbered points to lower-numbered points; White's will do the opposite. The two players move their pieces in opposite directions, so the 1-point for one player is the 24-point for the other.

PLAY

Each player rolls one die. Whoever rolls higher plays the number on his own die and the number on his opponent's die as if he had rolled them both. After that, players alternate turns and roll both dice at the beginning of each turn.

After rolling the dice a player must, if possible, move his pieces the number of points showing on each die. On a roll of 6 and 3, for example, a player has to move one piece six points forward and another one three points forward. The dice can be played in either order, and the same piece can be moved twice, as long as the two moves are distinct and legal.

A player must play both dice, except in the following situations:

- If a player has no legal moves after rolling the dice, because all of the points he might move to are occupied by two or more enemy pieces, he forfeits his turn.

- If he has a legal move for one die only, he has to make that move and then forfeit the use of the other die for this turn.

- If he has a legal move for either die, but not both, he has to play the higher number.

If a player rolls two of the same number (doubles) he plays each die twice. For example, if he rolls two 5s he has to move four pieces forward five spaces each. (As before, a piece can be moved multiple times as long as the moves are distinct.)

A piece can land on any empty point or a point that's already occupied by pieces of its own color. It can't move to a point that's occupied by more than one enemy piece.

The Bar

However, if a piece lands on a point occupied by only *one* enemy piece, called a "blot," the enemy piece is taken off the board and placed on the *bar*, the divider between the two sides of the board.

A piece that's on the bar can only re-enter the game through the opponent's home field, depending on a roll of the dice. A roll of 1 allows it to enter on the opponent's first point, a roll of 2 on the second point, and so on. Of course, the points must either be empty, already occupied by pieces of its own color, or occupied by an enemy blot, which would then be sent to the bar itself.

A player with one or more pieces on the bar can't move any of his other pieces until all the pieces on the bar have re-entered the board.

Bearing Off

When all of a player's pieces are in his home field (1–6 for Black, 19–24 for White), he can start removing them from the game, called "bearing off." A roll of 1 bears off a piece from the first point, a 2 from the second point, and so on. A number can't be used to bear off pieces from a lower point unless there are no pieces on any higher points. For example, a roll of 4 can move a piece on the fifth or sixth points closer to the first point—but won't bear them off. A roll of 4 *can* bear off a piece on the fourth, third, second, or first points.

SCORING

If a player has borne off some of his pieces by the time his opponent has borne off all of her fifteen, he loses a single game. If he hasn't borne off *any* pieces by the time his opponent has completely borne off, he has lost a *gammon*, which doubles what the game is worth—either 2 points or twice the number on the doubling cube (see Gambling on Backgammon). If a player hasn't borne off any pieces, and still has pieces on the bar and/or in his opponent's home board by the time his opponent has borne off all fifteen, he has lost a *backgammon*, which counts for triple a normal loss.

Gambling on Backgammon

Some backgammon sets come with a six-sided die, called a "doubling cube," that bears the numbers 2, 4, 8, 16, 32, and 64. Players who gamble on backgammon games use it to *double*, that is, demand that the game be played for twice the current stakes. The doubling cube is placed on the bar with the 2 side faceup to show that the game's value has been doubled. When challenged to a double, the opponent has to either accept the challenge or resign the game on the spot. After that, the right to *redouble* (double again) belongs exclusively to the player who last accepted a double. In this case, the cube is placed with the 4 faceup. The game is hardly ever redoubled above four times the original stake, but there's no theoretical limit to the number of doubles. Even though 64 is the highest number on the cube, the stakes can rise to 128, 256, and so on.

• • • • • • • • •

CHECKERS

Over the centuries the game has been scorned as "chess for women." Today, it's generally thought of as a game mostly played by kids—or old codgers sitting around a potbellied stove. But enthusiasts (including Edgar Allan Poe) have seen beyond the simplicity of the rules and think of it as profound.

EQUIPMENT

• An 8×8 checkerboard

• 24 wooden or plastic checkers (12 dark and 12 light). No matter what color the dark pieces are, they're called Black. The light pieces are always called White.

PLAYERS
2

OBJECT
To capture all the other player's pieces or to make it impossible for the other player to move.

SETUP

Each player starts with twelve pieces on the dark squares on the three rows closest to himself, the light corner square at his bottom right, as shown in the illustration.

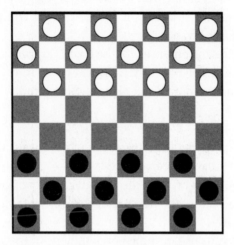

PLAY

Black always goes first, after which players take turns, moving forward—and forward only—one square at a time, diagonally, and only on the dark squares.

Players can jump diagonally forward over one or more enemy pieces, which are then removed from the board, i.e., captured. Players can't jump over their own pieces.

Play continues until one player loses all his men or can't make a legal move.

Capturing

When a piece jumps over an opponent's piece onto an empty space beyond it, the jumped piece is removed from the board.

Capturing is mandatory: If an opposing piece is next to and forward of any of a player's pieces and the space beyond it is empty, the player has to make the jump. If there's more than one choice on the board at the same time, the player can choose among them.

Multiple Jumps

Multiple jumps are mandatory, too. If any jump lands a player in a place where there's another opposing piece with an empty space beyond it, he has to make that jump—and continue to make jumps as long as he can, in a forward direction.

Crowning

When a piece reaches the opposite side of the board, the opposing player must crown that piece with one of his captured pieces—i.e., if White lands on Black's side, Black places another White piece on top. The newly crowned double-decker king has a distinct advantage. Though it can still move only one square at a time, it can now move and jump diagonally *backward* as well as forward.

If a piece reaches the other side of the board (known as "king's row") in a multiple jumping move, its turn ends when it's crowned, even if—as a new king—it could then turn and make another jump.

STRATEGY

Keep your checkers away from the sides; move toward the center of the board where you'll have more options.

Games are frequently won by the first king, so try to get your men—or at least one man—across the board as quickly as possible while guarding your own king's row.

Don't keep all your first-row men back in hope of preventing an enemy piece from being crowned. A better idea is to keep two there, in the two squares that will guard the four squares in front of them.

You touch it, you moved it. In serious games, if the piece you've touched (and therefore moved) can't actually make a legal move, you forfeit the turn. But don't feel bad; in tournament play, you would have forfeited the game.

FYI

Traditionally, if a player didn't take a jump when one was available, his opponent had two choices: He could remove the piece that didn't make the jump from the board, or force the piece to take the jump. But American tournament play doesn't allow for removing the offending piece—the piece is simply forced to make the move.

VARIATIONS

Giveaway Checkers is played under the same rules as regular checkers—but the object is to be the first player to *lose* all your pieces.

In **Diagonal Checkers**, players set up the board on the diagonal from the right-hand corner—two pieces on the dark squares closest to the corner, four in front of them, then six—so that the two opposing sides face each other across the diagonal from the upper right to lower left.

Italian Checkers is played like American Checkers, except that the board is rotated 90 degrees, so a light square is on the lower left-hand corner rather than the right, and kings can only be captured by kings. Also, if you have a choice of jumps you have to make the one that will capture the greatest number of pieces; if the number of captured pieces is equal, you have to capture a king rather than an ordinary piece.

Spanish Checkers is played like Italian Checkers, except that a king can move any distance along a diagonal, if not blocked. And a king can make long jumps over a piece, any distance beyond the captured piece, if the way is clear of pieces.

International Checkers (aka International Draughts, Continental Checkers, Polish Checkers) is the world's most popular version of checkers. The board is bigger (10×10) with twenty pieces per player placed on the first four rows. Pieces can only move forward, but they can capture backward. Kings have much more power, including the ability to move as far as they want along empty squares to capture, and even turn corners mid-play. A piece that lands in the back row has to continue a possible jump, but can't become a king until it lands on king's row at the end of a move or jump.

Canadian Checkers, played on a 12×12 board with twenty-four pieces, follows the same rules as International Checkers.

Spanish Pool and **German Checkers (aka Damenspiel)**, played on an 8×8 board, follow all the rules of International Checkers, except that instead of being made kings, pieces that make it to the opponent's first row are made queens. Queens can move as far as they want along any diagonal.

In **Turkish Checkers**, also played on an 8x8 board, the pieces move straight forward or sideways and kings move like rooks in chess (on both light and dark squares). Each player starts with sixteen pieces in the second and third rows—the king's rows are empty. Capturing is mandatory, and a piece has to stop on king's row to be crowned.

ORIGINS

Checkers is named for the pattern of the board it's played on.

Draughts is what the game is called in some parts of the world, based on the old-fashioned spelling of "drafts." As a verb, draft means to pull, as in carts pulled by draft horses, draft beer pulled from kegs, and civilians pulled into the military draft. So Draughts in the game sense is so called from the pieces being pulled across the playing board.

Computerized Checkers

An IBM researcher wrote the first computer program that could play checkers; it learned from its opponents and adjusted its strategy accordingly. Eventually the strongest machine player, Chinook, the brainchild of a team from the University of Alberta, won the man vs. machine checkers title in 1995. The best computer programs can still beat all humans.

· · · · · · · · ·

CHESS

You're never too young to learn how to play chess: Most world chess champs started playing the game by the time they were six years old.

EQUIPMENT
- A chessboard

- A full set of chess pieces for each player: 8 pawns, 2 knights, 2 bishops, 2 rooks, 1 queen, and 1 king

PLAYERS
2

OBJECT
To attack and capture the opponent's king.

SETUP
The chessboard is set up with the light square in the lower right corner at each player's right hand.

The line of White chessmen across the bottom row is called the "first rank." The White pawns are lined up in the second rank, and so on up to the seventh and eighth (Black's side of the board).

The *files* are perpendicular to the ranks: They run in the same direction the pieces are facing.

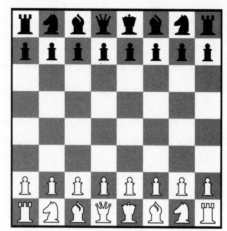

PLAY

White always goes first. Players alternate turns until one of the two kings is immobilized or captured.

Check

When a player moves one of his pieces so that the opponent's king could be captured in the next move, he calls "check," a warning to the other player that his king is under attack but has at least one way of escaping. The player whose king is under attack has three options:

- move the king out of danger

- capture the attacking piece

- move one of his pieces to a space that will protect the king

Checkmate

If none of the above options is possible, the player has been *checkmated* and loses the game.

Stalemate

If a king isn't under attack, but the only available moves would place him under attack, that player has been stalemated and the game ends in a draw.

MEET THE CHESSMEN

Here are the basics of the chess pieces—what they do, where they go, and how they get there.

The Pawn

The *American Heritage Dictionary of the English Language* defines "pawn" as "a person or an entity used to further the purposes of another," and that pretty much sums up the life of a pawn. Pawns are the expendable pieces on the board, but learning how to use them to your advantage can give you a head start in a game.

Placement
The eight pawns are lined up along the second rank.

Moves
A pawn normally moves ahead one space at a time, but is allowed to move two spaces ahead (as long as the spaces aren't occupied) on its first move only.

Captures
Pawns can capture other pieces, but only on the diagonal, if the piece to be captured is one square forward and to the left or right. A piece that's captured is removed from the board.

Special Moves
A pawn that advances all the way to the opposite side of the board is *promoted* and immediately replaced by a previously captured piece: a queen, rook, bishop, or knight of the same color. This is usually called "queening," because the piece chosen is nearly always a queen. Another special pawn move is called "*en passant*," described on page 17.

The Queen
The queen is the most powerful piece in the game. The experts say she's more valuable than all eight pawns combined.

Placement
The queen starts the game on the center space of the first rank, on the square of her own color.

Moves
She can move in any straight line: up or down, diagonally, or side to side over as many spaces as she likes.

Captures
The queen captures by landing on a space occupied by an enemy piece and removing it from the board.

The Bishop

Each player has two bishops, one that moves only on light spaces, the other that moves only on dark.

Placement

The bishops begin the game on either side of the king and queen.

Moves

The bishops move straight along diagonals as far as they can in one direction per move. They're not allowed to jump over other pieces, and can only move to or through unoccupied squares, unless they're capturing an enemy piece.

Captures

The bishop captures by landing on a space occupied by an enemy piece and removing it from the board.

The Rook

Chess began in India, where *rukh* meant chariot. The first rook was an elephant carrying a small tower, so it's also called a "tower" or "castle."

Placement

The rooks occupy the corners of the first row.

Moves

A rook can only move in straight lines, never on the diagonal, and only in one direction at a time.

Captures

The rook captures by landing on a space occupied by an enemy piece and removing it from the board.

Special Move

See "Castling," on page 16.

The Knight

The knight moves in mysterious ways—and has been doing so since before the seventh century. He's the only piece that can jump over the others.

Placement

The knights occupy the spaces between the bishops and the rooks in the first row.

Moves

The knight moves in an L-shape: one square forward and two squares to either side, or two squares forward and one to the side. Unlike other chess pieces, the knight ignores any pieces in the path of its move, "jumping" directly to the destination square. And because it's the only piece that can move over occupied spaces, it can move at the beginning of the game before any pawns have moved to make way for it.

Captures

The knight captures on the square where he finishes his jump, by landing on a space occupied by an enemy piece.

The King

The king is the prize, but his movements are limited. This makes him vulnerable when checkmate time arrives.

Placement

Next to the queen in the center of the first rank on the opponent's color square.

Moves

The king can move in any direction—forward, backward, sideways, or diagonally, *but only one square at a time.* And he can't move to a square that would put him *in check,* that is, make him vulnerable to capture.

Captures

The king captures by landing on a space occupied by an enemy piece.

SPECIAL MOVES
Castling

Used only occasionally, castling can remove a king from danger and move its rook toward the center of the board. Each side can perform one castling move per game, with these restrictions: The king and its rook can't have been moved before in the game, and the squares between the two pieces are empty.

First, move the king two squares along the first rank toward the rook. Then jump the rook over the king to the square beyond it. Even though two pieces are moved, castling counts as one move.

En Passant

A fairly obscure type of capture, *en passant* can be used only when a pawn uses its first-move option to advance two squares instead of one, and in doing so passes over a square that's attacked by an enemy pawn. That enemy pawn, which would have been able to capture the moving pawn if it had advanced only *one* square, is entitled to capture the moving pawn "in passing" *as if* it had advanced only one square. In the diagram below, the Black pawn has just moved to its present position, so the White pawn can capture it as if it had moved only one space. The White pawn then moves to the space (X) that the Black pawn jumped over.

The en passant option to capture has to be exercised on the move immediately following the double-square pawn advance.

STRATEGY
Knights

Think of them as claustrophobic. Knights work best in the center of the board; they shouldn't be placed along the border of the board (and never in the corners) because it restricts their movement and they can be too easily captured.

Pawns

If your opponent has an isolated pawn, you can try to block its path by placing a piece right in front of it, and then attack it from the side with a rook. The same can be done with your opponent's pawns that were "left behind."

Two pawns of the same color on the same file are also weak, especially so if they're isolated, because they can't protect each other and because one hinders the other's advancement. Three pawns in one file are even worse. Don't let it happen.

Pawns are most powerful in groups. If you're looking for a strong pawn, check out the "passed pawn," which—especially if they're advanced—by the endgame have been passed by enemy pawns and therefore can't be hindered by them. A passed pawn on the sixth row is roughly as strong as a knight or a bishop and could even decide the game.

Bishops

Because a bishop always stays on squares of the color it started on, if one of them is captured, it makes it a lot tougher to attack or defend squares of that color.

If you only have one bishop left, it's a good idea to move your pawns to squares of the *other* color so they don't block the bishop when it's time for him to move.

Rooks

Keep pawns out of their way: Rooks are powerful on files that don't contain pawns of their own color.

Rooks on the seventh row can be very powerful—they can attack pawns that can only be defended by other pieces, not by other pawns, and they can lock in the enemy king. A pair of rooks on the seventh rank is often a sign of a winning position.

In the endgame, if there's a passed pawn that's a candidate for promotion, the rooks generally belong *behind* the pawn rather than in front of it.

King

During the middle of the game, the king should mostly stay in a corner behind his pawns. But as the rooks leave the first row, there's a danger of an enemy rook invading the first row and checkmating the king, so you have to move one of the pawns in front of the king to counter the threat.

In the endgame, the king becomes a strong piece. With a reduced number of pieces, checkmate becomes less of an immediate concern, and the king should be moved toward the center of the board.

VARIATIONS

These are good games for beginners, or for dabblers seeking a little variety.

The Pawns Game: The object is to get one of your pawns all the way across the board to your opponent's first row—using pawns only, and starting them on their usual squares,

The Queen and Pawn Game: The Black queen starts at her usual black square and the White pawns at theirs. All White needs to do is get one of his pawns to the other side of the board.

White goes first as usual, but be sure that first move is a smart one! (Hint: There's only one pawn you can move that will prevent the queen from taking the pawn directly in her path in her first move.)

The King and Pawn Game: Both kings and pawns start on their usual squares. Tip: Get your king out onto the board quickly and start capturing those pawns!

The more seasoned player can try the following variations.

Giveaway Chess: Also known as Losing Chess, the object of this unorthodox variation is to *lose* all your pieces. The moves are all the same. The king has no special status and can be taken like any other piece. A player who can take an opponent's piece must do so.

Random Chess: All the pieces along the first rank start on squares that they would *not* be on in a regular game, arranged randomly, say, from left

---

FYI

- There are 169,518,829,100,544,000,000,000,000,000 ways to play the first ten moves.

- A project in New Brunswick, Canada, in the 1990s used chess to teach math to students in grades 2 through 7. The average problem-solving score in the province increased from 62 percent to 81 percent. The game is now taught in schools in thirty countries worldwide.

- Theoretically, the longest chess game possible is 5,949 moves.

- The word "checkmate" is from the Persian *"shah mat,"* which means "the king is dead."

to right: king, rook, queen, bishop, bishop, knight, rook, knight. The two opposing sides must be the same.

Two-Move Chess: Each player makes two moves at a time—except when a player puts his opponent's king in check on his first move; then, only one move is allowed. A player in check has only one move to get his king out of check. All other rules apply.

Progressive Chess: This is an excruciatingly challenging variation. White makes one move in his turn, Black has two moves, White has three, Black has four, and so on. When a player puts his opponent's king in check, his turn ends, he has no more moves in that turn. A player in check has only one move to get out of check.

Trivia

- The Grand Masters who learned chess before the age of six include Bobby Fischer, Boris Spassky, Gary Kasparov, and Anatoly Karpov (who started when he was four). This is not to mention the precocious Polgar sisters Susan, Sofia, and Judith, two of whom have earned the Grand Master title, the other of whom shocked the world by defeating a string of Soviet Grand Masters when she was fourteen.
- The legendary Ray Charles learned Chess in a hospital while quitting his heroin addiction cold turkey in 1965.

You Touch It, You've Moved It

Don't fiddle with your chessmen. If you touch a piece you *have to* move it. The only exception to this rule is if by some oversight, you move your king into checkmate.

· · · · · · · · ·

CHINESE CHECKERS

The game has nothing to do with China. It was given its name in the United States in the 1930s to make it sound more exotic. And even though the playing surface is in the shape of the Star of David, it has nothing to do with Judaism, either. The game as we know it today was first released in Ger-

many in the late nineteenth century, where it was called "Stern-Halma" because it's like the older Checkerslike game of Halma except that the designer reshaped the playing surface as a star (stern, in German).

EQUIPMENT
- Chinese Checkers board

- 6 sets of 10 colored marbles

PLAYERS
2–6

Two players: Each player can play one, two, or three sets of marbles. If one set is played, the pieces go into the opponent's corner. If two sets are played, the pieces can go either into the player's own opposite corners or into an opponent's corner. This should be decided before the game begins. If three sets are played, the pieces go to the opponent's corner.

Three players: The players can play one set or two sets of marbles each. If one set is used, the game pieces are moved across the field into an empty corner. If two sets are used, each player starts with two color sets at opposite corners.

Four players: The same as the six-player game, except two opposite corners are unused.

Five players: Each player takes one triangle, except that one player moves his pieces into an empty corner. Because this is an advantageous position, usually a weaker player (e.g., a young child) would take that position.

Six players: Each player takes one triangle.

OBJECT
To be the first player to move all 10 marbles across the board and into the opposite triangle.

SETUP
The ten marbles are arranged as a triangle in the starting position in one of the corners of the star.

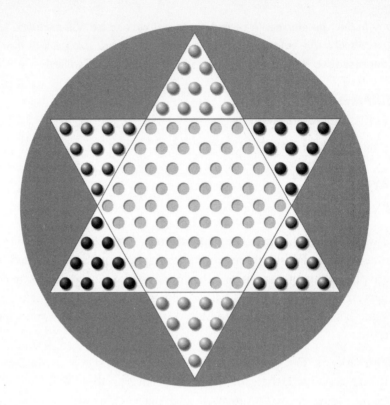

PLAY

The player who goes first can move a marble from his first row to an adjacent hole, or jump over a marble in his first row with a marble from his second row.

Play continues clockwise. Once marbles are in the center, players can begin to jump their marbles over adjacent marbles in any direction, as long as there's an empty hole directly beyond it where the marble at play can land. Unlike checkers, when a marble is jumped over, it isn't removed.

Any player's marble is eligible to be jumped over, even the player's own. Players can make a series of jumps—as many as they can or want to

---

FYI

Some players have moved a marble all the way from their starting triangle, across the board, and into the opposite triangle in only one turn!

during a turn, and can even move their marble into triangles belonging to other players on their way across the board.

Once a marble has reached the opposite triangle, it can't leave. It's still free to move, but only within the triangle. The first player to occupy all ten holes of his or her destination triangle or triangles is the winner.

·········

DOMINOES

There are two basic forms of the game: draw and block. In the former, when a player can't make a play, she can draw more dominoes; in the latter, when a player can't make a play, it's tough tooties, she's stuck with what she's got.

Herewith, the basics of Draw Dominoes to get you started. Followed by some interesting variations.

EQUIPMENT

- A set of dominoes

- A big surface to play on

PLAYERS
2–4

OBJECT
To be the first player to get rid of all his dominoes.

SETUP
A final score is decided on; playing to 50 or 100 points is standard, though some old hands at the game play to 61 points. The dominoes are turned facedown, then "shuffled," i.e., mixed around by one or all players.

Players draw their dominoes: *Two players* draw seven each; *Three or four players* draw five each.

As the dominoes (also called "bones") are drawn, players stand each on edge, facing themselves, so that the other players can't see them. The dominoes that are left, collectively called the "boneyard," are moved to one side to make room for play.

PLAY

The player who has the highest double (6-6, 5-5, and so on) lays it faceup in the center of the playing surface. If no one has drawn a double, the "heaviest" tile can start: 6-5, then 6-4, 6-3, and so on. Play continues clockwise.

Let's say the first domino is a 5-5. The next player has to match it with another 5, and lay that tile down so that the 5-5 is crosswise, at right angles to it.

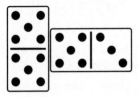

The next player can add to either end of the layout, by laying a 3-3 crosswise to the 5-3 or any domino with five pips on the other side of the 5-5, crosswise.

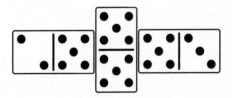

The play moves clockwise (or back and forth when there are two players) as players continue to add to either end of the layout.

Dominoes can be added at angles, too, especially when the line gets too close to the edge of the table. But only at one of the two ends.

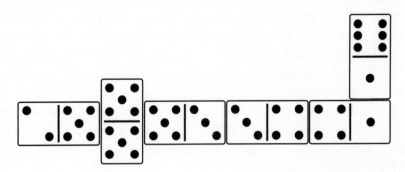

If a player can't match either of the open ends, she draws one at a time from the boneyard until she gets one that can be used. However, two dominoes must always remain in the boneyard. The unusable dominoes she picks up are added to her hand. If a player doesn't have a play and the boneyard is empty (except for the last two), that player passes until he can play in his turn.

Play continues until either one player uses her last domino—at which point she calls "Out!" or "Domino!" and the game is blocked: The boneyard is empty and no more plays can be made.

SCORING

The winner—either the player with no dominoes left or the player with the "lightest" hand (the lowest number of pips on her remaining dominoes)—is awarded the total number of pips in all the other players' hands.

The next hand is led by the player to the left of the previous first player, until a player or team reaches the agreed-upon number of points.

TEAM PLAY

- In a four-player game where players are divided into two teams, teams can be decided on by draw: The two players who draw the heaviest dominoes are one team. The player who drew the heaviest domino goes first, setting any domino in his hand.

- Partners play across from each other.

- When one partner gets rid of her dominoes, the opposing team's pips are counted and added to the winning team's score. If a game is blocked, the team with the lightest hand wins.

- If a blocked game turns out to be a draw, neither team scores.

RULES

- If a player draws too many dominoes, one of them is chosen at random by another player and returned to the boneyard.

- If a player realizes that he's drawn too few dominoes, he can draw one from the boneyard.

- If a player accidently exposes one of his dominoes to an opponent, he has to show it to all the other players.

- If a player misplays (places the incorrect number next to another) before the next play, he has to take the domino back and play another. If his misplay is discovered after the next player has taken a turn, the misplay stands.

VARIATIONS

Block Dominoes differs from the draw game in that there's no drawing from the boneyard. If you can't play a domino during your turn, you have to pass.

In **Cross Dominoes**, four players draw seven dominoes. Play starts with the highest double; but instead of playing in a single line only, players add bones both at the ends and at the perpendicular, thus forming a cross. And there's a catch: The original cross of five dominoes has to be completed before any other bones can be played.

Double Cross takes Cross Dominoes one step further: The cross has to be completed as in the previous game, but now a double has to be played on one "arm" of the cross before any other bones are played.

Maltese Cross is a killer: Double Cross times four. Doubles have to be be played on each arm of the cross before play can continue.

In **Blind Hughie (aka Billiton, Blind Dominoes),** two to five players draw five dominoes each and arrange them facedown in a row without looking at them, either horizontally or vertically with their long sides touching.

The first player turns over his "top" domino (the one at the far left or the one closest to the player) and sets it in the middle of the table. The next player turns over his top domino; if it can be played, the player sets it next to the first domino and turns over his next domino. And so on, until he turns over a domino that can't be played. That domino is placed facedown at the "bottom" of his row of dominoes and the player to his left goes next.

If at any time a player turns over an unplayable *double*, it goes to the bottom of the row, but is left faceup.

Variation: Instead of beginning the game with five dominoes apiece, divide the dominoes as equally as possible among all the players. If all the dominoes are dealt, the 6-6 begins the game. If there are leftover dominoes, one of them is turned over and used as the beginning domino.

Matador is more than a draw game—players can draw from the boneyard even if they have a domino that can be played.

The layout is a straight line; doubles aren't laid crosswise. There are four "matadors" in a set: the three tiles whose two ends add up to seven (6-1, 5-2, 4-3) and 0-0.

Dominoes are played so that the sum of the open end and the new end touching it add up to seven. If one of the open ends is a 3, for example, any bone with a 4 can be placed next to it—including the 4-4. If a 4-2 is played, the 4 is placed against the 3 and the 2 becomes the new open end.

A blank blocks an end because there's no 7 domino. That's where the matadors come in. The only play that can be made at a blank end is with a matador.

As mentioned, even if you have a playable domino in your hand you can draw from the boneyard, as long as it's your turn and two dominoes remain in the boneyard. It's usually better to draw one or more fresh dominoes than to play your last matador—it may save the game for you later on.

Bergen is a scoring game. Players draw six dominoes each. The player with the lowest double goes first. The next player has to lay down a matching domino perpendicular to the first. Play moves clockwise, players adding to the line on each end and so on. If a player can't match an end, she can draw from the boneyard until only two dominoes remain.

Points are scored while players are setting dominoes: **a triple-header** (3 points) for playing a double that matches the pip count at the other end of the line; **a double header** (2 points) for playing a domino with a pip count that matches the domino at the other end of the line; 1 point for playing all your dominoes.

The game has to end in Domino (one player has none left) if the points are going to be awarded. In the case of a blocked game, the player with the fewest number of pips in her hand is the winner and scores exactly one point.

The first player to reach 15 wins.

Tip: Keeping score is easier if every player gets fifteen chips before the first round. Then, as they score points, players can discard the corresponding number of chips. The first player to discard all fifteen chips is the winner.

Muggins (aka All Fives) is also a scoring game for two or four players. Players draw five dominoes (four players) or seven dominoes (two players). The object is to lay down dominoes so that the two ends add up to a multiple of five (5, 10, 15, or 20).

The first player can lead with any domino in his hand; if he plays a domino whose count is divisible by five, he scores that total. The next player has to match one of the ends. If the end of his domino and the other end add up to a multiple of five, the player scores that number of points. Or, if the ends in play are 2 and 4, a player can set the 4-4 crosswise and score 10 (4 plus 4, plus 2). All the pips on crosswise doubles are included in the count, too, scoring the total of their pips, e.g., 6-6 counts as 12, 5-5 as 10, and so on.

Players have to play if holding a matching domino. But if a player doesn't have a play, he can draw from the boneyard until he finds a bone that will play or until the boneyard is empty except for the two dominoes that have to remain.

When he finds a bone that will play he has to lay it down, at which point his turn ends. If he empties the boneyard (except for those last two) without finding a match, he has to pass.

Trivia

Matthias Aisch of Germany holds the Guinness record in domino stacking. He successfully stacked 726 dominoes on a single supporting domino on December 28, 2003. The stack remained standing for an hour. You can access a photo of Mr. Aisch and his amazing construction via www .recordholders.org/en/records/domino.html.

If you'd like to have a go at Mr. Aisch's record, here are the rules:

- The dominoes should be of standard commercial dimensions and weight. The minimum permitted dimensions are 39×19×7 mm (1⁹⁄₁₆" × ¾" × ¼").

- The bottom domino is placed in a vertical position.

- The other dominoes are placed horizontally on the top of the single vertical one.

- The stack must remain standing for at least one hour.

- Last but definitely not least: No adhesives allowed.

You might want to contact the folks at Guinness, too, to see what else you need in the way of witnesses, etc.

The player who goes out wins additional points based on the pips still in other players' hands, rounded to the nearest multiple of five. If play is blocked, the lightest hand wins and earns points as above.

All Threes is played just like Muggins, except that points are earned for multiples of three.

Fives and Threes is similar to Muggins and All Threes, but points are scored for multiples of five and multiples of three at the open ends, which are worth one point each. Muggins games can be played to 100 points—or 31, 61, or 121 points using a cribbage board to score.

STRATEGY

- If you're new to dominoes, take a good look at the set before you play. You'll see there are seven suits (6, 5, 4, 3, 2, 1, and blank), each of which appear on seven tiles: e.g., 6 appears with itself, 5, 4, 3, 2, 1, and blank. If you're inclined, you can try to keep track of the tiles that have been played and what you have in your hand, and you'll know what your opponents have, too, by the bones they *don't* play.

- Hang on to the bones that will give you the most options, that have the most variety, number- and blankwise.

- It's not a bad thing to have to draw from the boneyard early in the game—it's a way of increasing the variety in your hand. But later in the game, try to get rid of your "heaviest" (high-numbered) bones because if you don't go out first, you could be stuck with them.

- If you have a lot of one number (say four 5s) try to position them on both ends of the layout (this is known as "blocking") so that the other players have to dig in the boneyard.

SOLITAIRE DOMINOES

Domino Solitaire is like a lot of solitaire card games—it's easy to learn, but hard to win. Turn up one domino, then deal yourself five more. Using the dominoes in your hand, match the ends of the starting domino, then keep adding to the two ends of your layout. Once you've played your five dominoes, draw five more. If at any time you don't have a domino in your hand to play, you've lost the game. The game is won when you succeed in playing all dominoes.

Count Them Out is an easy game for the kiddies. Lay out all the dominoes in a line, faceup. Starting on the far left, touch each domino as you

---

Nicknames

Dominoes have nicknames, too, some of which are obvious. The others? Don't ask us!

0-0: Bingo, Saturday Night
1-1: Snake Eyes (from craps), Double Aces, Grandma's Peepers
2-2: Double Deuces
3-3: Poison Ivy, Spanish Curse
5-5: Gold Nuggets
6-6: Boxcars (from craps) and—our favorite—Hairy Belly (Texas slang)

---

count from zero to twelve. If the total number of pips on the domino is the same as the number you're calling (zero equals the 0-0 domino, 5 equals the 3-2, and so on), take it out of the line. When you've finished counting, close up the spaces, if any, and start counting from zero to twelve again from the next set of twelve dominoes. Continue until all the dominoes have been counted out.

Grace's Patience is easy to play but a challenge; don't expect to win very often. Lay out all the dominoes faceup and end-to-end in a long line. When you see an adjacent matching pair (the 6-6 next to 6-4, e.g.) take those two dominoes out of the line. Keep doing this until all twenty-eight dominoes have been removed.

Five Piles is played something like the classic Solitaire card game Klondike. Draw three dominoes and put the remaining twenty-five face-down in five piles of five. Then turn the top domino on each pile faceup. If the pips on any two of them add up to 12, discard them. You can also work from the three dominoes you drew at the beginning, but work from the five piles first if you can. The object is to discard all twenty-eight dominoes.

You can play **Concentration** with dominoes, too. It's like the card game, but with a math component that makes it even more of a challenge. Two to six can play. Lay out all the dominoes in a 4×7 rectangle. Players turn over two dominoes per turn and try to match dominoes whose pips add up to 12, like 6-6 and 0-0 or 2-4 and 5-1. A player who makes a match removes the two dominoes from the layout, puts them in front of himself, and goes again. If the two tiles don't match, the player's turn ends.

When all the dominoes have been turned over, players count up one point for every domino. The first player to score more than 50 points wins the game.

· · · · · · · · ·

GO

The Chinese invented it, but it's the Japanese version that's more widely played in the West.

EQUIPMENT
- A board marked with a grid of 19 lines by 19 lines (including the edges)
- 181 black stones
- 180 white stones

PLAYERS
2

OBJECT
To surround more territory than your opponent.

SETUP
The board is empty.

PLAY
Black plays first. Players take turns placing a stone on a vacant intersection of lines with the idea of staking out their own territories and venturing into each other's in attempts to capture their opponent's pieces.

Once a stone is played, it's not moved—until and

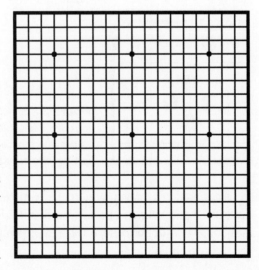

unless it's surrounded and captured, in which case it's removed from the board as a prisoner.

Capturing

After placing a stone, a player can capture and remove from the board any opposing stone or solidly connected group of stones surrounded by his own color. Stones are solidly connected only horizontally or vertically—*not* diagonally.

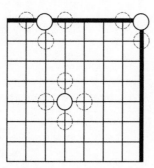

Figure 1 shows three White stones with their liberties (empty adjacent points) marked in dotted lines. Notice how the stones on the edge of the board have fewer liberties than those in the center.

Figure 2 illustrates the same stones, now threatened by Black: Each White stone has only one liberty left.

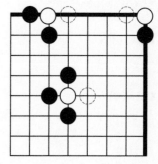

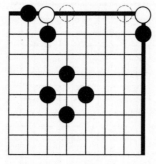

Figure 3 is an example of what the board would look like if Black enclosed one of the White stones, thereby capturing it. The captured stone has been removed from the board.

Occasionally a player will make a move that simultaneously causes both Black and White to be surrounded. In that case, the stones belonging to the player who made the move remain on the board and the opponent's group is captured.

FYI

It's generally agreed that the game had its beginnings in China or the Himalayas about 3,000 to 4,000 years ago; the Chinese name for it is *wei-ch'i*, which means "surrounding game." The game developed more slowly in China than in Japan; it languished during Mao's Cultural Revolution because it was regarded as an intellectual pursuit. Today, it's being reintroduced in schools in China.

The game spread via Korea to Japan, where it was renamed *i-go*, or *go*. By the thirteenth century, the game was a favorite pastime of the samurai.

There are just a few other rules governing placement of stones:

- A stone can't be played on a particular point if doing so would re-create the board position after the same player's previous turn. This is known as the Ko rule.

- A player may not "commit suicide," that is, play a stone into a position where it would have no liberties or form part of a group that would thereby have no liberties, unless, as a result, one or more of the stones surrounding it is captured.

Passing

A player is permitted to pass when it's her turn, and can resume play on a later turn. When both players pass in succession, the game is over.

SCORING

The player with the most territory wins. The final scoring differs between the Chinese and Japanese versions.

FYI

Go is one of the easiest games to learn, but it has an endless array of strategic and tactical possibilities. It's been described as being like four Chess games going on together on the same board.

Chinese

A player's territory is equal to the sum of the points he occupies and the empty intersections surrounded by his stones, or by his stones and the edge of the board.

Japanese

Occupied points don't count as territory but captured stones are worth 1 point each to the capturer.

In general, the two scoring methods turn out to be comparable, as long the number of nonpassing moves in the game has been largely equivalent.

VARIATIONS

- Playing on a a 9×9 or 13×13 board is a great way to learn the game.

- A silly idea for varying the game—especially if you don't have an official set: Make your own board and use M&M's as playing pieces. Then, when you capture your opponent's pieces, you can eat them.

·········

TIDDLYWINKS

You can't learn Tiddlywinks without learning a whole new vocabulary— words like "squidge" and "squop" . . . not to mention "tiddly."

EQUIPMENT

- A set of Tiddlywinks: Each of the four colors (Blue, Green, Red, and Yellow) has 4 small winks and 2 large winks that are known as "shooters" or "squidgers."

- Cup

PLAYERS

2 or 4

OBJECT

To land all your winks in the cup.

SETUP

Players decide if they'd prefer to play with a time limit of twenty minutes for singles games or twenty-five minutes for partners.

To decide who starts, one wink of each color is played toward the cup by "squidging" the wink, pushing the edge of the shooter down against the edge of a wink so that it flies up and forward. The color that lands nearest the cup goes first. If two players tie, they try it again. Once the winks are returned to their corners, the game begins.

Blue always partners with Red and Green always partners with Yellow. At the start of the game, each color is placed at a corner of the mat so that Blue is opposite Red and Green is opposite Yellow. The colors have to be arranged in alphabetical order going clockwise (which makes it easier to remember whose turn it is). So if Green wins the start, Green goes first, then Red plays, then Yellow, then Blue, then Green again, and so on.

PLAY

Starting from the corner, the first player squidges a wink at the cup. If it lands in the cup (known as "potting the wink") he gets another turn. If it misses the cup, the player to his left goes next. On subsequent turns, a player can choose to squidge a new wink or one that's already been played. Winks have to be played from where they land.

RULES

- If a wink is covered, even very slightly, by another wink, it's "squopped." A squopped wink can't be played until it's unsquopped. If the squopped wink is a player's last wink, he has to wait until it's free.

- If a wink balances on the rim of the cup, it's counted as potted and is put in the cup.

- If a wink is leaning against the cup, the player has to try to dislodge it by shooting another wink at it. If it's the player's last wink, he has to wait until another player dislodges it; then he can reshoot it.

- If a wink goes off the playing surface, it has to be reshot from its corner starting area on the player's next turn. A player can also "send off" a partner's or an opponent's wink by squidging it, but in that case, no shot is lost.

Play continues until one player "pots out," that is, lands all of his winks in the cup. This is followed by a period in which all squopped winks are uncovered by moving them (or the winks squopping them), keeping them the same distance from the cup. All players try to pot out, playing in turn as before. Any winks that are squopped during this round are immediately freed; no winks can be played because all the unpotted winks are squopped; or an agreed-upon time period—twenty minutes for singles games, twenty-five minutes for partners—has been reached, after which each color has a further five rounds, up to and *including* the color that that started the game.

SCORING

Here's where the "tiddlies" come in. At the end of the game, table points (known as tiddlies) are scored as follows:

- Potted winks are worth 3 tiddlies.

- Winks on the mat (unsquopped) score 1 tiddly.

Squopped winks don't score. Neither do winks that haven't been played at all.

Trivia

The French call the game *Jeu de Puce*—game of fleas—because of the high-jumping winks.

Homemade Tiddlywinks

If you don't have a set, you can play the game with coins and a small cup or shot glass—or even a jar lid.

The earliest patent application for "Tiddledywinks" was filed by Joseph Fincher in 1888, but the modern game didn't take off until a group of British undergraduates at Cambridge took it up in the 1950s. The game spread across the Atlantic in 1961 when Oxford undertook a tiddlywinks tour of the U.S., where the game took root at the Massachusetts Institute of Technology.

The record for the farthest wink shot is 31 feet, 3 inches (9.52 m), scored by Ben Soares of the St. Andrew's Tiddlywinks Society at Queen's College Tournament, Cambridge, England, on January 14, 1995.

The color that wins the most tiddlies or potted out first gets 4 game points. The second color gets 2 points and the third 1 point. In the event of a tie, points are shared—e.g., if two players score 5 points, they each get 2.5.

In the case of a pot-out, 1 bonus point is added to the winner's score and deducted from the loser's score. If the winner and the loser are on the same team, the 1 point is cancelled out.

VARIATION

Some sets come with a fold-out playing surface that looks like a bull's-eye: The target cup is set in the center, which is marked 25, and the rings that extend out from it are marked 20, 15, 10, and 5. In a "target" game like this, each wink can be shot only once. At the end of the game players score the number of points corresponding to the ring their winks land in. If a wink is touching two rings the player scores the points from the lower ring. Play is to a certain number of points (200, 300, 500), or each game can be scored individually.

· · · · · · · · ·

WARI

This is the simplest of the ancient African seed-sowing "mancala" games. If you get hooked, there are more than a hundred variations to try—a lot of which are played on the same board. AKA Ayoayo, Awale, Our i, Warri, Adji-Boto, Awari, and Awele

EQUIPMENT

- A mancala board or 14 small bowls (6 bowls plus 1 scoring bowl for *each* player)

- 48 playing pieces (small beads, seeds, or dried beans)

PLAYERS

2

OBJECT

To capture more beads than one's opponent.

SETUP

If using bowls, put six of them in front of each player, and one at each end to store the captured beads, so that each player's "capturing" bowl is on her right. Place four beads in each of the six bowls.

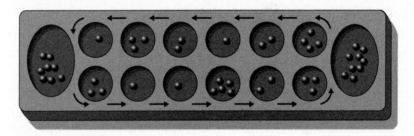

A game in progress. The large holes at either end are for captured beads. Play moves counterclockwise.

PLAY

The first player scoops up all four beads from any one of the six bowls in front of her and, moving counterclockwise, "sows" them consecutively by placing the first bead in the first pit to the right of the pit from which the beads were taken. The rest are placed one at a time in the bowls directly following each other, bypassing the "capturing" bowls at each end.

Players take turns and as the game continues, the opportunity for capturing comes into play.

Capturing

If a player's last bead drops into a bowl that contains either one or two of his opponent's beads, those beads are captured and placed in the player's capturing bowl. In addition, any time a player makes a capture, she can also capture the beads in the preceding bowls as long as the bowls are on the opponent's side of the board and as long as they contained only one or two beads before the player added hers.

Note: If a player picks up from a bowl with more than eleven beads in it, she places a bead in each bowl until she comes to the original bowl she scooped the beads from. She skips that bowl and continues sowing beads. If the same turn takes her around again (and again), she always has to skip the original bowl.

A player isn't permitted to capture all the beads on an opponent's side in one move; she can make a move that would do it, but can't pick up the beads. (But see Variation below.)

Play continues until:

- A player has captured more than half the forty-eight beads

- A player has captured *all* her opponent's beads.

- A player has no moves to make because all of her bowls are empty and there is no move her opponent can make that will put beads in his bowls. (Players who can are expected to make moves that will put one or more beads in their opponent's bowls, but if such a move is impossible, the player with the beads makes whatever moves she can to capture her own remaining beads, at which point the game ends).

- The remaining beads will continue to move with no captures possible for either player. In this case, the two players divide up the remaining beads, no matter which side of the board they're on.

SCORING

The player with the most beads wins. The game is tied if both players end up with twenty-four beads or if both players have an equal number of captured beads and the remaining beads can continue to move with no captures possible for either player.

STRATEGY

It's only common sense, but try to keep three or more beads in each of your bowls to protect your beads from being captured.

If you have a lot of beads in one bowl, wait to play them until you can capture a maximum number of your opponent's beads.

VARIATION

Grand Slam allows a move to capture all of an opponent's beads, typically called—you guessed it—a "Grand Slam." After such a move, the opponent no longer has any beads, so the current player then also captures all the beads in her own territory, ending the game.

Trivia

African slaves brought a version of Wari, called Awari, from Africa to Surinam, in South America. The game is played at funerals the day before the body is buried to entertain the body's spirit, which has yet to depart this world. Play stops at sundown for fear that the dearly departed will join the players and fly away with their spirits.

BRAINY GAMES

ANAGRAMS

BOTTICELLI
Vermicelli
Bratislava
Protozoa

FICTIONARY

GHOST
Two-Way Ghost

HANGMAN

IMPRESSIONS

JOTTO
Four-Letter Jotto
Six-Letter Jotto
Mastermind Jotto
Foreheads

PASSWORD

REVERSALS

TWO-MINUTE ALPHABET

··········

ANAGRAMS

For those who like their words scrambled.

EQUIPMENT
A set of letter tiles from a Scrabble or Upwords game.

PLAYERS
2+

OBJECT
To make as many long words as possible by anagramming the letter tiles.

SETUP
Shuffle the tiles facedown in the middle of the table. The player who picks the tile closest to the beginning of the alphabet goes first.

PLAY
One by one around the table, each player turns over a tile, leaving it in place. When four letters have been overturned, play can commence. From that point, any player who sees a word that can be made from the over-turned letters calls out that word, takes the tiles, and places the word in front of himself. Words have to be at least four letters long.

Play continues. As more tiles are turned over, another player can steal that word by taking it and mixing its letters with one or more of the up-turned tiles, forming another word. For instance, if the word CAPES is in play and there's a Y faceup among the tiles, a player can say, "Spacey," take CAPES from the other player, then set the word SPACEY down in front of herself.

Players can also anagram and add to their own words.

Play continues until all the tiles are faceup and no one can create or steal any more words.

RULES

- The letters of the original word have to be mixed when new letters are added: A player can't simply pluralize a word by adding an S at the end, or add a few letters at the beginning of a word, so that the original word retains the same meaning, like adding RE to APPEAR to make REAPPEAR. It *is* allowable, though, to add RE to TURN, for instance, to make the word RETURN.

- Once a word has been used, it can't be re-created in the same game by another player.

- If two players call out their words at exactly the same time, the longest word gets preference. If the two words are the same length, the other players can vote for the word they think is the most inventive. If there are only two players, the word that comes first alphabetically wins.

- Players have the right to challenge words they think have been made up; a dictionary will prove things one way or another.

SCORING

There are two ways to score. Decide before the game which method to play by.

- By simple letter count; the player who has the most tiles wins.

- By squaring (multiplying by itself) the lengths of each player's words so that the creation of longer words, as opposed to lots of short words, is rewarded.

HISTORY

The art of scrambling letters has been around as long as there have been alphabets. The ancient Greeks and Hebrews thought that anagrams could lead them to the secret of life. Medieval astronomers used anagram codes to hide their discoveries. France's King Louis XIII was such a fan that he appointed a Royal Anagrammist to his court—and paid him royally for his services.

· · · · · · · · ·

BOTTICELLI

Twenty Questions for the intelligentsia.

PLAYERS
2–8

OBJECT
To guess the identity of the person the "Thinker" is thinking of.

SETUP
One player (the Thinker) thinks of a person—living, dead, or mythical—that he thinks the other players will recognize.

PLAY
The Thinker gives a clue using the first letter of the famous person's last name (or the first letter of a full name if it's someone like Aristotle or Madonna).

Let's say the Thinker has started the game with "I am B." The other players have to guess the secret person's identity by asking questions in this way:

"Are you the actor who played the Godfather in the movies?"

To which the Thinker would answer, "No, I'm not Marlon Brando."

The second player might ask: "Did you give your father forty whacks?"

"No, I'm not Lizzie Borden."

"Are you a Visigoth princess?"

If this question stumps the Thinker, the player who asked it has to first give the name of the person he was guessing ("Brunhilde"), and then gets to ask a question that can be answered with "yes" or "no."

The game continues in this way until someone asks a question that makes the Thinker think the questioner has guessed correctly. But at this point, all the Thinker has to do is say, "Yes, I am," then wait for the guesser to tell him who he's thinking of. If the guesser is wrong, the game is still on and the other players now have a good clue to work with.

Once someone guesses correctly, it's his turn to be the Thinker.

FYI

Sandro Botticelli was the Renaissance artist who painted the famous *The Birth of Venus*, aka *Venus on a Half-Shell*. But it's lost to history as to why the game is named for him.

Tip

Good questions to ask early in the game are as broad as you can make them, like, "Are you living?" or "Are you male?" Then you can get more specific as the game goes on: "Are you an American?"; "Are you in the arts?"; "Are you a movie star?"; or "Are you a superstar?"

VARIATIONS

These variations were dreamed up by three Berkeley science/math guys: David Gedye, David Anderson, and Richard Kraft.

Vermicelli is played with the names of foods: everything from Twinkies to Crêpes Suzette.

Bratislava is played with geographical names, from nations, rivers, mountains, and neighborhoods to the planets and beyond.

Protozoa is played with the names of living things, typically only the common names of species. (But when some science types play, they allow kingdom, phylum, class, order, family, or genus. Yipes!)

· · · · · · · · ·

FICTIONARY

Individual house rules may vary when playing Fictionary, but play usually proceeds like this.

EQUIPMENT

- A large dictionary

- Pencils or pens for each player

- Note cards, index cards, or identical pieces of paper for each player

PLAYERS

3+

OBJECT

To write definitions of unknown words that will fool your opponents, and to try to figure out what the correct definitions are.

SETUP

A Chooser can be assigned to play throughout the whole game, or players can take turns, moving in a clockwise fashion.

PLAY

The Chooser picks an obscure word from the dictionary, pronounces it, and spells it. If a player is already familiar with the word, he or she should say so and the Chooser will choose another word.

If a word has more than one definition listed, the Chooser should, in general, pick the first definition as the one to use.

Once each player has heard the word, he or she writes a plausible definition of it, initials it, and submits it to the Chooser. The Chooser—who has written the correct definition on his piece of paper—reads the definitions as they're handed to him and checks them over to make sure that he can understand them. If he can't, he can speak privately with the author and clarify the definition, so it sounds credible when he reads it aloud. The Chooser then shuffles the definitions, including his own.

The Chooser then reads all the definitions aloud (but not the initials), in any order, and can read them a second time if asked. Now it's time to vote: each player (except for the Chooser) votes for the definition he or she thinks is correct. Players are not permitted to vote for their own definition.

Players earn 1 point if they vote for the correct definition, and 1 point for each vote the other players cast for the definition they wrote. The Chooser earns 1 point if no one selects the correct definition.

Play proceeds with the dictionary going to the player to the left of the Chooser, which starts a new turn. A full circuit of the dictionary constitutes a round.

VARIATION

Players can vote for their own definition in a twist on the original game. They won't get points for doing so, but that vote can encourage other players to vote for that definition as well (and the player, of course, would get those points).

·········

GHOST

There's nothing spooky about it—except when you have to admit that you've been stuck with adding the last letter of a word.

PLAYERS

2+

OBJECT

To keep adding letters to a word that's being built—but *not* to finish the word by adding the last letter.

PLAY

The first player gives a letter, the second player adds one, and the third player adds another. From that point on (because three-letter words don't count) the players have to make sure that the letters they add won't finish spelling a word.

Let's say the first two letters were C and A. Since three-letter words don't count, the third player would be safe in adding a T.

If the fourth player adds a C, making it C-A-T-C, the player who goes next might think she has no choice but to finish the word by adding H to make CATCH. *But* if she thinks of the word CATCALL, she can add an A instead.

If the next player thinks she's bluffing, he can challenge her. But once she proves herself correct (with or without the help of a dictionary), the game ends and the challenger is penalized with a G, the first letter of GHOST.

If, on the other hand, the challenger added an L, the next player would be faced with C-A-T-C-A-L. At this point, he has three choices:

- Challenge the previous player (if proven wrong, he will earn a G).

- Bluff and add a letter, making believe he has a particular word in mind (if challenged, he will earn a G).

- Surrender and add the last L, thereby finishing the word (earning a G).

The player to the first player's left begins the next word. When a player gets all five letters of GHOST, he's out of the game and isn't allowed to speak to any of the remaining players. The last survivor wins.

RULES
No hyphenated words or proper nouns are allowed.

VARIATION
In **Two-Way Ghost (aka Super Ghost)**, letters can be added to the beginning of a word as well as the end. In the previous example, a player might add a P to the front of CAT, going for HEPCAT.

·········

HANGMAN

The game that TV's Wheel of Fortune *is based on.*

EQUIPMENT
- Pencil

- Paper

PLAYERS
2+

OBJECT
To guess the correct word before the Hangman draws an entire hanged man.

SETUP
One person is chosen to be the Hangman for this round. She thinks of a word and writes dashes on a piece of paper to indicate the number of letters in the word. Somewhere on the same piece of paper the Hangman draws a gallows—nothing fancy, just a series of lines that represent a gallows that the hanged man can hang from.

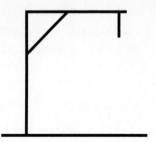

PLAY

Each of the other players suggests one letter in turn. If the letter is in the word, the Hangman writes it on the corresponding blank or blanks, in as many places as it appears, (e.g., if a player tries for E and if there's more than one in the word, the Hangman writes all the ES on the dashes in their correct places.

Every time a player guesses a letter that *isn't* in the word, the Hangman draws one of the elements that make up the hanged man:

A circle for his head

A vertical line below it for his torso

A left arm

A right arm

A left leg

A right leg

The game is over when the guessing players complete the word, or guess the whole word correctly—or when the Hangman completes the hanged man.

If the Hangman stumps the other players, he gets another turn as

Hangman. If one of the other players correctly guesses the word, that player gets to be the Hangman for the next round.

VARIATIONS

To add to the number of guesses, some players begin with no diagram at all, and start by drawing the parts of the gallows. More fun, though, is to start with the gallows and add more detail to the hanged man—like a hat, a bow tie, shoes, etc.

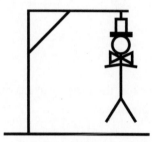

Try adding only *one* letter when it's guessed, even if there are more than one of them in the word (e.g., when someone guesses T in the word FLUT-TER).

You can use common phrases instead of single words, giving the category of the phrase (e.g., "Fictional Animal" for FELIX THE CAT).

Tip

For guessing purposes, it might help you to know that the most common letter in the English language is E, followed by T, A, O, I, N, S, H, R, D, L, U. (Of course, there are thousands of words that don't contain any of these letters, but it couldn't hurt to know, could it?)

·········

IMPRESSIONS

*A longtime parlor game favorite, it was featured in John Updike's novel,
Couples. AKA Analogies, Essence, If I Were a . . .*

PLAYERS
2+ (but better with 4+)

OBJECT
To guess what famous person the other players have decided you will be
by interpreting their "impressions."

SETUP
One player leaves the room; or if the group is large, two people can leave
the room, with the second person helping the first. The remaining players
decide on a famous person whom the player will be. This can be anyone
living or dead—from Cleopatra to Arnold Schwarzenegger to Abraham
Lincoln. When a person has been decided on, the other players call the
missing player(s) back into the room.

PLAY
The returning player then has to ask the question, "If I were a
_____, what would I be?" The answers given must be "impressions,"
nothing specific.

For instance, if the group decided on Madonna, the answer to "If I were
some kind of reading material . . ." couldn't be *Sex* (Madonna's 1992
book)—that's too specific. The answer would have to be something more
like "a ten-year-old Victoria's Secret catalog" or "a tabloid article" or even
"the Torah," referring to her interest in the kabbalah.

A question like, "If I were a form of transportation, what would I be?"
could be answered, "A roller coaster (referring to her career)" or "A long,
white limousine (her lifestyle)."

OTHER SUBJECTS

Color

Flower

Period in history

Beverage

Animal

Body of water

Bird

Biblical figure

TV show

Time of year

Type of architecture

RULES

Remember, the only wrong answers are the ones that are too specific.

· · · · · · · · ·

JOTTO

If this word game reminds you of Mastermind, that's because the brand-name game is a nonverbal spin-off.

EQUIPMENT

• Pencil

• Paper

PLAYERS

2

OBJECT

To guess the opponent's secret word.

SETUP

Each player picks a secret word of five letters (no proper names allowed) and writes it down without letting the other player see it. Beginners can also write the alphabet in a column to keep track of what's been guessed for their own words and their opponent's.

RULES

The game can be played with words that have repeated letters, like SPELL or ZIPPY or even POPPY, as long as both players agree beforehand.

PLAY

Taking turns, players try to find out the other's word by saying a five-letter word.

Let's say that Player 1 has chosen the word NAVEL. If Player 2 guesses "Venom," Player 1 has to answer, "Three" because V, E, and N are in the word NAVEL. If, when it was her turn again, Player 2 guessed, "Knave," Player 1 would answer, "Four."

Every time a player gives a word, she writes it down; then, when the other player answers with the number of letters that were correct, the player writes down the number next to the word.

Play continues back and forth until one of the players guesses correctly.

VARIATIONS

Four-Letter Jotto is a good version for beginners.

Six-Letter Jotto makes for a more difficult game.

Mastermind Jotto adds the rule that players respond only to letters that are in the right place. Say you're playing the six-letter version, and your opponent's word is FIESTA. If you guessed FEISTY, you'd be told you'd guessed three letters correctly—the F, S, and T—but not the I and the E, because they're in different positions.

Foreheads is the silly version of Jotto. Four players or more try to guess the words that are written on labels stuck to their foreheads.

FYI

It's possible to get an answer of "five" in five-letter Jotto and still not have the right answer, but at least then you know that you've hit on an anagram of the word.

Each player writes a four-letter word on a Post-it–type sticky label and sticks it on the forehead of the player to her right. The players can see all the words except the one on their own foreheads.

In turn, players start by saying a four-letter word made up of letters that they see on the other players' foreheads. By paying attention to the letters that the others guess that *don't* appear in any of their words, you can gradually build up an idea of your own. Let's say you can see three words: BLUE, SODA, and TIME. You say, "Lots," four of the letters you see before you. When it's BLUE's turn, he says, "Damp." You can see a D, A, and M, but no P, so you know your word has a P in it. The SODA player says, "Tear." Now you've got an R to work with.

Players get only one try to guess their own words. If the guess is correct, they win; if it's incorrect, they can stay in the game, but they lose their chance to win: They can't guess again.

STRATEGY

Vary your guesses so that they're not just a letter or two away from each other. For example, if you guess SLATE and are answered with "Two," don't guess SKATE the next time to see if one of the letters is L or K. Instead, guess a completely different word, like PINKY—you'll get more clues in fewer guesses.

·········

PASSWORD

The original of the long-running TV game show of the same name.

EQUIPMENT

- Pencil

- Paper

PLAYERS

4 or 5 (Four players divide up into two teams; with five players, one person can act as emcee.)

OBJECT

To get another player to correctly guess a word by giving clues that suggest the word.

SETUP

If there's an emcee, she collects the words that each team writes out for the other team to solve, and keeps track of the number of clues it takes for a player to guess a word.

If you're playing without an emcee, each player writes a few words on small pieces of paper and holds on to them until it's time to give the other team a word. Each team keeps track of the number of clues it takes to guess a word.

PLAY

The first player is given a word and has a few moments to decide how to play it. Let's say the word is "picture." She might give clues like "photo" or "frame" or "drawing," depending on the direction her partner seems to be going in.

When the word has been guessed, the other team takes its turn. Then the first team goes again, reversing the roles of clue-giver and guesser this time. The second team has its try, and at the end of this round, the scores are announced.

SCORING

At the end of the round (after four words have been guessed) the scores are added up. Lowest score wins the round.

VARIATION

The game can be played with a larger group, without teams: One player is chosen to be the clue-giver and gives the first clue to all the other players. The first player to guess the word gets a point and takes over as clue-giver for the next round. If no one gets it on the first clue, a second clue is given. And so on.

RULES

- No gestures allowed! But facial expressions and voice inflections are okay (e.g., in trying for the word "wedding," you might draw out the word "engagement" at the end to signify something that *follows* an engagement).

- No part or variant of the word can be used (e.g., "frozen" for "antifreeze").

- Proper nouns are allowed as clues (e.g., "Charles" for "prince").

- It's okay to repeat a clue for emphasis.

- No hyphenated words as clues (e.g., "hard-boiled").

·········

REVERSALS

A good way to play is to spring it on your game-mates without letting them know about the reversal at the end.

EQUIPMENT
- Pencil

- Paper

PLAYERS
2+

OBJECT
To write down the names of famous people whose names begin with each letter of the alphabet.

SETUP
Players write the alphabet, A–Z, in a column down the left-hand side of a piece of paper.

PLAY
Round One
Players write down the names of famous people whose first names begin with each letter of the alphabet.

   A: Al Sharpton

   B: Bette Midler

C: Charles Atlas

D: David Letterman

. . . and so on.

Round Two

When everyone has finished their list as best they can, they reverse the initials of the person they wrote on each line. So next to "A: Al Sharpton," the player has to think of a person whose initials are "S.A."

And so on down the line.

The player who fills in the most names on both lists wins.

·········

TWO-MINUTE ALPHABET

Anyone who's seen the TV show Whose Line Is It Anyway? *in its UK and/or American version will recognize this game: The show calls it "90-Second Alphabet."*

EQUIPMENT

A timer or wristwatch with a second hand

PLAYERS

2+

OBJECT

To keep adding to a conversation by using sentences that begin with consecutive letters of the alphabet.

SETUP

Players decide on a topic or situation—having a baby, being saved by a lifeguard, registering to vote, and so on.

PLAY

Starting with a random letter of the alphabet, players take turns complet-ing a conversation by starting each sentence with a consecutive letter of the alphabet.

Here's an example. The topic: going to the chiropractor.

"**I** need a little adjustment, Doc."

"**J**ust sit over there."

"**K**eep your hands off me!"

"**L**ook, I've got to touch you or it won't work."

"**M**y back hurts too much."

"**N**ow, now, just relax and let me . . . twist you!"

"**O**uch!"

"**P**ut your arm behind your head . . ."

"**Q**uit that!"

"**R**elax, I told you to relax!"

"**S**o you can hurt me again?"

And so on, through the alphabet all the way to z, then A through H. Players have two minutes to complete the twenty-six sentences. If they manage it, they score 10 points apiece. If one them gets stuck, he scores a −1 point, and the game begins again with a new topic and a new letter.

VARIATIONS

The game can be played with teams of two or three. One team goes first, and the other team suggests the topic and the letter of the alphabet that starts the round.

There are two ways to score the game:

- Play can end at two minutes, at which point the other team gets a chance to play. The winner is the team that goes the farthest in the al-phabet.

- Play can extend until the entire alphabet is finished; the winning team is the one that finishes in the least amount of time.

FAMILY GAMES

BATTLESHIPS

BUZZ
Buzz, Fizz

CATEGORIES
Two-Handed Categories

COFFEEPOT

CONNECT THE DOTS

CONSEQUENCES
Honeymoon Consequences

DEADPAN

I WENT TO THE MARKET
The Alphabet Game
I Packed My Bag

IN PLAIN SIGHT

JACKS

PICK-UP STICKS

TABLE FOOTBALL

TIC-TAC-TOE

TWENTY QUESTIONS
Animal, Vegetable, or Mineral

UP, JENKINS!
Up, Jenkins Upmanship

WORD LIGHTNING

·········

BATTLESHIPS

The game is thought to have been created by British POWs in Germany during World War I. It was first marketed to the public in 1931 as Salvo.

EQUIPMENT

• Pencil

• Paper

• A book or a piece of cardboard to serve as a barrier between each player's grids

PLAYERS

2

OBJECT

To find and sink the enemy's fleet.

SETUP

Each players draws two side-by-side 10×10 grids (or marks off 10×10 squares on graph paper) and labels one of them MY SHIPS, the other ENEMY SHIPS.

Across the top of each grid a player writes the letters A through J and the numbers 1 through 10 down the left side of the grid. Where the numbers and letters cross will serve as the coordinates: A1, A2, and so on to J10.

Then, after putting up a barrier so their opponents won't see, both players "place" their fleets either horizontally or vertically on their MY SHIPS grids (leaving at least one space between any two ships) by inserting a string of A's for aircraft carrier, B's for battleship, D's for destroyer, etc., in the appropriate number of squares.

The Ships

The number and variety of ships vary from game book to game book. Here's one arrangement:

One aircraft carrier—5 squares
One battleship—4 squares
One destroyer—3 squares
One submarine—3 squares
One cruiser—2 squares

PLAY

The first player "fires a shot" by calling out the coordinates of a square. The other player looks at his MY SHIPS grid to see if the square is occupied by any of his fleet. If it isn't, the player declares it a "miss." But if it is, the player declares a "hit" and identifies the type of ship. In either case, he marks the grid with an X.

The player who fired the shot either records a miss in the appropriate square in his ENEMY SHIPS grid (by marking it with a slash) or records a hit by marking the square with a letter that identifies the type of ship: B for Battleship, C for Cruiser, etc. Once all the squares of a ship have been hit, that ship is "sunk."

Players continue to take turns firing shots until one player completely destroys the enemy fleet.

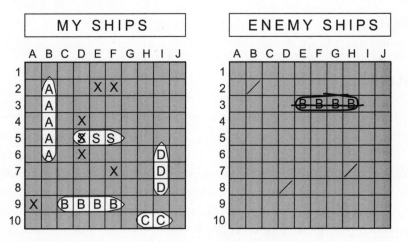

The MY SHIPS grid records six misses and a hit on the submarine. The ENEMY SHIPS grid shows three misses and one battleship destroyed.

STRATEGY

Don't try to scatter your hits. You'll get better results by concentrating your shots in one area at a time.

VARIATIONS

Battleships has lots of variations having to do with the size of the grids, the numbers and sizes of the ships, the number of shots allowed during a turn, when the hits are announced, and so on.

In one version, the first player gets a certain number of shots in one turn, often seven or eleven. When all the shots have been fired, the defensive player calls out the location of each shot and whether each was a hit or a miss, but doesn't identify the type of ship. The number of shots a player gets is reduced by the number that corresponds to his ships that were sunk in a previous round (e.g., minus five for an aircraft carrier, minus four for a battleship, and so on).

In another variation, the defensive player does *not* declare the location of each shot, only the names of the ships and the number of hits on each during that round.

FYI

The Milton Bradley Company published its ever-popular version of the game in 1943. It featured these ships:

An aircraft carrier—5 spaces

A battleship—4 spaces

A cruiser—3 spaces

A submarine—3 spaces

A destroyer—2 spaces

Before and since 1943, various versions have been marketed as *Combat*, *Broadsides*, *Warfare Naval Combat*, *Swiss Navy*, *Sunk*, *Convoy*, and *Wings*.

· · · · · · · · ·

BUZZ

A kids' game that quite a few grown-ups find intimidating.

PLAYERS
2+

OBJECT
To count to 100 while saying "buzz" when you're supposed to.

PLAY
In sequence, players count off, substituting the word "buzz" for every five or multiple of five: one, two, three, four, buzz, six, seven, eight, nine, buzz . . . and so on to 100.

A player who slips and says a number instead of "buzz" (or says "buzz" when she isn't supposed to) has to leave the game. The last player left is the winner.

VARIATIONS
You can use any number (except 1, of course) to be your buzz number.

In **Buzz, Fizz**, players have to say "buzz" for every multiple of one number, and "fizz" for every multiple of another. If you chose 5 and 7, for instance, the counting off would go like this: one, two, three, four, buzz, six, fizz, eight, nine, buzz, eleven, twelve, thirteen, fizz, buzz . . . and so on.

When the count gets to 57, the player has to say has to say "buzzty-fizz." And 75 is "fizzty-buzz."

·········

CATEGORIES

It's also known as "Guggenheim," but whether the game is named for the prominent New York family—or one of them invented it—is lost to posterity.

EQUIPMENT
• Paper

• Pencil

PLAYERS
2+

OBJECT
To score the most points by thinking of words that the other players won't think of.

SETUP
Each player should construct a 5×5 grid on a piece of paper. The players agree on five categories, the names of which are written along the left side of the grid. Next, the players agree on a five-letter word with no repeated letters; the five letters are written across the top of the grid, above each of the five spaces.

Players decide on a time limit of five to fifteen minutes.

PLAY

Players fill in each space in a category with a word or phrase that begins with the letter at the top of the grid, trying to think of entries that the other players won't think of. For instance, if the category is Animals and the letter is B, the word "bear" might spring to mind first. But a player would probably be better off trying "baboon" or "buffalo" or "burro" because less common words will score more points.

SCORING

When time is up, each player reads her word lists aloud and the other players keep track of their scores.

A word or phrase scores one point for every other player who *did not* write it on his list. So in a game with six players, if only only one player named "burro," it would score five points. If two players wrote "burro," it would score four points—one point for each player who didn't write it in.

If everyone wrote "bear," no one would score a point for that square.

VARIATIONS

Two-Handed Categories is for two players. The one who finishes first (and whose entries are acceptable to the loser) is the winner.

In a similar game, also called **Categories**, players decide on a list of categories (usually ten or more) and write them in a column down the left

---

FYI

Categories was the basis for the commercial games Scattergories and Facts in Five.

---

side of a piece of paper. A letter of the alphabet is chosen at random and players have to think of one entry for each of the categories that starts with that letter.

A word that no one else has thought of gets two points; a word that one or more players have also written down gets one point. The player with the most points is the winner.

The same categories can be used again in the next round after a new letter is chosen.

Here are some suggestions for categories to get you started. There are millions more!

Geographical names

Newspapers and magazines

Fruits and vegetables

Parts of the body

Car makes and models

Things that are green (yellow, purple, etc.)

Gems and minerals

Book titles

Sports

Games (or, specifically, card games, children's games, board games, etc.)

Words that contain the letter Q

Insects

Prescription drugs

Famous people who are known by one name

Mountain ranges

Things you can buy at Home Depot

Scientists and inventors

Items of clothing

·········

COFFEEPOT

The only game we know of that's named after a household appliance.

PLAYERS
3+

OBJECT
To guess the verb that the other players have decided on.

SETUP
One player is chosen to be "It" and leaves the room while the other players think of a verb: sleep, dance, shop, fight, ski, and so on.

PLAY
When It comes back into the room, he tries to guess the verb that the others picked, but he has to ask questions by substituting the world "coffepot" for the unknown verb. Here are some examples:

Do I coffepot?

Do people coffeepot outdoors?

Can you coffeepot sitting down?

Do fish coffeepot?

The questions have to be answered truthfully with "yes," "no," or "I don't know."

It can try for the word anytime during play. When It gets the answer, the person who answered the last question becomes It for the next round.

VARIATIONS
Use compound verbs: play tennis, brush your teeth, drive a car, watch TV, ride a horse, dig a hole in the ground

The game can be played with just two people, too—one player thinks of a verb, the other has to guess it.

· · · · · · · · ·

CONNECT THE DOTS

Stake out your own territory in this simple—but subtly analytical—game. AKA Boxes

EQUIPMENT
- Paper

- Pencil

PLAYERS

2

OBJECT

To connect the dots on a grid to make the most boxes.

SETUP

Make a square grid of dots (4×4) on a sheet of paper.

PLAY

Players take turns drawing either a horizontal or vertical line between two dots. (Diagonal lines aren't allowed.) A player *has to* add a line when it's her turn, even if it will give the other player the opportunity to add the fourth side to a box when it gets to be his turn.

When a player finishes off the fourth side of a box, he writes his initials in the square and takes another turn.

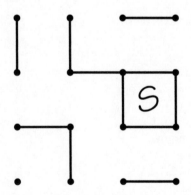

The game is over when all the dots are connected. The player with the most squares wins.

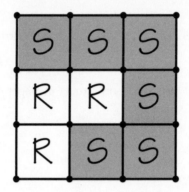

ADVANCED PLAY

Once you've got the hang of it, try bigger grids, like 5×5, 6×6, and so on.

· · · · · · · · ·

CONSEQUENCES

Based on an old parlor game in which the first player would write a phrase on a sheet of paper, fold the paper to conceal part of it, and pass it on to the next player to continue the story . . .

EQUIPMENT

- Pencil
- Paper

PLAYERS

3 or 4

OBJECT

To draw a composite figure.

PLAY

The first player draws the head and neck of a real or imaginary figure (human or animal) at the top of the paper, then folds the paper so the next player can only see a few of the bottom lines of it.

The second player adds a torso to what she can see of the first drawing, then folds the paper so that the last player can only see a few lines of her drawing. (If there are four players, the torso can be divided into upper and lower torso to be drawn by the second and third players.)

The drawing is passed to the last player, who has to draw the legs and feet. After he's done, the last player unveils the finished monster—er, figure—which should look pretty silly by now.

VARIATION

Honeymoon Consequences is played with a twosome.

Trivia
Surrealist artists of the 1920s used the game to create a number of serious works of art. They called the game *"cadavre exquis"*—Exquisite Corpse. To see some of these bizarre drawings visit: www.cyberstars.com/ron-mike/history.html.

· · · · · · · · ·

DEADPAN

Like TV's Make Me Laugh, only you're the stand-up comedians and the contestants.

PLAYERS
3+

OBJECT
To keep from smiling or laughing.

SETUP
Players sit in a circle. One player is chosen to go first.

PLAY
The first player does something like patting the person to his left on the head, who pats the person on his left on the head, who pats the person on his left on the head—all the way around the circle.

The round begins again. This time, for instance, the first player chucks the person to his left under the chin, and so on around the circle again.

In subsequent rounds, the first player blows in the second player's ear, or punches him in the arm, or tweaks his nose, and so on.

Any player who smiles or laughs is out of the game. The last person left is the winner.

·········

I WENT TO THE MARKET

The growing list is easier to remember if everyone stays in the same place, say, around a table. If you play it in a car, don't let the driver play—it's way too distracting.

PLAYERS
2+ (but the most fun is with at least 6 people).

OBJECT
To remember a growing list of words.

PLAY
The first player has to come up with something that can be bought at a market that begins with A. She says, "I went to the market to buy artichokes."

The second player has to say, "I went to the market to buy artichokes . . ." and has to add an item that starts with B. So he says, "artichokes and Brazil nuts."

The third player chooses "Cheerios" for his C word, saying, "I went to the market to buy artichokes, Brazil nuts, and Cheerios."

The fourth player has to say the same thing and come up with a D word. And so on—all the way to Z.

If a player can't think of an item that starts with his or her letter—and no one else can, either—the letter is skipped and the game continues with whatever letter follows it. But if someone else *can* come up with a word, the player who couldn't think of one is out of the game, and the player who follows him can use the word.

A player is out if he can't remember the chain. Any players left at the end of the alphabet have to restart the same chain, but this time they have to go backward: from Z to A.

The last person left in the game wins.

STRATEGY
As each player says a word, try to build an association. Imagine the first player from the example eating an artichoke, for instance. And pay atten-

tion: As each player repeats all the words, you can cement them even
more firmly in your mind.

VARIATIONS

The Alphabet Game is similar, but not restricted to market items—any
category will do. For example, car makes and models; things that are green;
TV shows; dog breeds; desserts—any broad category will do. You don't
have to say "I went to the market," just memorize the growing list of words.

I Packed My Bag (aka I Packed My Bag for Boston) is another memory game, but the items aren't usually in alphabetical order and therefore
harder to remember. Players have to include any appropriate item—or not
so appropriate—by saying, "I packed my bag and in it I put . . ."

·········

IN PLAIN SIGHT

*You can add another level by making participants think they're playing a
simple memory game instead of warning them that they'll have to find the
stuff, all of it hidden in plain sight.*

EQUIPMENT
- A tray containing at least 15 small, ordinary items

- Pencil

- Paper

PLAYERS
3+

OBJECT
To find all the items that are hidden in plain sight.

SETUP
The players are shown fifteen to twenty small items and given as much
time as they need to examine them.

All the players leave the room while one person hides the objects "in
plain sight": a silver ring on a silver tray, a coin sitting in the bottom of a

glass bowl, a paper clip attached to a lamp cord, a chopstick stuck in a pot-ted plant, a wooden matchstick lying on top of a wooden frame, and so on.

Once the items have all been planted, the players are called back into the room, and given a pencil and a piece of paper.

PLAY

The players go around the room looking for the hidden objects. When they see one, they have to write down its position—and be very careful not to give away its position to the other players.

The first player to find all the objects wins.

VARIATION

If the players number six or more, the game can also be played with two teams.

·········

JACKS

Not as innocuous as you'd think, the game is a descendent of "knuckle-bones," which was played—in ancient Greece and, with variations, in China, Haiti, and the Ukraine—with real bones.

EQUIPMENT
- A set of 5 jacks
- Ball (The ball should be bouncy—the ball that came with the set works fine, though some players prefer bigger balls like Pinkies, aka Spaldeens.)

PLAYERS
2+

OBJECT
To pick up jacks in the time it takes to bounce a ball.

PLAY

The first round is called "onesies." The first player throws the five jacks on the ground, then picks up the ball in one hand and throws it into the air. While the ball is in the air, and with the same hand, the player picks up one jack and catches the ball before it hits the ground. The jack is then put into the other hand. This is repeated until all the jacks have been picked up.

To start the "twosies" round, the player throws the jacks on the floor, throws the ball up, but this time has to pick up two jacks at a time (until, of course, the third and final throw when only one jack is left). When the last jack is picked up, the player goes again but this time with three jacks (threesies), then four (foursies), and finally fivesies, in which the ball is thrown up and all five jacks have to be picked up at the same time before the ball is caught.

If a player misses the ball or doesn't pick up the required number of jacks, the turn is over and the next player has a try. The player who manages to get furthest in the sequence wins.

VARIATIONS

There are as many ways to play as there are kids who've played Jacks—and that includes your grandfather. Here are a few:

• Play the game with ten, fifteen, or twenty jacks instead of five.

• Bounce the ball instead of throwing it up.

• Players have to clap their hands before the pick-up. In this case, of

---

Who Goes First?

You can always give it the old "eeny-meeny-miney-moe," but the "pros" do it this way: A player throws five jacks into the air with one hand and tries to catch as many as possible on the *back* of the same hand. The jacks that were caught are then thrown up again from the back of the hand and as many as possible are caught in the palm of the same hand. The other players do the same, and the player who catches the most jacks starts play.

Or try this: If you're playing with more than five jacks, throw the jacks up and make a dish of your two hands, thumbs together, to catch the jacks on the backs of your hands. Then repeat and turn your palms up, pinkies together, to see how many you can catch.

course, you have to put your picked-up jacks on the ground instead of in the opposite hand.

- In another variation, the opposite hand has to be used in alternating rounds.

·········

PICK-UP STICKS

In North America, the game has been traced back to Native Americans, who played it with straws of wheat and passed it on to English settlers. But another school of thought attributes it to a Chinese game called Spillikins or Spelicans. AKA Jackstraws

EQUIPMENT
- A set of pick-up sticks

PLAYERS
2+

OBJECT
To pick up as many sticks as possible without disturbing any others.

SETUP
One player holds all the sticks upright in one hand with the bottoms of the sticks touching or nearly touching the playing surface and releases them so that they fall into a pile.

PLAY
The first player tries to remove a stick from the pile. If she succeeds in picking up a stick without moving any of the others, she goes again. But if

---

Tip

If you can't find a stick that looks like it can be lifted up directly, try pressing down on one end and taking hold of the other end when it rises.

any of the other sticks move during the process, her turn is over, and play passes to the next player.

Play continues until all the sticks have been picked up.

SCORING
Players count the number of sticks they've retrieved; the player with the most sticks wins.

VARIATIONS
The helper stick, usually black, is set aside before a game begins. All the players can use the helper stick to help them remove other sticks.

In another version, the helper stick is released with the rest of the sticks and the player who successfully takes it out of the pile—and *only* that player—can then use it.

Some players prefer to assign point values to the different colors, in which case players should agree in advance on how many points are needed to win the overall game (usually 500 points):

Black—25 points

Red—10 points

Blue—5 points

Green—2 points

Yellow—1 point

. . . .

TABLE FOOTBALL

You don't have to be a jock to enjoy this version of football. AKA Paper Football

EQUIPMENT
- A long table to serve as the playing field

- A paper football. Here's how to make one: Take a piece of 8½×11 paper (typing paper, notebook paper) and fold it into thirds the long way.

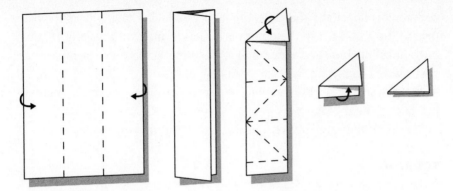

Fold one corner down to the opposite edge, making an angle at the top. Fold the angle straight down along its edge.

Repeat previous steps all the way down the paper until you can't fold anymore.

Tuck the excess paper into the open end. The "football" should be a 3×3×4-inch triangle.

PLAYERS
2

OBJECT
To score touchdowns and field goals.

SETUP
Players sit at opposite ends of the table.

PLAY
Players take turns finger-flicking the football down the table, trying to get it to the edge of the other end of the table. If part of it hangs over the edge, the player scores a touchdown, worth 6 points.

If a shot falls short of the end of the table, the other player receives possession of the ball and gets to shoot at his own goal from that point.

If a shot goes off the side of the table it's "out of bounds." The other player gets to shoot from the point at which the ball went over the edge.

Field Goals
If a shot goes entirely off the far end of the table, the other player gets to kick a "field goal" worth 3 points. Holding the football so that it stands up

between his finger and the table, the field-goal kicker finger-flicks the ball toward the goal—which the other player has formed with his fingers, tips of thumbs touching and index fingers pointing up so they resemble goal posts, wrists resting on the edge of the table.

If a player scores a touchdown, he can go for an extra point, executed just like the field goal.

Play continues until a predetermined score or time limit is reached.

SCORING

Touchdown—6 points

Field goal—3 points

Extra point—1 point

VARIATION

Some experts play with a smaller, fatter football made by folding the paper in half, then half again, and then following the instructions listed earlier.

·········

TIC-TAC-TOE

One of the game's original names was Tit-Tat-Toe, based on the saying "tit for tat" as in "Oh, yeah? I'll get you for that!" AKA Noughts and Crosses (zeroes being "noughts" in the UK and elsewhere).

EQUIPMENT

- Pencil

- Paper

PLAYERS

2

OBJECT

To write in three x's or o's in a row.

SETUP

Draw four intersecting lines to make a 3×3 grid. Players decide who'll be x and who'll be o.

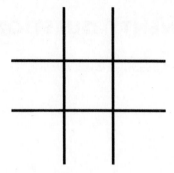

PLAY

x and o take turns writing their letters in the grid. The first player to get three x's or o's in a row—going across, up and down, or diagonally—wins the game. The loser gets to go first in the next game.

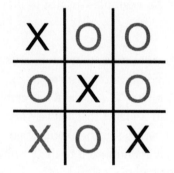

VARIATIONS

Try playing a game so that the first player to line up his x's or o's *loses* the game.

　　Increase the number of squares: four by four, five by five, and so on.

· · · · · · · · ·

TWENTY QUESTIONS

Animal, Vegetable, or Mineral's closest relative. AKA I'm Thinking of Something

PLAYERS
2+

OBJECT
To find out which person, place, or thing another player is thinking of.

SETUP
One player thinks of a specific person, place, or thing and tells the other players when she's ready to play. Players decide whether to play to a certain score—100 points, for example—or just to play it loose.

PLAY
The player(s) asks twenty questions that can be answered by "yes" or "no." The *answerer* answers each question in turn.

   The first question is often, "Is it animal, vegetable, or mineral?" (Animal: anything [other than a plant] that's alive, from single-cell organisms to humans; Vegetable: anything in the plant kingdom; Mineral: anything made of minerals, from a grain of sand to the Empire State Building.) Another question that's particularly helpful is *"Is it bigger than a breadbox?"*

   If a questioner guesses the object, that questioner wins and becomes the answerer for the next round. If twenty questions are asked without a correct guess, then the answerer has stumped the questioners and gets to be the answerer for another round.

Tip

The most effective way to play is to ask questions that will split the field of remaining possibilities roughly in half each time.

SCORING

If the other players can't figure out what the secret object is after twenty questions, the answerer gets 20 points.

VARIATION

The game **Animal, Vegetable, or Mineral** is the teensiest bit different. In it, the answerer *tells* the questioners at the very start of the game whether the object is animal, vegetable, or mineral.

Trivia

Twenty Questions started as a radio show in the 1940s, was simulcast on radio and television starting in 1949, and went on to become a prime-time staple on the pioneering Dumont channel in the 1950s.

FYI

Funnyman Steve Allen first thought up the question, "Is it bigger than a breadbox?" while he was a panelist on the TV quiz show *What's My Line?* in the 1950s. Of course, these days a lot of people have never seen a breadbox so it's hard for them to figure out how big one is. If you're one of them, imagine a box about the size of a small microwave oven.

·········

UP, JENKINS!

A rousing game, the perfect diversion to follow a big family dinner.

EQUIPMENT

• A long table

• A quarter or silver dollar

PLAYERS

8+

OBJECT

To guess which player has hidden the coin.

SETUP

Players choose two captains and divide into two equal teams. The teams sit along each side of the table, facing each other; the captains sit at the ends of the table. The captains decide whether to set a time limit or a target score: ten minutes or 10 points, for instance.

PLAY

Teams take turns hiding a coin. The captain of the first team gets the coin and passes it under the table to the second person on his team. Players continue to pass the coin back and forth from one player to another, being careful not to let the other team guess which player has the coin at any given moment.

After counting slowly to ten, the captain of the opposing team calls, "Up, Jenkins!" At this signal, the players on the team with the coin raise their hands over their heads with fists clenched. The captain then calls out, "Down, Jenkins!" and the players slap their hands down, palms flat on the table, keeping the coin hidden.

Now the opposing team has to guess which player has the coin. After conferring, the captain of the opposing team names a player and says, "Show up." The player he's named has to lift up both hands to show if the coin is on the table.

SCORING

If the coin is there, the opposing team gets 1 point; if it isn't, the first team wins the point.

If a time limit was set, the team with the most points when time runs out wins. If a point limit was set, the first team to reach it wins.

STRATEGY

The team with the coin can't make a sound after they hear "Up, Jenkins!"—that way they can't drown out the sound of the coin hitting the table. What they should strive for instead is to slam their hands down hard and in unison so that the coin can't be heard.

VARIATION

In **Up, Jenkins Upmanship**, players have to guess not only who has the coin, but which hand—right or left—it's under.

·········

WORD LIGHTNING

A great travel game, too . . .

EQUIPMENT

- Pencil

- Paper

- A wristwatch or clock

PLAYERS

2+

OBJECT

To think of as many words as possible that begin with a certain letter in one minute.

PLAY

Players take turns assigning each other a letter of the alphabet. While one player is thinking of as many words as possible within the time limit, the other player or players are keeping count of the words and watching the clock.

Play continues until the players have had an equal number of turns. The player who thought of the most words wins.

PARTY GAMES

BABY SHOWER GAMES
Baby Biz
Baby Face
Baby's First Portrait
The Bag Game
The Diaper Game
Feed the Baby
Feeding Time
Hey, Good Looking
I Love My Teddy Bear
Potato Push
Sniff, Sniff
So Big Ribbon Game

WEDDING SHOWER GAMES
The Date Game
The Newlywed Game
Old What's-His-Name
Purse Bingo
Rice Is Nice
Smoochy Songs
Wedding Dress
Wedding Night

· · · · · · · · ·

BABY BIZ

EQUIPMENT
- Ten or so baby objects that aren't easily identified, e.g., a nose syringe, a temperature strip, a breast pump, a teething ring, and so on.

- Paper

- Pencils

PLAYERS
6+

OBJECT
To correctly identify the most baby items.

SETUP
Give each player a piece of paper and a pencil.

PLAY
Show the players the baby equipment and ask them to write down their guesses as to what each object is, or is for. The player with the most correct answers is the winner.

Tip
When the game is over, put all the baby items in a basket and present them to the mother-to-be.

·········

BABY FACE

EQUIPMENT

- A baby picture of each guest

- A piece of poster board

- Pencils

- Paper

PLAYERS

6+

OBJECT

To correctly match each guest with her baby picture.

SETUP

Attach the baby pictures to the poster board, each with a number next to it.

PLAY

Ask the guests to figure out which baby picture goes with which guest. The guest who gets the most right wins.

·········

BABY'S FIRST PORTRAIT

EQUIPMENT

Enough paper plates and crayons to go around.

PLAYERS

6+

OBJECT

To draw the best baby portrait.

SETUP

Give each player a paper plate and a crayon.

PLAY

Putting the plate on top of her head, each player has to draw a picture of a "baby." When everyone is done, the player whose portrait is judged the best wins.

·········

THE BAG GAME

EQUIPMENT

One paper supermarket bag or small shopping bag for each guest.

PLAYERS

6+

OBJECT

To be the first player to remove the bag on her head.

SETUP

Give each guest a bag and ask her to place the bag over her head.

PLAY

Now ask the players to each take off something they really don't need. Most of them will take off a ring or a shoe or a bracelet.

Whoever takes off the bag first is the winner. But the other players don't know that: Keep asking the ones who are still wearing bags to take more things off for a few rounds. If they still don't get it, tell them to take the bag off their heads—*that's* the thing they really don't need!

·········

THE DIAPER GAME

EQUIPMENT

A baby diaper for each player.

PLAYERS

6+

OBJECT

To get the diaper with the messy "surprise."

SETUP

Create a "poop" inside one of the diapers using chocolate, baby food prunes, or anything else that would look like a good "mess," then refold it. Put all the diapers in a basket or on a tray.

PLAY

Pass the basket to each guest. Tell them they'll each need a diaper to play the next game—but that no one should open their diaper until the signal is given. Once everyone has a diaper, ask the guests to open their diapers at the same time. The one with the "surprise" in her diaper wins.

·········

FEED THE BABY

EQUIPMENT

For each team:

- 1 pudding cup
- 1 spoon
- 1 garbage bag
- 1 blindfold

PLAYERS

6+

OBJECT

To be the first team to finish its pudding.

SETUP

Divide the players into teams of two. Dress each player in a large plastic bag in which holes have been cut for their arms and legs. Then blindfold each player.

PLAY

At a signal, each player has to feed the pudding to her partner as fast as she can. The team that finishes their pudding first wins.

·········

FEEDING TIME

EQUIPMENT

- 8 or more jars of different baby foods

- Enough plastic spoons to go around

- Paper

- Pencil for each player

PLAYERS

6+

OBJECT

To correctly identify the most baby foods.

SETUP

Put a little of each food on a disposable plate with a number written beside it. Give each guest a spoon, a piece of paper, and a pencil.

PLAY

Pass the plates around the room. Guests have to taste the food on each numbered plate and write down the correct taste next to the number it's been given. Whoever has the most right answers wins.

Be sure to keep a master list of which food is which.

This is a good time to have a camera at hand—some of the faces the players make will be priceless.

Instead of putting the food on paper plates, you can cover the labels on the jars of food, number the jars, and pass *them* around instead.

·········

HEY, GOOD LOOKING!

EQUIPMENT
- 10 or so baby items, such as a diaper, bottle, pacifier, etc.

- Pencils

- Paper

PLAYERS
6+

OBJECT
To remember the most about what the mother-to-be is wearing.

SETUP
Arrange the baby items on a tray. Give each player paper and pencil.

PLAY
Ask the mother-to-be to pass the tray around and then to leave the room. Once she's gone tell the players to write down as many things as they can remember about what the guest of honor was wearing (color of her outfit, hair accessories, earrings, shoes, etc.) The player who has the most correct answers wins.

·········

I LOVE MY TEDDY BEAR

EQUIPMENT
A teddy bear

PLAYERS
6+

OBJECT
To kiss a teddy bear, then kiss the player on the left in the same place.

SETUP
Make sure that the guests are sitting in a relatively continuous circle. Encourage them to be creative as you tell them what to do.

PLAY
The first player has to kiss the teddy bear—anywhere on his body—then pass the bear to the person on her left, who has to do likewise, and so on around the circle.

When that round is done, tell the player who started the first round that she has to kiss the person to her left in the same place that she'd kissed the teddy bear. For instance, if she'd kissed the bear on the nose, she now has to kiss the player to her left on the nose.

It's important that you don't tell guests about the second round beforehand. And if you encourage players to be creative during the first round, the second round will prove hilarious.

·········

POTATO PUSH

EQUIPMENT

- 2 pairs of panty hose

- 2 medium potatoes

- 2 medium to large oranges

PLAYERS

6+

OBJECT

To be the first player to gets her orange across the finish line.

SETUP

Establish a "racecourse" with a well-defined beginning and end, ten to twelve feet long.

Pick two players to compete against each other.

Put a potato in one leg of the panty hose and tie the other leg around the waist of each racer so that the potato hangs down between her legs.

Place an orange on the floor in front of each player.

PLAY

Each racer has to swing her potato so that it hits the orange to push it forward. The first one to get to the finish line wins.

·········

SNIFF, SNIFF

EQUIPMENT
- 10 or so diapers

- 10 or so different scents (vanilla, baby powder, Worcestershire sauce—whatever you can find around the house)

- Paper

- Pencils

PLAYERS
6+

OBJECT
To correctly identify the scent in each diaper.

SETUP
Pour or rub each diaper with a different scent. Give each guest a piece of paper and a pencil.

PLAY
Pass the diapers around and let each guest sniff them and write down the scents. Whoever guesses the most scents correctly wins.

·········

SO BIG RIBBON GAME

EQUIPMENT
- A spool of ribbon
- Scissors

PLAYERS
6+

OBJECT
To make the closest guess as to how much ribbon will go around the expectant mother's belly.

SETUP
The expectant mother stands in the middle of the room so that all the guests can take a good look at her belly.

PLAY
The spool of ribbon is passed around and each player has to cut off the amount of ribbon that she thinks will go around the expectant mother's belly. The player who guesses most accurately wins.

WEDDING SHOWER GAMES

· · · · · · · · ·

THE DATE GAME

PLAYERS
6+

OBJECT
To be the player whose birthday is the closest to the wedding day.

SETUP
Make sure all the guests are in the same room.

PLAY
Starting with the person sitting to the left of the bride, each guest tells her birthday. The guest whose date is closest to the wedding wins a prize.

· · · · · · · · ·

THE NEWLYWED GAME

EQUIPMENT
• Paper and pencil for each guest

PLAYERS
6+

OBJECT
To get the most correct answers to questions about the bride and groom.

SETUP

Before the day of the shower, the hostess or one of the guests should prepare a list of questions about the bride and groom. For example:

When is the wedding day?

Where is the wedding reception?

Where are the bride and groom going on their honeymoon? Be as specific as possible.

Within a certain number of months, how long have the bride and groom been together?

Where did they go on their first date?

Where were they when they first kissed?

Where did they meet?

What first attracted the bride to the groom?

What first attracted the groom to the bride?

On a scale of zero to five, how much does the bride like her in-laws?

On a scale of zero to five, how much does the groom like his in-laws?

PLAY

The guests and the bride-to-be write down their answers, then compare them. The guest with the most correct answers wins.

VARIATION

Call the groom before the shower and ask him the same questions. After the game, the hostess can report on how the groom's answers compared with bride's.

·········

OLD WHAT'S-HIS-NAME

EQUIPMENT
A clothespin for each guest

PLAYERS
6+

OBJECT
To get the most clothespins by catching the other guests mentioning the groom's name.

SETUP
Give each guest a clothespin as she arrives and tell her *not* to mention the groom's name during the shower, but to listen for the other guests to "slip up" and say his name.

PLAY
If Guest A catches Guest B saying the groom's name, Guest B has to give up her clothespin to Guest A. At the end of the shower, the person with the most clothespins is declared the winner.

·········

PURSE BINGO

EQUIPMENT
- Paper

- Pencils

- All the players' purses

PLAYERS
6+

OBJECT
To get the most points based on the contents of one's purse.

SETUP
Make a list of common and uncommon things that can be found in a woman's purse (or select from the list below), assigning each item a point value. Each guest should have her purse on her lap.

PLAY
As the hostess calls out each item on the list, any guest who has that item in her purse pulls it out and gives herself the appropriate number of points.

Bingo Master List
The scores are suggestions. Feel free to vary them.

2 points
Wallet
Pen
Credit card receipt

3 points
Ten-dollar bill
Supermarket discount card
The player's own business card

5 points
Toothpick
Postage stamp
Mirror
Photo of a male relative

10 points
Rubber band
Hand lotion
Flashlight

15 points
Library card
Sunscreen
Matches
Dental floss

20 points
Nail polish
Toothbrush
Band-Aid

25 points
Whistle
Condom
Scotch tape

Play continues until each item has been called. The guest with the most points wins.

VARIATIONS

The bride holds the "master list" and decides what "item" should be found. The first guest to present that item receives the points for that round. Each guest can keep her own score or someone can be the designated scorekeeper.

·········

RICE IS NICE

EQUIPMENT

- 2 pounds of uncooked white rice

- 15–20 paper clips

- 1 large bowl

- 1 blindfold

- A timer or a watch with a second hand

PLAYERS

6+

OBJECT

To find the most paper clips.

SETUP

Put the rice and paper clips in the bowl. Mix well and place the bowl on a table. Establish a time limit (one to two minutes) for each turn, then blindfold each guest.

PLAY

The blindfolded guest tries to find as many paper clips as possible. Whoever finds the most paper clips wins.

. . . .

SMOOCHY SONGS

EQUIPMENT

- 8–10 slips of paper

- Paper

- Pencils

- A bowl large enough to hold the slips of paper

PLAYERS

6+

OBJECT

To be the team that comes up with the most songs.

SETUP

Write a different wedding word on each slip of paper (e.g., MARRIAGE, RING, HONEYMOON, etc.) and put them in a bowl. Divide the guests into two teams.

PLAY

Team A draws a slip of paper and has to sing at least five words of a song that includes that word. Say they've drawn LOVE. They might sing, "But will you love me tomorrow . . ." Now Team B has to come up with a song that includes that same word. Team B might sing "Love, love me do, you know I love you . . ." Then the turn goes back to Team A, and so on until one of the teams can't come up with another LOVE song. In that case, the other team gets one point.

Next, it's Team B's turn to draw a word. Play continues until all the words have been used. The team with the most points wins.

....

WEDDING DRESS

EQUIPMENT
Rolls of white toilet paper

PLAYERS
6+

OBJECT
To design the winning wedding dress out of toilet paper.

SETUP
Divide the guests into teams of three to five people and give each team a roll of toilet paper.

Each team chooses a model and designs a "wedding dress" out of toilet paper. Accessories are allowed (earrings, bouquets, wedding ring, etc.), but they have to be made out of toilet paper.

PLAY
The teams have five minutes or so to dress their "bride," after which the real bride picks the winner.

Don't forget to be "camera-ready" for this one.

·········

WEDDING NIGHT

EQUIPMENT

- A suitcase

- Items of clothing and/or accessories (sunglasses, men's underwear, bra, pajamas, etc.)

- A blindfold

PLAYERS

6+

OBJECT

To put on all the clothes in the suitcase while blindfolded.

SETUP

Put all the items in the suitcase.

PLAY

Tell the bride that the wedding is over and it's her wedding night. The place where she and her new husband are spending the night loses all electricity and the bride has to get ready for her wedding night in complete darkness.

Blindfold the bride, hand her the suitcase, and tell her she has to put everything in the suitcase on over her clothes.

Be sure to have a nice reward for the bride after this one. How about a pretty frame for the Polaroid you'll be taking when she's done getting dressed?

PARLOR GAMES

BINGO
Bingo with Cards

BUNCO

CHARADES
Fortune Cookies Charades
Headlines Charades
Beginner's Charades
Adverbs
Action Spelling

HOLLYWOOD CONNECTIONS

JELLY BEAN TASTE TEST

MOVIE TITLES

PROVERBS

SARDINES

SCAVENGER HUNT
One-Upmanship Scavenger Hunt
Downtown Scavenger Hunt
Kiddie Scavenger Hunt

SHOUT IT OUT!

SPIN THE BOTTLE

WHO AM I?

BINGO

A do-it-yourself version of the popular game played in church basements all over North America.

EQUIPMENT
- Paper
- Pencils
- 100 small pieces of paper
- A container for the numbers: a hat, a bowl, or a big jar
- Markers to put over the numbers: pennies, buttons, checkers, etc.

PLAYERS
3+

OBJECT
To be the first to fill in a row of numbers horizontally, vertically, or diagonally.

SETUP
Write the numbers 1 through 100 on the small pieces of paper and put them in the container.

Make Bingo cards by drawing a 5×5 grid on a piece of paper. Write the letters B-I-N-G-O across the top. Then choose numbers at random and write them in each square according to the following parameters:

Row B: any numbers between 1 and 20

Row I: 21 to 40

Row N: 41 to 60

Row G: 61 to 80

Row O: 81 to 100.

B	I	N	G	O
4	30	49	63	88
17	26	53	72	92
9	33	60	79	83
11	40	44	61	90
2	22	51	74	94

Give each player about 20 markers and leave a pile of extra markers close by.

Choose one person to be the Caller for the first game.

PLAY

The Caller mixes up the small pieces of paper, takes one out and reads the number to the players. A player who has that number on her card puts a marker on it. The Caller continues calling numbers until a player has filled one row with markers either horizontally, vertically, or diagonally.

According to custom, that player yells, "Bingo!" and wins the game.

HISTORY

The game, supposedly invented by an Italian nobleman, is still played in Italy, where it's known as *Tombola*.

VARIATIONS

Players have to fill up the whole card before calling "Bingo."

Bingo with Cards requires a deck of cards and chips (75 for 2 players; 108 for 3 players; 138 for 4 players; 165 for 5 players; 189 for 6 players) or pennies (100 or more) to play.

Game 1: Players are dealt five cards. One at a time, the dealer turns up cards from the rest of the deck. If a turned-up card matches in rank, the player puts chips that equal the numerical value of that card on every one of his cards that matches; thirteen chips on a king, twelve on a queen, etc.

The first player to have chips on all five of his cards wins the other players' chips. In case of a tie, the winners share the total number of chips.

Game 2: Players ante to a pot. All players, including the dealer, are dealt five cards. From another fifty-two-card deck, the dealer turns up cards one by one. When a player's card is matched, that card is turned facedown. The first player to turn over all his cards wins.

• • • • • • • • •

BUNCO

It's not just a game—it's practically a cult. Twelve members take turns hosting monthly or weekly get-togethers at which they eat, drink, gossip, and generally have an uproarious time. The rules vary wildly; here are the basics.

EQUIPMENT
- 12 personal score sheets
- some scratch paper
- Pencils
- 3 tables
- 9 dice
- 1 bell

PLAYERS
12

OBJECT
To roll as many dice as possible that match the number of the round.

SETUP

The host assigns numbers to the three tables: #1 (aka the "head table"), #2, and #3. She places paper and pencil and three dice on each table, and puts a bell on table #1.

Players contribute a designated amount of money—$4 or more—at the beginning of each set of six rounds. For the first round, they either select their seats randomly or by draw (e.g., from a facedown array of the twelve score sheets, each of which has the numbers 1, 2, or 3 written in the corner). Players sitting opposite each other are partners for the first round.

Each table needs a scorekeeper—someone who volunteers or is elected by the roll of a die—to keep track of points scored by teams during a round.

If the host has not already done so, the players write the numbers 1 through 6 in a column on their score sheets.

PLAY

The scorekeeper at the head table rings the bell to signal the beginning of the round. The scorekeeper at each table goes first, rolling the three dice. In each round, a player is trying to roll the number that corresponds to the number of the round—the number that's "up" for the round.

So, in Round One, the player is trying to roll as many "ones" as possible. If a player rolls a one, she scores 1 point. If she rolls two ones, 2 points. If she rolls three ones, it's a "bunco," worth 21 points.

Every time a player rolls the number that's up for that round, she rolls again. When and if she fails to roll the number that's up, she passes the dice to the player to her left.

While trying to roll buncos, players can score extra points by rolling three of a kind of a number that isn't up. Threes of a kind score 5 points, and the player rolls again.

There are two ways to win a round: A player can roll a bunco (aka "true" or "natural" bunco). When a player rolls a natural bunco, she shouts out "Bunco!" and the scorekeeper at the head table rings the bell; or a team can win the round by rolling a total that adds up to 21 points or more (aka baby bunco). As soon as they reach 21, the scorekeeper for their table calls, "Bunco!" and the scorekeeper at the head table rings the bell.

Once the bell is rung, all play stops. The teams with the most points at the two non-bunco tables are declared winners.

In case of a tie at either table, there's a "roll-off." To determine who goes first in a roll-off, each player rolls all three dice. High total will roll first (but doesn't score for the roll). Points are scored for rolling buncos and numbers that correspond to the round just completed. The first player to reach 5 points wins.

The winners at each table put a "W" next to the 1 on their scorecards, the losers write in an "L." A player who scored a bunco adds a "B" to her "W"—her partner does not.

Before the next round begins, the players rearrange their seating, taking their scorecards with them.

The Table 1 winners stay there; the losers move to Table 3.

The Table 2 winners move to Table 1.

The Table 3 winners move to Table 2.

The teams that stay at the same table break up as a team; one of them shifts to the right or left so that each will be partnered with someone new. The new arrivals become their new partners. The next five rounds are played just like Round One, except that in Round Two the number two is up, and so on.

Six rounds make a "set." Most bunco groups play four sets per get-together. When the four sets have been completed, the top winner is the player with the most "W's."

If there's a tie, the player with the most W's *and* B's wins the game. If there's *still* a tie, there must be a roll-off: Points are scored for rolling sixes (the round just completed) and buncos. The first player to reach 5 points wins.

FYI

Food and drink are important ingredients in Bunco. Groups develop their own menus—everything from soda and munchies to four-course dinners—and establish timing for breaks between sets to refresh drinks or serve dinner or dessert.

Besides the boxed versions of Bunco that include bells, dice, score sheets, and even a fuzzy die, the game has spawned cookbooks, T-shirts, coffee mugs, time clocks, and a welcome mat. If you want to catch the Bunco wave, start at www.worldbunco.com.

PRIZES

A player is eligible to win only one prize per session. Here's an example from a group that contributes five dollars apiece.

Most Wins	$20.00
Most Buncos	$15.00
Last Bunco	$10.00
Most Baby Buncos	$ 5.00
50/50 prize (wins = losses)	$ 5.00
Fewest Wins	$ 5.00

VARIATIONS

Probably because the game spread largely by word-of-mouth, Bunco has more variations in its rules than any other game in this book. Here are a few.

Instead of being numbered 1 to 3, the tables are labeled "Head," "Middle," and "Losing."

As players win buncos during the four sets, they're given a special prize to hold (a fuzzy die seems to be the most common). At the end of the final set, the player who's holding it gets the "Last Bunco" prize.

When someone rolls a bunco, the other players scramble to grab for the dice. Each die is worth an extra point to the players who snag it.

Some groups design elaborate scorecards that include the number for all four sets, with their group logo/name at the top.

Some groups play with a "wipe-out" (e.g., after the first round, if a player rolls three ones, she and her partner lose all their current points in that round).

If a round is won by a non-natural bunco, the other tables keep playing until one team at each table scores a bunco of either type. Their bunco doesn't earn them a "B," though. Just a "W."

HISTORY

Bunco has a shady past: A crooked gambler from England brought it to San Francisco during the gold rush under the name "Banco." Eventually, the game was renamed Bunco (also spelled "Bunko"). Combined with a Bunco card game, the two began to be played in the late 1900s in what were called "bunco parlors"—at which point the word "bunco" entered the language as a synonym for "swindle or cheat." The first police "bunco squads" were established to raid bunco parlors during Prohibition. As the parlors closed down, at-home bunco spread to the suburbs. Today, the game is mostly played by women—not gold miners.

·········

CHARADES

Also known as "The Game," because in 1930s and 1940s America, it was "the" parlor game. And maybe still is.

EQUIPMENT

- Pencils

- Paper

- A stopwatch or watch with a second hand

OBJECT

To act out a phrase in the shortest amount of time.

PLAYERS

6+ (two teams of 4 or 5 or more is ideal)

SETUP

Players divide up into two teams. Each team goes to a separate room and brainstorms to come up with the names of movies, songs, books, TV shows, plays, or famous phrases or quotations that the other team will have to act out.

They write their choices (as many as there are members of the other team—more if they have time) on small pieces of paper, fold them up, and return to the "parlor."

FYI

The two-minute time limit can be extended for new players or younger children.

One person is designated Timekeeper. Each team member has two minutes to convey his charade to his team.

PLAY

The first player selects a charade that the other team has chosen. He has up to one minute to read it to himself and think about how to best act it out. He signals to the Timekeeper when he's ready to begin.

Without making a sound or using props of any kind, and with the help of the signals (see sidebar below), he acts out his charade. The Timekeeper keeps track of the time it takes each player to convey his charade.

If the playing team doesn't get the correct answer within the two minutes, the Timekeeper calls "time" and the player tells his teammates what the charade was.

The teams alternate until each team member has had a turn.

SCORING

The Timekeeper adds up the minutes at the end. The lowest score wins.

The Signals

There are some standard signals and shortcuts to help the speech-deprived player get his message across.

First, define the category:

Book title: Unfold your hands as if they were a book opening.
Movie title: Look through one hand rounded like a lens while your other hand cranks an old-fashioned movie camera.
Play title: Open your hands as if you were spreading a theater curtain open.
Song title: Open your mouth as if you're singing.
TV show: Draw a rectangular TV screen in the air in front of you.
Quote or Phrase: Make quotation marks in the air with your fingers.

Next, to convey things like:
The number of words in the title. Hold up the number of fingers (e.g., five if it's a five-word charade).
The word you want to work on first. Hold up the number of fingers again (e.g., three if it's the third word).

The number of syllables in the word. Lay the number of fingers on the inside of your outstretched forearm. If you're going to work a word syllable by syllable, let your team know which syllable you're working on: Lay the corresponding number of fingers on your arm again (e.g., two if it's the second syllable).

If you decide to act out your charade as **the entire concept**, sweep your arms up and around in a big circle.

When someone makes a correct guess, point at your nose with one hand, and at the guesser with your other.

"Sounds like" (going for a rhyme with the word or syllable): Pull on your earlobe, then act out the rhyme.

"More" or "longer version" (e.g., if someone says "run" and you want them to say "running"): Stretch out an invisible piece of taffy between your hands.

"Shorter version": Chop the air with your hand.

If you're looking for the **"past tense"** of a verb: Wave your hand over your shoulder toward your back.

The **"small word"** sign is given by holding your index finger and thumb sideways and about an inch apart. (Works for "a," "an," "it," "is," "of," and the rest.) Sometimes the word "a" is signaled by steepling fingertips together,

"I" is signaled by pointing at your eye.

The **"T"** sign—one index finger upright, the other across the top—signals "the," "this," "that," "than," and a slew of others.

Even though the use of props is forbidden in serious play, pointing to a woman in the group for "her" or "she" or to a man for "him" or "he" is okay.

VARIATIONS

The game can be played with team captains, who can be decided on at the beginning of the game (by draw or election). The captains draft their teams taking turns back and forth.

Fortune Cookies Charades is played by saving the fortunes (you can buy the cookies by the bag and serve them to your guests) and using them for a rousing round. No pencils needed.

Headlines Charades takes more prep work: Start collecting interesting/ridiculous headlines—the best are from the tabloids.

Beginner's Charades is just the game modified for children. No teams, no timing. Each person thinks of a charade, writes it down, and signs it. The charades are selected from the pile and the person who wrote it down isn't allowed to play. The player has to convey his charade to the whole group (except for the person who wrote it down) until they get it. Beginners can be helped along by the more seasoned players.

Adverbs (aka In the Manner of the Word) uses adverbs as the charade—you know, those words that end in "ly." One player leaves the room. The remaining players come up with an adverb—*sweetly, clumsily, defiantly, hopefully,* and so on.

When the first player is called back, he asks the other players to do something—answer the door, play the piano, clean up the room, throw an imaginary pitch—in the manner of the word.

When he guesses the right adverb, he names the player who helped him the most to figure it out. That player is next to leave the room.

Action Spelling is a silly game. First, let the group decide on movements or sounds (no letters or words) that will stand for every letter of the alphabet: Steepled fingers for A, a buzz for B, looking through binoculars for C (see), and so on. Then see if your audience can guess the word you're trying to spell.

Trivia

A long time ago, in a galaxy far, far away (the 1950s), charades was a popular prime-time game show called *Pantomime Quiz*. In it, two teams of four clever celebrities acted out charades that were sent in by home viewers. Some of the players of the time: Carol Burnett, Howard Morris (a Sid Caesar sidekick), and Tom Poston (who played George Utley on *Newhart*).

·········

HOLLYWOOD CONNECTIONS

A game for movie mavens. And just like in Hollywood, it's who you know.

EQUIPMENT
A reference book like *Leonard Maltin's Movie Guide* or access to www.imdb.com.

PLAYERS
2+

OBJECT
To link actors and actresses by the films they've been in.

SETUP
The players agree on the number of points they'll end the game with. 1 point is cutthroat (and can be over in a flash), 3 makes for a short game, 5 is more leisurely. One player is selected to start.

PLAY
Player 1 says, "Dustin Hoffman." Player 2 has to come up with an actor who has appeared in a film with Dustin Hoffman. Thinking of *Rain Man*, Player 2 says, "Tom Cruise." Now it's Player 3's turn: he says, "Renée Zellweger," (thinking of *Jerry Maguire*). Notice that the movies are never mentioned, just the actors.

Thinking of *Bridget Jones' Diary*, Player 4 says, "Hugh Grant." It's Player 1's turn again. Let's say that Player 1 can't think of a movie that Renée Zellweger and Hugh Grant appeared in together. He has two choices: ignore the connection and say "Julia Roberts," or challenge Player 4 to name the movie. If Player 4 was bluffing, and can't name a movie that Renée Zellweger and Hugh Grant appeared in, she loses a point. If she tells Player 1 that she was thinking of *Bridget Jones' Diary*, Player 1 is free to check the answer. Once he agrees that Player 4 made a legitimate connection, Player 4 gets a point.

Let's say that Player 4 had said, "Clark Gable" instead of "Hugh Grant."

If Player 1 challenged and it was proven that Renée and Clark had indeed never been in a move together, Player 1 would get the point.

The player who got the point starts the next round, choosing a new actor. Once a name has been used as a link or a bluff, that name is out of play and can't be used again.

Play proceeds until one player—the winner!—has reached the agreed-upon number of points for the game.

·········

JELLY BEAN TASTE TEST

Have you tried the banana cream pie?

EQUIPMENT
- Gourmet jelly beans
- Small bowls
- Pencil
- Paper

PLAYERS
4+

OBJECT
To guess the most flavors.

SETUP
The jelly beans are separated, and each flavor is placed in a separate bowl.

PLAY
As the host passes the bowls around one by one, she announces a number (1 for the first bowl, etc.) The players have to taste that jelly bean and write the correct flavor next to the number.

When all the jelly beans have been tasted, the host goes through each number and the players say aloud what flavor they've guessed.

The player who makes the most correct guesses wins.

·········

MOVIE TITLES

Conveniently adaptable for TV shows and song titles, too.

PLAYERS
2+

OBJECT
To think of movie titles that start with the last letter of the movie named by the previous player.

PLAY
One player starts by naming a movie—any movie. The next player has to name a movie whose title begins with the last letter of the movie just named, and so on.

A player who can't come up with the name of a movie within a designated time limit—say, ten seconds—is out.

Here's an example:

The Godfather

Revenge of the Nerds

Sabrina

All About Eve

Edward Scissorhands

"The" in a title doesn't count, so *The Shawshank Redemption* could follow *Edward Scissorhands*.

. . . .

PROVERBS

A game that's as old and quaint as the proverbs and sayings it's played with. AKA Hidden Proverbs

PLAYERS
2+

OBJECT
To guess the hidden proverb.

SETUP
One person is chosen to be It, and leaves the room. The others decide on a proverb, a saying like, "The grass is always greener on the other side"; "A rolling stone gathers no moss"; or "Every cloud has a silver lining."

PLAY
When It comes back, he asks questions—any kind of questions—of the players, going clockwise around the room, such as, "What did you have for lunch today?" or "How's your uncle Louie?"

The first player has to answer the first question with a sentence that contains the first word of the proverb, the second player has to use the second word, and so on.

Here's an example of how it might work. Say the proverb is "The grass is always greener on the other side."

The first player has it easy. When It asks, "What did you have for lunch today?" all he has to do is put "The" in his answer: "A burger with all *the* trimmings and fries on the side."

When It asks, "How's your uncle Louie?" a player might say, "He just got a job at a cemetery. He has to keep the graves neat, trim the trees, mow the *grass*, and make sure the ghost doesn't scare away the visitors."

Play continues until It guesses the proverb. The last player to answer a question is It for the next round.

RULES

The hidden word has to stand by itself—don't try to hide "grass" in "grass-land," for example.

VARIATION

Instead of proverbs, you can use well-known sayings like in the following list.

Here today, gone tomorrow.

I can't believe I ate the whole thing.

Age before beauty.

A bird in the hand is worth two in the bush.

All that glitters is not gold.

Blood is thicker than water.

Don't count your chickens before they're hatched.

Handsome is as handsome does.

·········

SARDINES

A game of Hide & Seek with the emphasis on the former. Best played in-doors and in a big house with lots of good hiding places.

PLAYERS

4+

OBJECT

To find the Sardine.

SETUP

All the players assemble in one room and choose a person to be the Sardine.

PLAY

The Sardine leaves the room and hides—preferably in a place that's big enough to accommodate all the players. After a specified amount of time—say, a count of 50 or 100—the other players go looking for him or her.

The first player to find the Sardine hides in the same place. The next player to find them hides there, too, and so on until the last player finds everyone else hiding in that one place. The player who found the Sardine first gets to be the Sardine in the next game.

Tip

We're serious about finding a place that's big enough to accommodate everyone, so that once you're all together, you'll still be hard to find. And you'll probably need some giggle room.

· · · · · · · · ·

SCAVENGER HUNT

A great neighborhood party game for older kids and/or adults.

EQUIPMENT

- A list of items for each team

- A bag to carry them in

PLAYERS

6+ (at least 3 or 4 scavengers to a team)

OBJECT

To be the first team to find all the items on the scavenger list.

SETUP

Each team is given the same list of items, and told to return with as many as they can find within a certain amount of time—a half-hour or even two hours, depending on the length of the list.

PLAY

Teams go door-to-door in the neighborhood, asking for the items on their list, and return within the time limit with as many items as they can find.

Any team that doesn't return within the stated time limit is disqualified.

Here are some ideas to get you started:

Easy List

Feather

A size 10 shoe

Unburned candle

Ace of spades

Magazine that's more than a year old

Dead plant

Harder List

Egg cup

Pencil shorter than 2" long

Blue candle

Receipt for more than $100

Photo of John F. Kennedy

Mystery novel by an author with three names (or a middle initial)

Garden statue (1 extra point for a gnome!)

VARIATIONS

In **One-Upmanship Scavenger Hunt**, teams get exactly the same list and compete to see who can come back with the

Highest bouncing ball

Longest winter scarf

Fattest magazine

Biggest stuffed animal

Oldest penny

Downtown Scavenger Hunt can be played in the business section of a small town, neighborhood, or your local mall. The items on the list should be things that don't need to be bought, such as

Business card that's signed by the manager of a store

20% OFF sale sign

Coffee container with top

Restaurant menu signed by the manager

Free sample of anything

Kiddie Scavenger Hunt is played in a house or yard. You'll need at least 14 objects that can be easily hidden—a teddy bear, a cheese grater, a dictionary, and so on. When a team finds an item, they put it in a bag and cross it off their list. The team that finds the most items in a set amount of time wins.

· · · · · · · · ·

SHOUT IT OUT!

Big crowd in a big space? Here's your game.

PLAYERS
10+ (two teams of at least 5 players)

OBJECT
To guess the phrase that the other team is shouting.

SETUP
Each team decides on a common phrase that has the same number of words as members of the team. One word is assigned to each player.

The teams stand as far away from each other as they can get.

PLAY

At a given signal—and at exactly the same time—the first team shouts their words all together. The other team has to guess what the phrase is. If they don't get it on the first shout, the shouting team can try again. If they still don't get it, the shouting team takes one more turn at shouting.

Teams take turns, and after a given number of rounds, the team with the highest number of points wins.

SCORING

If a team correctly guesses the other team's phrase on the first shout, they're awarded 3 points; second shout, 2 points; third shout, 1 point. If a team can't guess the phrase at all, the shouting team gets 1 point.

·········

SPIN THE BOTTLE

Who hasn't played it?

EQUIPMENT
• A soda bottle

PLAYERS
4+

OBJECT
To kiss and be kissed.

SETUP
The players sit in a circle—traditionally on the floor—with a bottle lying on its side in the middle.

PLAY
One player spins the bottle. If, when the bottle stops, it's pointing to a member of the opposite sex, the spinner kisses that person. If not, the spinner spins again.

A player who's just been kissed gets to be the next spinner.

·········

WHO AM I?

The perfect icebreaker for a big party.

EQUIPMENT
- Name tags that have been filled out with the names of famous people, dead or alive.

- Pins or tape

OBJECT
To find out "who you are."

SETUP
As guests enter, the host pins or sticks a name tag on their backs without letting them see the name.

PLAY
Players ask questions of the other guests to try to find out who they are supposed to be. The rules are simple.

Only questions that can be answered "yes" or "no" are allowed.

Once a player thinks he knows who he is, he can ask the host if he's right. If he's right, he can take his tag off. If he's wrong, he goes back into the crowd to ask more questions.

Questions to Help You Get Started
Am I . . .

female?

living?

an historical figure?

a fictional character?

an American?

famous for my looks?

famous for my talent?

famous for my charm?

VARIATIONS

Sometimes the game is played with one extra rule: A player can ask only three questions of one person at a time. Then she has to move on to ask her next three questions of another person.

Tips

Don't forget to cover up the mirrors in the party room!

Some overachievers who've already guessed who they are may want another name so they can go back and try again. Have extras nametags on hand just in case!

If mostly couples are coming to your party, fill out the name tags with famous couples and distribute the name tags randomly. Besides figuring out who they are, your guests also need to find their name tag partners. But if their partners haven't figured out who they themselves are yet, the player in the know is not allowed to tell them.

Here's a short list to get you started.

ADAM AND EVE

MARC ANTONY AND CLEOPATRA

ARNOLD SCHWARZENEGGER AND MARIA SHRIVER

BILL AND HILLARY CLINTON

HUMPHREY BOGART AND LAUREN BACALL

DAGWOOD AND BLONDIE

MURDER GAMES

KILLER | MURDER

MAFIA

Werewolf

·········

KILLER

Best played while the participants are going about their business at a weekend house party, on vacation, or in a college dorm.

EQUIPMENT
Playing cards equaling the number of players, one of which is the ace of spades

PLAYERS
6+

OBJECT
If you're the Killer, to get away with murder.
    If you're not, to stay alive and try to guess the identity of the Killer.

SETUP
The cards are set facedown on a table and each player chooses one, being careful not to let anyone else see their card. The player who chooses the ace is the Killer. The number of kills he is allowed to make should roughly equal one-third of the number of players, a number that is decided before play begins:

    6–7 players—2 kills

    8–10 players—3 kills

    11 players or more—4 kills

Players decide on a time for a meeting, at which time all participants must show up—dead or alive. The meeting should be scheduled for a few hours to a full day after the game begins.

PLAY

The Killer flashes the ace of spades to a victim, who must remain frozen for one minute before resuming what he was doing. During that time he is not permitted to speak or move. After a minute he can go on about his business, *without revealing to anyone that he's been killed.*

If a player is unlucky enough to witness a kill—and the Killer knows it—the Killer has to kill the Witness if he has any kills left. But if the Killer doesn't have any kills left, the Killer is the unlucky one, sure to be accused by the Witness, who has to wait until the meeting to tell the other players what he's seen.

SCORING

At the meeting, the victims speak first. But they're only allowed to say when and where they were killed—nothing more. They cannot tell anyone who killed them.

After the other players discuss and compare notes regarding each other's whereabouts, they vote on who they think the Killer is.

If they're correct, the Killer confesses and the correct guessers each score a point. If they're incorrect, the Killer gets 1 point for each wrong guess.

Trivia

We know of a family who played this game for years, with their five children and scads of friends on weekends and holidays. After the kids grew up, the parents would go away with other couples for long weekends, and they'd play a new game every day.

One of their guests went down in Killer history for the Crapper Caper by sliding the ace of spades under the bathroom door while Father Steve, a priest friend, was taking care of his business.

Then there was the Killer who taped the ace to the bathroom mirror: Whoever went into the bathroom was killed automatically. After three people went in and came out, the Killer ran in, removed the card, and got away with murder.

·········

MAFIA

With all due apologies to our friends in the business. We're just having a little harmless fun, fellas . . . heh, heh, heh.

EQUIPMENT

- Small pieces of paper: 1 labeled GODFATHER; 1+ labeled MAFIA (the number of Mafia in a game is typically one-third to one-quarter of the total group); and the rest blank (TOWNSPEOPLE).

- Larger pieces of paper on which certain roles are described.*

PLAYERS

7+

OBJECT

The Mafia's goal is to kill enough Townspeople to outnumber them; the Townspeople's objective is to find out who among them is Mafia and eliminate them all.

SETUP

A Moderator is chosen. Each player, except for the Moderator, draws one of the small slips of paper to find out if they are going to be Mafia or one of the Townspeople.

PLAY

The Moderator asks everyone to close their eyes and "go to sleep." This phase of the game is referred to as "Night."

The Townspeople keep their eyes closed while the Moderator tells the Godfather and the Mafia to look up so they know who their partners in crime are.

Special Roles

Moderators are all-powerful and can invent their own special roles as they're needed. But these roles are standard to the game.

The Doctor is one of the Townspeople. Before nightfall, the Doctor can choose one person to save. If this person is a Mafia target, she survives the Night, and the Moderator announces the next morning that there was an unsuccessful attempt on that person's life. If the player is Mafia, it doesn't matter. (Some Moderators allow the Doctor to save himself; others don't.)

The Guardian Angel is told the identity of the Mafia by the Moderator on the first Night. The Angel has to sleep when the Townspeople do, but during the Day, she can try to tell the Townspeople who the Mafia are. She has to do it without arousing suspicion, though, or she'll be killed for sure.

The Sheriff is also one of the Townspeople. Every Night, the Sheriff can investigate one person by pointing to that person. The Moderator will inform the Sheriff (by nodding or thumbs-up or down) whether that person is Mafia—*unless* he's the Godfather. The Godfather is immune to investigation. If the Godfather is investigated, the Moderator will see to it that he comes up innocent.

Extra Special Roles

If group size warrants it, the Moderator can add these Special Roles.

The Devil's Advocate is a Mafia player who investigates the Townspeople at Night, trying to figure out who the Sheriff is, and then trying to get him killed either through lynching or informing the Mafia of his identity. If investigated by the Sheriff, the Moderator will identify the Devil's Advocate as innocent.

The Witness can "peek" during the killing phase. Not a great role—you know what can happen to someone who witnesses a Mafia killing—but if played right, can have its rewards.

If the number of players is huge, you can add the roles of **Masons**, Townspeople who are aware of each other and who know for sure that they're innocent.

A **Serial Killer** or two can make things interesting: They operate on their own and win the game only if they're the last one left in the game. They're allowed one kill a Night just like the Mafia.

The Murder

The Mafia choose someone to kill by pointing and/or nodding, but with as little movement as possible so the players near them don't sense the movement.

The Moderator tells the Mafia to go to sleep and assigns roles to the Townspeople by waking them up individually and showing them the larger pieces of paper that describe their roles.

After that's done, "Day" begins. The Moderator wakes everyone up and announces who was killed during the Night. The dead player can observe the rest of the game, but can't participate.

The Lynching

The entire group, including the Mafia, now has to discuss which player should be lynched for the murder. The Mafia, of course, will lie to uphold their innocence, but eventually the group has to vote on who will be lynched. If a player wants to protest his innocence or reveal some information, he has to do it *before* the vote goes through. As soon as a majority vote decides on someone, that player is dead; like the murder victim, she can observe but not participate any further in the game.

After the lynching, the Moderator reveals whether the lynching victim was Mafia or Townsperson.

Night falls again and the Mafia choose another victim. The cycle of Night and Day repeats until either the Mafia have killed a majority of the Townspeople or the Townspeople have killed all of the Mafia.

VARIATIONS

At Night, the players can make noise by humming, tapping the table, rocking back and forth, etc., to cover up any accidental sounds.

Werewolf is the same game, only in this case it's Werewolves against Villagers, one of whom is a Seer. At night, the Werewolves choose a Villager to kill. When they've killed their victim, the Moderator tells them to close their eyes and asks the Seer to open his and point to someone he'd like to know about. The Seer points to a player and the Moderator signals if the Seer pointed at a Werewolf or a Villager. Like the Guardian Angel in Mafia, the Seer tries to throw suspicion on any Werewolves he discovers, but without revealing his role. The Seer can reveal himself at any time, if he thinks it's worth probable death to tell the other players what he's learned. The Villagers win if they kill all the Werewolves; the Werewolves win if they kill as many Villagers as there are Werewolves.

More Mafia

If you're inspired to investigate the game, you can visit The Graduate Mafia Brotherhood of Princeton University's website at www.princeton.edu/~mafia/.

· · · · · · · · ·

MURDER

The simplest of the murder games, it can be played in an hour or two— maybe less if you've got a crackerjack Detective. AKA Murder in the Dark

EQUIPMENT
Folded slips of paper (as many as there are players), one of which is marked with an x, another with an o. All the rest are blank.

PLAYERS
8+

OBJECT
If you're the Murderer, to get away with murder. If you're not, to discover who the Murderer is.

SETUP
The slips of paper are placed in a hat or bowl, then passed around the room. Each player draws a slip. The player who draws the o can announce to the other players that she's the Detective. But no one else can give any

sign as to the contents of their slips, especially the Murderer—the player who drew the x.

When play is about to begin, the Detective should make sure that all lights are off.

PLAY

The Detective lets the players settle down, discreetly turns off the light switch and goes to another part of the house to wait until she's called.

Players are free to move around the darkened room. When the Murderer is ready, he approaches another player and places one or both hands around the Victim's neck, holding on for a few seconds, then releasing his hold. The Victim screams and falls to the floor.

When the Detective hears the scream, she comes back into the room and turns on the lights. She inspects the crime scene and questions the players (except for the Victim— who is, after all, dead) as to their movements and anything they might have heard or sensed.

The players have to answer the Detective's questions truthfully—only the Murderer is permitted to lie. The only question he has to answer truthfully is "Are you the Murderer?"—at which point he is expected to break down and confess all.

The Detective tries to solve the case by seeking out inconsistencies in stories and watching body language. She's allowed two guesses to identify the murderer.

VARIATION

The Detective can be chosen by the group beforehand—someone that the other players agree would be a good choice. In that case, the slips of paper will only include one that bears an x.

STRATEGY

If you're the Murderer, try this: When the lights go out, hold on to someone's hand for the duration while you strangle your Victim with your other hand. You'll have the perfect alibi!

PARTY GAMES FOR KIDS

BLIND MAN'S BLUFF
Blind Postman

FIND THE LEADER

GOING PLACES

HOT POTATO
Musical Hot Potato

MUMMIES

MUSICAL CHAIRS
Musical Laps

PASS THE ORANGE

TELEPHONE

WESTERN UNION
Electricity

·········

BLIND MAN'S BLUFF

It was a naughty game in past centuries, an excuse for (ahem) touching one's other game-players. The Victorians put an end to that sort of nonsense—they played the game with long canes and identified each other by voice.

EQUIPMENT
• A blindfold

PLAYERS
6+

OBJECT
To guess the identity of another player.

SETUP
One player is blindfolded, spun around three times, and released while the other players scatter around the room.

PLAY
The blindfolded player tries to find and tag another player. Once a player is tagged, he has to stand still while the blindfolded player tries to figure out his identity by touch. If the blindfolded player succeeds, the identified player gets to wear the blindfold next.

VARIATIONS
Players join hands and move in a circle around the blindfolded player. When the blindfolded player signals by clapping his hands, the circle stops, and the blindfolded player points. Whoever is closest to where the blindfolded player is pointing has to step inside the circle and try to elude the blindfolded person.

In **Blind Postman**, one player is chosen to be postmaster, another to be the blind postman. The other players sit in a circle, either on the floor or in chairs; the blind postman stands in the middle.

The postmaster gives each player the name of a town that they're supposed to represent. Then he turns the blind postman three times.

The postmaster announces that a letter is going from one town to another. The players whose towns are called have to trade places before the blind postman takes one of their seats. If the blind postman finds a seat, the other player becomes the new blind postman.

As an added twist, the postmaster can also say how the letter traveled: either by air, sea, train, or car. The players whose towns are called have to change seats in a specific way; for example, if by air they have to hop; by sea, walk backward; by train, crawl; and by car, skip.

Origins

Similar blindfold games are mentioned in ancient Greek writings. Blind Man's Bluff was originally named Blind Man's *Buff*, as in "buffet," because those playful (ouch!) Elizabethans buffeted the blindfolded player with knotted ropes until he could identify another player.

·········

FIND THE LEADER

Another of those "somebody leaves the room" games—but a cute one.

PLAYERS
6+

OBJECT
To figure out who the leader is.

SETUP
One player, the outsider, is sent out of the room while the other players select a leader.

PLAY

When the outsider is called back into the room, the entire group is doing something like scratching their heads or tapping their feet. As the leader initiates different actions, the other players immediately follow his lead.

When the outsider guesses who the leader is, it's the leader's turn to be the outsider for the next game.

·········

GOING PLACES

A takeoff (excuse the pun) on Pin the Tail on the Donkey. And it's educational, too!

EQUIPMENT

- A large map of the world

- Airplanes cut out of light cardboard—1 for each player

- Thumbtacks or pushpins

- A blindfold

- A tape measure or ruler

PLAYERS

5+

OBJECT

To "fly" one's airplane the farthest from the departure point.

SETUP

The map is pinned or taped to a wall; the real-life location where the game is taking place is marked on the map as accurately as possible. This will be the departure point.

The players line up at the opposite end of the room, each holding an airplane with a thumbtack or pushpin in it.

PLAY

One by one, the players are blindfolded. They then cross the room, and pin the plane on the map as far as possible from the departure point—but still on the map. If the plane is pinned in the water, it's lost at sea, and that player isn't eligible to win.

The player who "flies" to the farthest point on the map wins.

·········

HOT POTATO

Who gets stuck with it? AKA Wonder Ball, Time Bomb

EQUIPMENT

A potato (or tennis ball, beanbag, or any potato-sized object)

PLAYERS

6+

OBJECT

To avoid being caught holding the "hot potato."

SETUP

One player sits in the center of a circle of other players, holding the potato.

PLAY

The player in the center throws the potato to one of the players and shuts her eyes, while the other players pass it around the circle in one direction as quickly as possible—as if it was *really* hot.

When the player in the center yells, "Hot!" whoever is holding the potato is eliminated.

The game continues until only one person is left—the winner.

VARIATION

In a more roughhouse version, the potato can be thrown randomly from player to player instead of passed in one direction.

Musical Hot Potato is played with music—the player holding the potato when the music stops is eliminated from the circle.

·········

MUMMIES

A silly game, but somebody's got to play it.

EQUIPMENT
• A roll of toilet paper for each team

PLAYERS
5+ (at least one player must be the judge)

OBJECT
To wrap your teammate in toilet paper, thus creating an award-winning mummy.

SETUP
Divide players into two teams, making sure there's at least one person left over to be the judge.

PLAY
One person or team wraps their teammate in toilet paper like an Egyptian mummy. The team that makes the best mummy—according to the judge or judges—wins.

·········

MUSICAL CHAIRS

The classic game was once known as "Going to Jerusalem." Author Laura Lee Hope describes it under that name in The Bobbsey Twins at School, *published in 1913. The kids (two sets of twins) play the game while Mrs. Bobbsey plays the piano.*

EQUIPMENT
- Chairs—one less than the number of people playing.

- Some source of music: radio, CD player, or even a live piano player.

PLAYERS
6+ (and one person to act as "deejay")

OBJECT
To be the person sitting in the last chair.

SETUP
Chairs are placed in a circle or oval, seats facing outward.

PLAY
When the deejay starts the music, everyone walks around the circle in a single line.

When the music stops, the players try to find a chair to sit in. The person who can't find an empty chair has to leave the game.

One chair is removed, and the music starts again. Play continues until there is only one chair. The player who sits in the last remaining chair is the winner.

VARIATION
Musical Laps is something of a nongame, but with the right group in the right mood, a lot of fun. In this version, you keep removing chairs, but no one has to leave the game. Everyone still has to find a place to sit, but with fewer and fewer chairs.

Help Stamp Out Musical Chairs!

The British Labor government has authorized a pamphlet urging teachers to ban the children's game of Musical Chairs on the grounds that it promotes aggression and allows the biggest and strongest children to win. The booklet's author, Sue Finch, says, "Musical statues (a game where everyone has to stand stock still when the music stops) is better because everyone wins."

·········

PASS THE ORANGE

Getting up close and personal with your fellow gamesters.

EQUIPMENT
- An orange

PLAYERS
5+

OBJECT
Not to drop the orange.

SETUP
Players stand in a circle.

PLAY
The first player tucks an an orange under his chin and, without using his hands, passes it to the next person, who has to take it under her chin (no hands!), and so on around the circle.

If a player drops the orange, he's out of the game. The last remaining player is the winner.

VARIATION
Two teams of at least four players each stand in straight lines facing each other. On the word "Go!" the players at the head of each line pass the orange to the second player, and so on down the line.

If the orange falls, it has to be returned to the player at the head of the line. The first team to get their orange to the end of the line wins.

·········

TELEPHONE

It's also been known as Chinese Whispers (probably because so much is lost in translation). AKA Gossip, Russian Scandal

PLAYERS

6+

OBJECT

To see how a phrase changes as it passes among a number of speakers.

SETUP

Players sit side-by-side in a circle or a line.

The player who's going first thinks of a message of at least ten words—anything from "Next month I'm going to Mexico with my parents and my sister" to "My next-door neighbor Joe belongs in an insane asylum."

PLAY

The first player whispers the message to the player next to her, who in turn whispers it to the player sitting next to him, and so on until the message has been whispered to the last player, who says the message aloud.

VARIATION

Get two messages going at once by starting one message to the right and another to the left at the same time.

·········

WESTERN UNION

First you'll have to explain to the kids what a telegram is . . .

PLAYERS
6+

OBJECT
To keep It from figuring out who's passing the message.

SETUP
Players join hands, forming a circle around It, who stands in the center and covers her eyes. One player selects another player in the circle as the recipient of a "telegram" and announces, "I'm going to send a telegram to (the name of the other player)."

PLAY
The sender squeezes the hand of one of the players on either side of her to begin transmission. It opens her eyes and tries to see the message being transmitted by squeeze. If It catches someone squeezing, that player becomes It and another round begins.

When the player announced as the recipient of the telegram gets the message (in the form of a squeeze) she says so, and the game begins again with the same person as It.

RULES
The direction of transmission can change at any time during play.

VARIATION
Electricity is Western Union without the telegram. One player sends a shock (in the form of a hand squeeze) around the circle until It figures out who's passing it.

CHILDHOOD GAMES

BEETLE

BUTTON, BUTTON,
WHO'S GOT THE BUTTON?

DROP THE HANDKERCHIEF
Duck, Duck, Goose

FOLLOW THE LEADER

HIDE AND SEEK
Cops and Robbers
Good Guys vs. Bad Guys
Cowboys and Indians

HONEY, DO YOU LOVE ME?
Quaker Meeting

I SPY

MOTHER MAY I?

RED LIGHT, GREEN LIGHT

RED ROVER

SIMON SAYS

·········

BEETLE

The game was marketed by Schaper Toys in 1948 under the cuter name Cootie. AKA Bugs

EQUIPMENT

- One die

- Paper and Pencils

PLAYERS

2–6

OBJECT

To be the first player to draw a complete beetle.

SETUP

Each player gets a piece of paper and a pencil. The player who rolls the highest number on the die goes first.

PLAY

Players take turns rolling the die, one roll per turn.

RULES

Before a player can start drawing a beetle, he has to roll a 1 for the body. On his next turn, he can start adding other body parts.

Once he's drawn the body, a player can start adding other parts, according to what number he rolls.

Here's the list of numbers needed to add each body part.

- 1 for the body

- 2 for the head

- 3 for one leg

- 4 for one feeler

- 5 for one eye

- 6 for the tail

A player has to roll a 2 and add the head before he can add feelers (4) or eyes (5).

If a player doesn't roll a number he can use, he can't add to his drawing in that turn—he has to wait until his next turn to try again.

The first player to finish his beetle wins.

· · · · · · · · ·

BUTTON, BUTTON, WHO'S GOT THE BUTTON?

That "hotter, hotter . . . colder, colder" game.

EQUIPMENT
- A button

PLAYERS

2+

OBJECT
To find the button.

SETUP
One player hides the button.

PLAY
The players starts looking for the button, while the player who hid it tells the seekers whether or not they're getting close to finding it. If they are, the hider tells them, "You're getting warmer." The closer they get, the "warmer" they are. If a player gets very close, the hider will say, "You're hot!" If a player moves farther away, he's told, "You're getting cold . . . colder . . . freezing!"

VARIATION
Small children can play this game for hours, but if you ever need to motivate a little button-seeker, try hiding a piece of candy.

· · · · · · · · ·

DROP THE HANDKERCHIEF

You might know it better as A Tisket, a Tasket.

EQUIPMENT
• A handkerchief or a small piece of paper

PLAYERS
6+

OBJECT
To catch the player who's It before It can go around the circle and take your place.

SETUP
Choose one player to be It and give that player the handkerchief. The remaining players form a circle and hold hands.

PLAY

It walks around the circle saying,

> *"A tisket, a tasket, a green and yellow basket,*
> *I wrote a letter to my love and on the way I dropped it;*
> *A little girlie picked it up and put it in her pocket."*

At any time during the rhyme, It drops the handkerchief behind one of the players.

As soon as that player sees it, she picks it up and chases It around the circle, trying to catch It before It takes her now-empty place.

If the player tags It in time, It stays It. If the player doesn't catch up with It, she becomes the next It.

Trivia

Ella Fitzgerald recorded a hip version of "A Tisket, a Tasket" in 1938.

STRATEGY

The drop: The player who's It can be obvious (by starting to run as soon as she drops the handkerchief) or subtle about it (by dropping it and continuing to walk at the same pace).

VARIATION

In **Duck, Duck, Goose**, It walks around the outside of the circle, tapping each player on the head while saying, "Duck, duck, duck . . ." When It says, "Goose," that player chases It around the circle, trying to get back to her place before It does.

·········

FOLLOW THE LEADER

It's a good idea to set a time limit, so everyone gets a chance to be leader.

PLAYERS
2+

OBJECT
To follow the leader and do everything she does.

SETUP
One player is chosen to be the leader, and the others line up behind her.

PLAY
The leader takes off, and the other players follow, doing everything the leader does: hopping on one foot; climbing up and down stairs; singing a song; sitting for a moment, then jumping up; saying "Hello" to people in the street; and so on.

·········

HIDE AND SEEK

A-hunting we will go . . .

PLAYERS
3+

OBJECT
To come out of hiding and reach home base without being tagged by It.

SETUP
One player is chosen to be It. Boundaries and a place to use as home base are agreed on.

PLAY

It stands at home base, covers his eyes, and counts out loud to 50 or 100 while the other players hide. When he reaches 100, he calls out, "Ready or not, here I come!" And just in case any hiders are lurking close to home base, he adds, "Anyone around home base is It!"

While It goes hunting for hiders, the other players try to sneak back to home base without getting tagged. If they make it, they yell, "Home free!" If they don't, they're captured and have to stay at home base until another hider comes and frees them with "Alley, alley, oxen free!"

The game is over when/if all the hiders make it back without being tagged, or the last hider frees all the captured players.

In both these cases, It stays It for the next round.

If It catches all the hiders, the first hider he caught is the next It.

VARIATIONS

Hiding players can be "tagged" just by being spotted by It, who calls out the player's name and hiding place: "I see Brandon in the doorway!" In which case, Brandon has to surrender and proceed to home base.

Cops and Robbers, **Good Guys vs. Bad Guys**, and **Cowboys and Indians** are all variations on Hide and Seek; the difference is that no one person is It. Instead, the players divide up into two groups. The Cops seek the Robbers, the Good Guys hunt the Bad Guys, and the Cowboys go after the Indians.

Trivia

In 2002, a federal judge threw out a civil lawsuit filed by the parents of a New Jersey kindergartener who was suspended for playing Cops and Robbers at school.

Scot and Cassandra Garrick sued the Sayreville school district in June 2000 after their six-year-old son and three classmates were disciplined for playing the game and pointing their fingers as guns.

The couple took the case all the way to the Supreme Court, but the court refused to hear an appeal.

·········

HONEY, DO YOU LOVE ME?

Smile, and you lose the game.

PLAYERS
5+

OBJECT
To make another player smile.

SETUP
One person is chosen to be It. The other players form a circle around him.

PLAY
It picks a player and asks, "Honey, do you love me?" The player being questioned has to answer, "Honey, I love you but I just can't smile."

If that player smiles or laughs, she becomes It, and the former It joins the circle. If the player doesn't smile or laugh, It has to approach someone else in the circle until someone laughs or smiles.

The only thing the person who is It can't do to the other players is touch them.

VARIATION
In **Quaker Meeting**, It tries to make everyone laugh at once. To kick off a round, It says,

> *"Quaker Meeting has begun,*
> *No more laughing, no more fun.*
> *If you dare to crack a smile,*
> *You may have to walk a mile."*

Then It does anything she can think of—except touch one of the other players—to get someone to laugh. If someone laughs, It decides on a punishment, like having to sit in the corner until someone else laughs, or sing a silly song, or stand on one leg, etc.

After the laugher has completed the punishment, she becomes the next It.

If It doesn't make the audience laugh within a certain amount of time, the audience votes for a punishment for It, and a new It is chosen.

. . . .

I SPY

. . . with my little eye . . .

PLAYERS
2+

OBJECT
To guess the item that the other player has "spied."

SETUP
One of the players (the Spy) looks around and decides on an object within sight of all the players (a window, a lamp, a hat).

PLAY
The Spy announces the first letter of the object she's picked this way: "I spy, with my little eye, something that begins with (the first letter of the object)."

Let's say the letter is T. Each player gets a turn to ask a question.

"Is it a table?"

"Is it a television?"

"Is it a tree?"

The player who guesses correctly gets to be the Spy in the next game.

VARIATION
Instead of giving the first letter, you can give the color of the object or some other kind of hint, like "something that belongs to Bob," or "something that you can see through." Use your imagination.

·········

MOTHER, MAY I?

The game of baby steps and giant steps. AKA Father, May I?; Queen; Little Queen

EQUIPMENT

- A long, open space such as a field or driveway, or a big room or long hallway

PLAYERS

3+

OBJECT

To be the first player to get to Mother.

SETUP

Someone is chosen to be "Mother." The players line up in a straight line facing Mother, who's standing about ten feet away.

PLAY

The players move toward Mother by asking permission to take steps. For example, "Mother, may I take ten steps (baby steps or giant steps) forward?"

Mother answers, "Yes, you may" or "No, you may not," and the player has to obey. If a player moves when she hasn't been given permission, she has to go all the way back to the starting line. The first player to touch Mother becomes Mother in the next game.

Tip

The game is the most fun when players take different kinds of steps besides regular steps, giant steps, and baby steps—like frog jumps or bunny hops.

VARIATION

Instead of a player asking Mother for permission to move, Mother tells the players what move to make—but before moving, the player has to ask Mother for permission to make the move. For example, when Mother says, "Sarah, take three giant steps," Sarah has to ask, "Mother, may I?" Mother is allowed to change her mind—she doesn't have to give permission, and Sarah can't more until she receives permission from Mother. If a player forgets to ask permission, he has to go back to the starting line.

....

RED LIGHT, GREEN LIGHT

Also known as Stop and Go.

PLAYERS

3+

OBJECT

To tag It.

SETUP

One person is chosen to be It. The other players line up in a row at least thirty paces behind It.

PLAY

Facing away from the other players, It calls out one of three commands. "Green light" means that the other players can run toward him. "Yellow light" means the players can walk toward him. "Red light" means the other players have to freeze before It turns around. If It catches anyone moving, that player has to go back to the starting line. The first person to get close enough to touch It wins—and gets to be It in the next game.

RULES

If you're It, and you turn around *before* you say "red light," all the other players can take one giant step forward.

·········

RED ROVER

A slightly rambunctious game that has nothing to do with dogs named Rover.

PLAYERS

2 teams with at least 4 players each

OBJECT

To stop as many players as possible from breaking through your line.

SETUP

Players hold hands very tightly with their teammates and form a line facing the other team, with anywhere from ten to twenty paces between them.

PLAY

After deciding which team will go first, the first team chooses a player from the opposing team and inserts his name in this rhyme: "Red Rover, Red Rover, let _____ come over!"

The player they've called for has to run toward them and try to break through the clasped hands of two of the players. If he succeeds, he returns to his own team. If he doesn't, he has to stay with the opposing team; he joins hands with one of the players on either end.

The teams take turns calling Red Rover. The team that wins all the players wins the game. Or, if the game has to end at a certain time, the team with the most players wins.

·········

SIMON SAYS

Remember to do everything Simon says—not what he does.

PLAYERS
4+

OBJECT
To do everything that "Simon says."

SETUP
One player is chosen to be Simon. He or she stands facing the other players.

PLAY
Simon performs an action while giving orders to the other players. For instance, he might hold his nose and say, "Simon says hold your nose!" All the other players have to obey immediately.

But if he doesn't say "Simon says" before he gives the order, and just says "Hold your nose!" the players *must not* obey him. If they do, they're out of the game.

The last player standing is the winner and gets to be Simon for the next round.

STRATEGY
Simon can get even trickier—by scratching his head while saying, "Simon says tap your foot!"

KIDS' OUTDOOR GAMES

CAPTURE THE FLAG
Prisoner's Base

CHICKEN FIGHTS

FOX AND GEESE

HOPSCOTCH
Italian Hopscotch
Snail Hopscotch

JOHNNY RIDE A PONY

KEEP AWAY

KICK THE CAN

KING OF THE HILL

MARBLES
Ringer Variations
Boss Out
Pyramid
Bridgeboard
Miniature Marbles
Bun-hole
Cherry Pit

MARCO POLO
Big Toe Marco Polo
Fish Out of Water

PICKLE

RINGOLEAVIO

SHARKS AND MINNOWS

SKULLY

SPUD
I Declare War

STICKBALL
Fungo
Flies Are Up
Punchball
Over-the-Line

STOOPBALL
Roofball

TAG
Freeze Tag
Flashlight Tag
Relay Tag
Dragon Tag
Blob Tag
Statues
Ghost in the Graveyard
Hospital Tag
Floating Tag
Toilet Tag
Turtle Tag
Shadow Tag

UNDERWATER TAG

WATER BALLOON TOSS
Egg Toss

·········

CAPTURE THE FLAG

If a game's been around for more than 500 years, it must be doing something right. AKA Freedom, Drapeau (French for "flag")

EQUIPMENT
- A yard or other area divided into two territories separated by a boundary line
- 2 "flags" (bandannas or rags tied to sticks)

PLAYERS
8+ (2 teams of at least 4 players each)

OBJECT
To capture the enemy's flag and return it to your side.

SETUP
The teams assemble close together near the boundary line, showing their flags.

Each team has up to five minutes to place its flag at any point within 200 paces of the boundary. The flag must be visible. Teams call out when their flags have been placed.

A guard can be posted near the flag, but has to stay outside a twenty-five-step radius from it—*unless* an enemy gets inside the radius. In that case, the guard can go in after the enemy player.

A particular spot has to be selected to serve as Jail (a tree, a rock, a small defined area of land), where captured prisoners will be kept.

If the players wish, a time limit can be set.

PLAY
A signal is given for the start of the game. It's now up to each team to enter the other's territory and try to capture the enemy's flag.

Capture

A player can be captured by an enemy player holding him (by some part of his body—*not* by his clothes) long enough for the capturer to say "Caught!" three times. Then the capturer can bring the captured player to Jail.

Rescue

A prisoner can be released from Jail if one of his teammates touches him, but only if the prisoner is touching the Jail with a hand or foot. Then both can return to their own territory. Of course, if the rescuer is caught before he touches the prisoner, he has to go to Jail. *Important:* A rescuer can rescue only one prisoner at a time.

Capturing the Flag

If an enemy player captures the flag, it has to be carried across the boundary line back into that enemy's territory. If the player who has captured the flag is caught before he reaches home, the flag is set up at the point *where it was rescued* and the game continues.

If neither side captures its enemy's flag within the agreed-upon time limit, the team with the most prisoners wins the game.

VARIATIONS

In some versions of the game, spies can be sent into enemy territory during the period when the enemy is placing its flag.

Try playing a smaller version indoors on a rainy day. The flags can be any household items—toys, or pieces of clothing.

Prisoner's Base is the centuries-old game that Capture the Flag is based on. It was so popular in fourteenth-century England that King Edward III banned the game from Westminster Palace because it interfered with parliamentary activity.

In one version of Prisoner's Base, each team starts out with one prisoner, the object being to rescue him without getting captured by a member of the opposing team. If the rescuer makes it to the prison without being caught, he's safe there and can pick his own time to run with the prisoner back to their own side of the line. Of course, if the would-be rescuer is caught he also becomes a prisoner.

In another version, the two teams face each other. The captain of Team A dispatches a player to run toward the center of the field, at which point the Team B captain sends out one of his runners to catch the Team A player. Another Team A runner goes out to catch the B player, and so on until all the players are on the field. Each player can only capture one of the players who went before him, and can only be captured by players who entered the field after him.

·········

CHICKEN FIGHTS

The teams are most often coed: girls on guys' shoulders, but vice versa might be fun, too.

EQUIPMENT
- A swimming pool or shallow beach area where the water is waist- to chest-high.

PLAYERS
4+ (organized into teams of 2)

OBJECT
To knock a player off of his teammate's shoulders.

SETUP
Players divide into partners who are equal in size and strength so the teams are as evenly matched as possible; then they choose which of the two will sit on a teammate's shoulders.

PLAY
Players wrestle, push, pull, or splash each other, trying to knock another player off of his partner's shoulders and into the water. The last team to stay upright is the winner.

·········

FOX AND GEESE

If you live in the right climate, Fox and Geese is a great game to play in the snow, too. AKA Cut the Pie, Wheel Tag

EQUIPMENT
- A big expanse of pavement

- Chalk

PLAYERS
4+

OBJECT
To stay on the lines while trying to evade the fox.

SETUP
Create the playing field by outlining a big circle between fifteen and thirty paces across by drawing it with chalk. Divide the circle by adding six spokes running from the center of the circle to the edges, forming six pieces of pie. These lines will be the tracks that the players run on.

One player is chosen to be the fox.

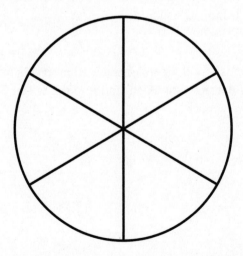

PLAY

The fox stands in the center of the circle, while the others scatter around the outside or on the spokes of the circle. At a signal, the fox takes off after the geese. Once the fox leaves the center of the circle it becomes home base, where the geese are safe from capture.

Everyone, including the fox, has to stay on the lines at all times during play. If two geese run into each other, one or both can turn around, or they can try to pass each other, but they can't step anywhere but on the lines. And jumping across corners is not allowed.

Play continues until the fox catches a goose or a goose steps off the lines, at which time the goose becomes the new fox.

VARIATIONS

Instead of switching roles with the fox when a goose gets tagged, each captured goose can join the fox in hunting down his prey. The last surviving goose is the winner.

When the fox catches a goose, the goose is out of the game. The game ends when the fox has eliminated all of the geese.

The game is much more riotous when it's played without a home base.

The game can be played in sand, too, by dragging a stick to create the wheel.

·········

HOPSCOTCH

Scotland had nothing to do with the game's origination. According to The Encyclopedia of Word and Phrase Origins, *the "scotch" in hopscotch comes from the fact that the lines of the grid are "scotched"—back when to "scotch" something meant to engrave it. AKA Potsy*

EQUIPMENT

- A Hopscotch court drawn on the pavement with chalk or mapped out with masking tape on a floor; the boxes should be about 18 to 24 inches square.

- 1 "potsie" (a flat stone, coin, or little beanbag) for each player

PLAYERS
2+

OBJECT
To be the first player to travel through the hopscotch court and back home.

SETUP
To determine who goes first, the players stand just below the bottom of the Hopscotch court and throw their potsies. The player whose potsie lands completely inside the highest number goes first.

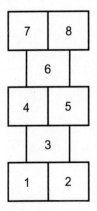

One of the simplest Hopscotch patterns, as played in New York City c. 1950. The potsie of choice was a wooden Dixie Cup spoon weighed down with tar scooped out from between squares of pavement.

PLAY
Standing at the bottom of and just outside the Hopscotch court, the first player tosses her potsie into box #1. If it touches one of the lines or lands outside the box, she loses her turn.

If it lands completely inside the box, she can go ahead, hopping on the same foot throughout, into the #2 square, then into the #3 box, straddling #4 and #5—left foot in #4, right foot in #5—hop on one foot into #6, straddle #7 and #8, turn in the air and land straddling #7 and #8, and move back through the squares in reverse order.

When she hops into box #2 she bends over and, still standing on one leg, retrieves her potsie from the #1 box. If she does so without touching down in the #1 box, or putting her other hand or foot down, she hops out and takes another turn, this time throwing the potsie into box #2, and so on.

If at any time a player steps on a line or out of the box, or misses a square, her turn ends and she has to begin again at that number when it's her turn again.

When a player gets to #7, she hops from #6 to #8, bends down to pick up the potsie, hops back into #6, and so on down the court. At #8, the player picks up the potsie standing in the #7, then turns around and hops/straddles down and out of the grid.

The first player to complete the course for every numbered square on the court wins the game.

Tip

The heavier your potsie, the better. If you're using a coin or a light pebble, you can weigh it down with old chewing gum—as long as isn't too sticky anymore.

HISTORY

The original Hopscotch courts were more than 100 feet long and used for military training exercises by Roman soldiers in full armor. Throughout the Roman Empire, which encompassed most of the known world at one point, children imitated the soldiers by drawing their own courts—and passed the game down through the generations.

Trivia

The record for the Most Hopscotch Games in 24 Hours was set at the Westin Regina Hotel, Cancun, Mexico, on January 12–13, 1998, by Ashrita Furman, an American who completed 434 games of Hopscotch in the time limit.

VARIATIONS

Italian Hopscotch is played like regular Hopscotch, with these exceptions:

- Players can land on REST with both feet.

- If the potsie lands in the first blank space, the player loses his turn and has to start on his next turn from the number he played before the bad toss.

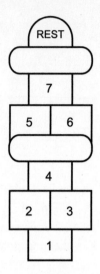

- If the potsie lands in the far blank space, the player loses his turn and has to start again from #1.

SNAIL HOPSCOTCH

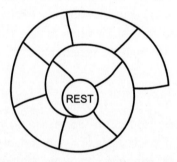

In **Snail Hopscotch**, no potsie is needed. The player hops on one foot through the course until she reaches the Rest, where she can put both feet down on the ground. During her return—still hopping—she can stop in any of the spaces with both feet and chalk in her initials or name. After that, the other players have to hop over her square. Of course, the next player gets to do the same, and so on.

·········

JOHNNY RIDE A PONY

Only the strong survive this rough-and-tumble kids' game. AKA Johnny on the Pony, Ride the Pony, Buck-Buck, Tony on the Pony, and many more.

PLAYERS
8+

OBJECT
To see how many kids the "pony" can carry.

SETUP
Players divide into two teams. One team will be the pony, the other team will be the riders.

Forming the Pony
The least strong player on the pony team stands with his back against a wall, bracing himself. The next pony player bends over and buries his head in the first player's stomach. The rest of the team lines up behind him—bending over, heads to one side—each holding the previous player at the waist, making a long horizontal line to form the pony's back.

PLAY
The rider team chants, "Johnny Ride a Pony, one, two, three," while one at a time, the riders run and jump as far forward on the back of the pony as possible, giving their team members room to land behind them. Meanwhile, the pony team bucks like a bronco to try to dislodge the riders.

If anyone on the rider team falls off or touches a foot to the ground, the pony team wins that round. If the rider team manages to land on the pony without touching the ground or being thrown off, it wins the round.

Either way, the teams switch places after each round.

HISTORY
It's thought that the game evolved from Buck-Buck, originally "*Bucca Bucca quot sunt hic?* (Buck, Buck, how many are these?)," a game in which

the rider would ask the question while holding up a finger or two. It was played in Europe and the Near East at least as far back as the seventeenth century.

· · · · · · · · ·

KEEP AWAY

One of those games that's been played for centuries all over the world, it's been especially popular in Russia, Australia, and Italy, and among Native Americans.

EQUIPMENT
• A volleyball, soccer ball, or similarly sized ball

PLAYERS
4+ (even-numbered teams are best)

OBJECT
To keep the ball in motion while keeping it away from the other players.

SETUP
Players divide into two teams and decide which team will go first.

PLAY
The player who gets the ball first passes it to a teammate who passes it to another, trying to keep it away from the opposing team.

SCORING
While the ball is being passed, the players count out each pass—"One, two, three"—and so on until the ball is intercepted. At that point, the new team starts the count at number one. When the other team intercepts, they start the count at one again.

After a certain time limit, the team that had the highest number of passes in one round wins the game.

SCORING VARIATIONS

When the ball is returned to a team, the team can continue the count where it left off when it lost the ball. The first team to reach a certain point total—say, 100—wins.

Or teams can make the object to play to a certain point total—say, 21—in one turn.

·········

KICK THE CAN

From the days before Toys "R" Us, when kids had to find their own toys.

EQUIPMENT

- An expanse of pavement

- An empty aluminum can

- A piece of chalk (optional)

PLAYERS

3+

OBJECT

To find all the hiders and bring them back to the area around the can.

SETUP

A small, specific area of the pavement is chosen—a manhole cover or a circle about three feet in diameter drawn with chalk. The can is placed in the middle.

One person is chosen to be It, another is chosen to kick the can.

PLAY

The kicker kicks the can as far as he can and the other players scatter to find hiding places. It has to bring the can back and put it in the middle of the circle. Once he's done that, he can start looking for hiders.

When It finds a hider, he runs back to the circle, bangs the can on the ground, and calls out the hider's name. But if the hider can make it back to the circle first and kick over the can before It gets to it, she's safe. If It makes it to the can first, the player whose name he called out is captured and has to wait inside the circle with the can.

While It is out looking for other hiders, a hider who's still free can release the captured hider by kicking over the can and calling out "Home free!"

The game continues until all the hiders have been captured. The first person caught becomes It in the next game. If jailbreaks keep the game going on too long, the first person who is caught three times becomes It and a new game begins.

VARIATION

When It brings the can back to home base at the beginning of the game, he has to count to 50 (or 100) with his eyes closed before he can start searching.

·········

KING OF THE HILL

The ultimate power trip for a nine-year-old. AKA King of the Castle, King of the Mountain

PLAYERS

2+

OBJECT

To pull the king off his hill.

SETUP

One person is chosen to be king. The king gets up on his hill (a mound of dirt, a box, a tree stump) or stands inside a chalk circle about three feet wide.

PLAY

One at a time, the other players try to pull the king off the hill (or out of the circle). The player who succeeds gets to be king in the next round.

RULES

Don't try to pull the king off by his clothes. If you do you'll become the king's prisoner and you won't able to play the rest of the round.

·········

MARBLES

First played with round pebbles, nuts, or fruit pits, the game wasn't called "Marbles" until someone started using actual chips of marble. This is the standard game, known as Ringer.

EQUIPMENT

- At least 6 marbles and 1 larger shooter marble for each player

- Chalk for drawing the circles

PLAYERS

2+

OBJECT

To capture the most marbles by hitting them out of the circle.

SETUP

Two circles are drawn, the inside circle about one foot across, the outside circle three to six feet across. Each player puts the same number of marbles in the inner circle.

To decide who starts, players can toss a coin or "lag"—that is, shoot or throw a marble from a straight line drawn along one edge of the big circle to a parallel line drawn along the opposite side (known as the "lag line"). The player who comes closest to the lag line, either in front of it or beyond it, goes first. The next closest goes second, and so on.

Shooting Marbles

To shoot a marble, put the big knuckle of the index finger on the ground. Place the shooter in the crook of the forefinger, with the thumb behind it. Then, aim and flick the shooter with the thumb. The movement has to be a flick—not a push with the hand.

PLAY

Shooting from any point around the outside of the circle, the first player "knuckles down" and flicks his shooter, trying to knock the other players' marbles outside the outer circle without letting his own shooter leave the outer circle.

If the player is successful, he shoots again from where the shooter came to rest.

If he fails to hit a marble out of the big circle, or his shooter ends up outside the circle, the turn goes to the next player.

If a player's shooter ends up in the inner circle, the turn goes to the next player—and the shooter becomes a target for the other players. A player who hits the shooter is entitled to all the marbles that the shooter's owner has won up to that point in the game.

The game continues until all of the original marbles have been knocked out. The player with the most marbles wins.

VARIATIONS

In a simpler version of **Ringer**, one circle about two to three feet across is drawn. Players try to knock the other players' marbles out of the circle, while making sure that their own shooter rolls out, too. Any shooter that's left inside the circle can be hit by another player. If it is, the shooting player wins all the marbles the shooter owner has won up to that point in the game.

Another version of **Ringer** is played at the annual National Marbles Championship in Wildwood, New Jersey. In it, thirteen target marbles are placed in the center of a circle ten feet across so that they form an x, one row of seven crossing the other in the middle. Like basic Ringer, players try to knock one or more marbles out of the ring, or to knock another player's shooter out of the ring. The shooter gets to keep any marbles he hits out of the ring. If he hits a shooter out of the ring, that shooter's owner is out of the game ("killed"), and has to surrender any marbles that he's won to the player who killed him.

A player who hits an opponent's shooter but doesn't knock it out of the ring can pick up any marble he chooses, and if his own shooter stays in the ring he continues to shoot. But he can't hit the same opponent's shooter again until he hits another shooter, he knocks a marble out of the ring, or he comes around to his next turn to shoot.

The game ends when the last marble is shot out. The player with the most marbles wins.

Boss Out can be played anywhere—no circle needed. The first player shoots or throws a marble. From the same spot, the second player tries to hit it. If he does, he wins the marble. If the two marbles are close enough, he can try to "span" them by placing his thumb on his marble and his index finger on the other, then trying to bring them together by raising his hand. If the two marbles hit, he collects both marbles.

If the second player misses, the first player can shoot at the second marble; if he hits it, he wins it. His own marble stays where it is and the other player has another chance to hit it. If more than two people play, after the first two miss, the third aims for either marble, and so on.

To play **Pyramid (aka Castle)**, you need a circle about one foot across. In the center of it, one player builds a pyramid by putting three marbles together and placing another on top of them. The object is to knock down the pyramid and collect all the marbles from it. If the shooter doesn't manage to knock the pyramid down in one try, the pyramid builder can claim one of the shooter's marbles.

Bridgeboard or **Nine Holes** is played with a board (or upside-down shoe box) with nine cut-out archways randomly numbered (and sized) from 1 to 9. Players try to shoot through the arches in numerical order, continuing their turn if they succeed. The first player to send her marble through all nine holes in the correct order wins.

Miniature Marbles is played on a miniature golf–like course that players can create from materials at hand: egg cartons, thimbles, pipe cleaners, parts from toy train sets, etc. Players take turns shooting their marbles over, under, around, and through the obstacles. The first player to complete the course wins.

"Pot games" are played with a hole in the ground. **Bun-hole** requires a one-foot-wide hole dug in the center of the playing field. Players try to get their marble as close as possible to the hole without going in. If your marble comes closest without going in, you win one marble from each player. Knocking your opponent's marble into the bun-hole is permitted.

Cherry Pit also requires a one-foot-wide hole, specifically in the center of a ten-foot circle. Each player places two to four marbles around the hole, up to about twelve in all. Then players take turns trying to knock marbles into the hole. As long as marbles keep getting knocked into the hole and the shooter stays in the ring, players may continue to shoot. If a player's shooter goes into the hole, he has to forfeit an agreed-upon number of marbles and place them around the hole to "buy back" his shooter.

FYI

- Almost every culture had some form of the game, from the ancient Romans to early Native American tribes.

- The British World Marbles Championship has been held every Good Friday in Tinsley Green, England, since the seventeenth century.

· · · · · · · · ·

MARCO POLO

As far as we've been able to find out, the great Italian explorer of the same name had nothing to do with the creation of this game.

EQUIPMENT
- A swimming pool

PLAYERS
3+

OBJECT
Not to get caught by "Marco" (the person who is It).

SETUP
The player chosen to be Marco goes to one end of the pool and closes his eyes.

PLAY
When Marco shouts "Marco!" all the other players have to answer "Polo!" Swimming in the direction of a voice, *with his eyes still shut*, Marco has to tag one of the other players. He can call "Marco!" as often as he likes, and as often as he does, the other players *must* answer "Polo!"

If a player fails to say "Polo," Marco can call their name and accuse them. If all the other players agree, the person who didn't call "Polo" becomes the next Marco.

VARIATIONS

In **Big Toe Marco Polo,** Marco has to stay in the pool but all other players can climb out on the edge as long as some part of their body (such as a big toe) stays in the water. They must still respond "Polo" when "Marco" is yelled.

Fish Out of Water is similar to the Big Toe variation, but in this case, if Marco calls "Fish out of water!" the person with the least amount of skin in the water is the next Marco. If two or more people are out of the water completely, the last person to get back into the pool is the next Marco.

· · · · · · · · ·

PICKLE

Played with a ball . . . not a green vegetable in sight. AKA Running Bases, Hot Box, Run Down

EQUIPMENT

- A ball

PLAYERS

4+

OBJECT

To reach base without being tagged.

SETUP

Pick two bases about ten to twenty steps apart and choose one player to guard each base. The other players will be the runners.

PLAY

The guards start the game by throwing the ball back and forth. Players run between the bases, while the guards try to tag them with the ball, either by touching them when they approach, or throwing the ball at them and hitting them.

Players are only safe while touching one of the bases. If a runner is hit or touched by the ball, he replaces the guard who tagged him, and that guard becomes a runner.

·········

RINGOLEAVIO

Fans of the game know how to say it and play it, but spelling it varies widely from neighborhood to neighborhood.

PLAYERS
8+

OBJECT
For one team to capture all the members of the opposing team.

SETUP
An area is selected to be the base (or jail), big enough to hold all the captured players—a park bench or stoop in the city, or a marked-off section of a driveway in the suburbs.

Players divide up into two teams—hiders and hunters.

PLAY
The hunters close their eyes and count while the other team hides. When the count is done, some of the hunters begin the search and some stay near the base to guard it.

When a hunter finds a hider, she grabs him, and if she can hold on to him long enough to yell, "Ringoleavio one, two, three!" the captured player has to go with the hunter back to the jail, where he'll stay until the end of the game—unless he's freed by one of his teammates.

To free a captured hider, a teammate has to touch the base and yell "Home free!"—the signal for all his captured teammates to scatter in all directions.

Play continues until all the hiders are caught. Then the two teams can switch roles; the hunters can be hiders, and vice versa.

VARIATIONS

The game can be played with jail wardens who are in charge of guarding the base and recapturing freed prisoners and/or general boundaries of play.

But if you're playing *without* specific boundaries, it's not considered good form to disappear into some out-of-the-way hiding spot for the duration of the game.

· · · · · · · · ·

SHARKS AND MINNOWS

Everybody into the pool!

EQUIPMENT

- A swimming pool or shallow beach area where the water is waist- to chest-high.

PLAYERS

4+

OBJECT

To swim from one side of a pool to the other without being caught by a "shark."

SETUP

The player chosen to be the shark stands in the middle of the pool; the other players, the "minnows," line up at one end.

PLAY

When the shark invites the minnows to come swimming, they start heading for the other side of the pool as fast as they can, trying to avoid getting caught by the shark.

But once the shark tags a minnow, the minnow becomes a shark and joins the original shark in the center trying to catch the remaining minnows. The last minnow is the winner and chooses who will be the shark in the next round.

RULES

Sharks have to stay in the center of the pool. If they venture outside the center to chase a minnow, that catch is not legal, and the minnow is allowed to swim away.

·········

SKULLY

The rules of the old street game—and the design of the boxes—vary from neighborhood to neighborhood. This version seems to be the most common one. AKA Skullsies, Skelly, Skelsies, Skilsies, Bottlecaps, Deadbox

EQUIPMENT

- 3 × 3-foot grid

- Chalk

- Bottlecaps weighted down with coins and melted crayons

PLAYERS

2–6

OBJECT

To shoot a bottlecap through a series of numbered boxes until the center box—#13, the "skull"—is reached, then to reverse direction all the way back to #1.

SETUP

Draw the skully grid on a sidewalk, driveway, or basement, then mark a starting line outside the box, a few inches away from the #1 box.

PLAY

From just behind the starting line, the first player finger-flicks (holds the tip of his middle finger back with his thumb to form a circle, then flicks the bottlecap with his middle finger as it releases) his upside-down bottlecap toward the #1 box. If he doesn't make it on this first turn, the next player starts.

If a player gets his cap completely inside the #1 box, without touching

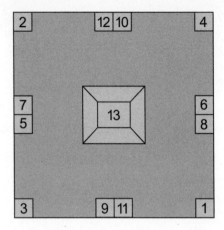

any lines, he's completed "ones." From any position in the #1 box, he tries for the #2 box—"going for twos." As long as he gets his cap inside the next box in one try, he keeps going. When and if he fails, the next player takes a turn.

Once a player has gotten into the #2 box, he can take advantage of another way of advancing in the game: hitting another player's bottlecap no matter where it is inside the box. If he manages on his turn to hit an opponent's cap, he's awarded his next box (as if he'd shot it in), and his turn continues. If he hits *two* other caps in one shot, he gets two extra boxes; if he hits three caps, he gets three boxes; and so on.

Play proceeds as the players get closer to the center box. If a cap lands in the area that borders the #13 box (aka No Man's Land), the cap is stuck there until another player hits it out.

The first player to make it to #13 and back to #1 wins the game.

VARIATIONS

If a player lands in No Man's Land, he loses three turns instead of waiting until another player knocks him out of the box.

Some skully diehards play a version in which any player who makes it back to the #1 box and out becomes a killer. On his next turn, he can re-enter the grid and hunt the other caps. If he hits a non-killer cap three times in a row, that player is out. If he hits a killer once, *that* player is out. But it's dangerous work. A non-killer can become a killer by simply hitting a killer's cap. The last remaining killer wins the game.

·········

SPUD

As far as we can tell, this game has nothing to do with potatoes and didn't originate in Idaho.

EQUIPMENT

- A big expanse of pavement

- A high-bouncing ball

PLAYERS

4+

OBJECT

To run fast enough to avoid getting hit by the ball.

SETUP

Players choose who'll be the first Caller and gather around the ball.

PLAY

The Caller slams the ball down on the pavement, bouncing it as high as he can, at the same time calling out the name of one of the other players. The player whose name is called has to catch the ball while the other players run away as fast as they can.

When the player catches the ball, he yells, "Spud!" and all the fleeing players have to freeze in their tracks. The Catcher is allowed to take three steps toward one of the other players (usually the closest) and tries to hit him with the ball. If he succeeds, the hit player gets an "S"—the first letter of SPUD. If he misses, he himself gets an "S."

The player who got the "S" is the Caller in the next round. Play continues until one player gets all four letters of SPUD.

VARIATION

I Declare War is similar, except that each player takes the name of a country and the caller announces the country instead of a player's name by calling out, "I declare war on . . ." then throwing down the ball while naming the country.

·········

STICKBALL

Originally a street game played in New York City and environs, it's still played by nostalgic grown-ups who learned it as kids.

EQUIPMENT

- Traditionally, a city side street

- A rubber ball (preferably a Spaldeen, aka pinky)

- A sawed-off broomstick or mop handle

In suburbia in the 1960s and 1970s the Spaldeen and stick gave way to tennis balls and real bats.

PLAYERS
4+ on each team

OBJECT
To score the most runs.

SETUP
Order of play and field positions are decided on, depending on the number of players. Four players: pitcher (and third baseman); first baseman; second baseman (and short centerfielder); and outfielder.

With more players, other fielding positions could be added, such as third baseman, centerfielder, another outfielder, and a catcher.

One sewer cover in the middle of the street serves as home plate, the next sewer cover is second base. First and third are opposite each other near the curbs on each side of the street—a car door handle, a fire hydrant—whatever is in or near the right place.

PLAY

Basic baseball rules apply. If a ball is hit out of play (onto a roof, into a backyard, or—Babe Ruth forbid—through a broken window), that batter is out.

VARIATIONS

Fungo is Stickball played without a pitcher. The batter throws the ball up with one hand and either hits it on the fly or lets it bounce once before hitting it.

Flies Are Up (aka Flies Up, Hit the Bat, Cherry) is a simplified version of Fungo. The batter hits the ball to the fielders; whoever catches the ball on the fly gets a turn at bat.

In another version, the batter hits the ball, then places the bat on the ground in front of himself. The fielder who caught the ball rolls it at the bat from the place where he caught it. If the ball hits the bat and pops up into the air, the batter tries to catch it. If he does, he bats again. If he doesn't, the player who caught and rolled the ball takes a turn up at bat.

Punchball is played without a stick. All the rules of Stickball apply, but the batter uses his fist or open hand to hit the ball.

Over-the-Line started in 1953 as a sand baseball game, but has since evolved into a street or diamond game with as few as three players to a team. Each team has a pitcher or pitches to itself. If played on a diamond, half the diamond is fair and half foul: For a right-handed batter, the right side (facing the batter) is foul; for a lefty, it shifts to the left. On the street, the whole street is fair, but parked cars, for instance, can be considered part of foul territory. The lines are decided on before the game starts—a pole or streetlight or someone's shirt can signify the lines—one each for singles, doubles, triples, and home runs. If a ball that isn't caught by a fielder passes one or more of the lines, an imaginary runner ends up on the corresponding base. Other imaginary runners already on base move up the same number of bases.

Trivia

Willie Mays and Phil Rizzuto are among the major leaguers who learned the basics of baseball playing stickball. It's said that Willie was a four-sewer man, meaning he could hit the ball a distance of four manholes from the plate.

·········

STOOPBALL

The word "stoop" comes from the Dutch name for a small porch. In New York (the former New Amsterdam) it came to mean the steps leading up to an apartment building and the perfect setting for a street game.

EQUIPMENT

• A sidewalk next to a stoop

• A high-bouncing ball

PLAYERS

2+

OBJECT

To score the most points by throwing a ball at the stoop and catching it on the fly.

PLAY

The first player throws the ball against the steps. If the ball bounces back and the player catches it on the fly, he wins 10 points. If it bounces once, the player gets 5 points. If the ball bounces more than once, the player is out, and the next player is up.

A game is usually played to 100 points.

VARIATIONS

Roofball is Stoopball's suburban cousin, played against an angled roof. The server stands about twenty feet away from the roof and hits the ball with his hand to serve. The other player has to catch the ball before it hits the ground.

A similar version is played with a larger, softer ball. In this case, the players have to keep the ball going by hitting it either on the fly or letting it bounce once—but only once.

Most serious Roofball fans turn their noses up at the Roofball that's more like a game of catch—with a house in between. Players stand on either side of a two-sided roof so that neither can see the other. The only clue that a catcher has that the ball is coming is hearing the other player yell "Eevy ivy over!" as he throws the ball.

·········

TAG

You might think that Tag evolved out of the hunter vs. prey situation, but some of the best minds in game history think that the game has its roots instead in the long-ago days when evil spirits roamed the earth and could bring us down with just a touch.

PLAYERS
5+ (all Tag games are best played with lots of kids)

OBJECT
If you're It, to tag someone. If you're not, to keep from being tagged.

SETUP
Players designate a spot as a base where they can be safe for a short period while they catch their breath, and decide how long a player can stay there. The decision also has to be made as to whether or not tagging back (immediately tagging the player who just tagged you) is allowed.

One player is chosen to be It.

PLAY
It runs around and tries to tag another player. When he does, he calls out "You're It!" The tagged player becomes It and has to tag someone else.

VARIATIONS
Freeze Tag Players have a few seconds to scatter before It takes off after them. When he touches them, they have to freeze like a statue until an unfrozen player tags them. This "melts" the ice so they can move again. The game is over when It freezes all the players.

If the game takes too long because the frozen players keep getting defrosted and It can't keep up, you can change the rules so that once you're frozen you stay that way.

Flashlight Tag This is a nighttime variation of Tag, only in the Flashlight version, the player who's It doesn't tag with his hands, but with a flashlight. When the light shines on another player, he's It.

Relay Tag Players hand off a ball or Frisbee (or some other object that won't break if it's dropped) while It tries to tag whoever is carrying it.

When It finally catches the player who's holding the object, that player becomes the new It.

Dragon Tag Three or four players link arms, forming a chain—the dragon. They run around trying to catch as many players as they can by forming a circle around them.

When a player is completely circled, he becomes part of the dragon and now helps capture other players. The game is over when everyone has been tagged and is part of one long dragon.

Blob Tag (aka Amoeba Tag) Instead of circling other players as in Dragon Tag, Blob taggers join hands or arms to tag other players who then join the chain. The "blob" continues to grow until the final player has been tagged.

Statues Players stand at a starting line about thirty to fifty paces away from and facing It.

It turns his back and counts out loud to 10 while the other players start to walk or run toward him. As soon as he reaches 10, It swings around to face them. If he catches anyone moving, even the tiniest bit, he sends them back to the starting line. Then he turns around and counts to 10 again. And again.

When a player gets close enough to tag It, everyone runs back to the starting line while It chases them. If they all make it back without being tagged, It stays It. But if It tags someone before they get back to the starting line, the game is over, and the player who was tagged becomes It for the next game.

Ghost in the Graveyard Best played outdoors after dark. It—the "ghost in the graveyard"—runs away from the group to hide while the other players stay at their "base," close their eyes, and count out loud, "One o'clock, two o'clock, three o'clock . . ." all the way to "Midnight!"

The group then goes in search of the "ghost." If a player sees him, he yells, "Ghost in the graveyard!" That's the cue for all the players to run back to base. If the ghost catches one of them, that player is the ghost in the next round.

Hospital Tag (aka Poison Tag) When It (known as "Mr. Yuck" in some neighborhoods) tags a player, that player is "wounded." Not only does the tagged player become It, he also has to chase the other players with one hand on his wound, wherever he was tagged. A variation on this one has everyone as It when the game starts. A player is out when he gets three "wounds." The last surviving player is the winner.

VARIATIONS

Floating Tag (aka Hang Tag) A player can't be tagged as long as her feet are off the ground, whether she climbs a fence, jumps up on a chair, or hangs from a tree limb.

Toilet Tag (aka Squat Tag) A player can't be tagged if he squats down.

Turtle Tag A player can't be tagged if he drops to the ground with his arms and leg in the air like an upside-down turtle.

Shadow Tag A player is tagged if It steps on his shadow.

· · · · · · · · ·

UNDERWATER TAG

The basic kids' game takes to the water.

EQUIPMENT

- A swimming pool or shallow beach area where the water is waist- to chest-high

PLAYERS

4+

OBJECT

For the player who's It, to tag another player. For the other players, to avoid being tagged.

SETUP

One player is chosen to be It.

PLAY

It gives the signal to begin, and tries to tag any player who isn't completely underwater, the only place that is completely safe.

It can chase the other players until they tire out, or wait until the players who are underwater need to come up for air.

When It tags another player, that player becomes the new It.

·········

WATER BALLOON TOSS

One of those great games played at family picnics.

EQUIPMENT
• Water balloons

PLAYERS
4+ (an even number)

OBJECT
To toss a water balloon back and forth without breaking it.

SETUP
Players pair off into teams of two and line up facing their partners about five feet apart, one player on each team holding a water balloon.

PLAY
At a signal, players toss the water balloon to their partners. The players whose water balloons haven't popped take a step back and toss the water balloon again. The other players are out of the game.

The game continues until there's only one team—the winners—left.

VARIATION
Egg Toss is played with raw eggs instead of water balloons.

TRAVEL GAMES

·········

ARE WE THERE YET?

This'll keep them quiet for a while.

EQUIPMENT
- A map or atlas of the United States

PLAYERS
2+

OBJECT
To complete an imaginary trip by spotting the appropriate license plates.

SETUP
Select two states, one as the starting point, the other as the destination—say, Maine and Florida.

PLAY
Each player has to spot a license plate from the state where the race begins, then find a license plate from an adjoining state along the route, and so on.

It's up to each player to decide their route: For example, if Maine is the beginning state, either a New Hampshire or Vermont plate would help them get started.

Only one player can claim each license plate. If the players both need an Ohio plate the first player to spot one can claim it; the other player has to find a different Ohio plate.

The first player to complete the race wins.

VARIATION
Each player has to take the same route, which is decided at the beginning of the game.

·········

COUNTING COWS

The classic kids-in-the-car game that isn't as boring as it sounds.

PLAYERS
2+ (competing individually or in teams)

OBJECT
To get the most points by counting the most cows.

PLAY
Each player or team chooses a side of the car to look out of, and starts counting cows.

If the car passes a cemetery, and one of the players on the other side calls out, "Your cows are buried," the players on the cemetery side of the car lose all their cow-points and have to start all over.

The game ends when the destination is reached or at the end of a pre-determined time limit. The person or team with the most cows wins.

SCORING
Players/teams get 1 point for every cow they count.

STRATEGY
Distracting the other team is allowed, even encouraged. For example, when you see some cows coming up on your opponents' side of the car, or a cemetery is up ahead for your team and you don't want the other team to notice it.

VARIATIONS
White horses or bulls can count as a bonus, as long as it's decided before the game begins.

·········

FORTUNATELY, UNFORTUNATELY

A creative game that can be played anywhere.

PLAYERS
2+

OBJECT
To keep thinking of alternating phrases that begin with "fortunately" or "Unfortunately."

PLAY
One player starts by making up a sentence beginning with "fortunately." For example, "Fortunately, I'm hungry and the restaurant is only two miles away." The next player has to make up a sentence that relates to the first sentence but begins with "unfortunately." So she might say, "Unfortunately, they only serve liver and onions." The third player has to follow with a "fortunately" sentence, say, "Fortunately, I *love* liver and onions." And so on.

Players continue alternating between fortunate and unfortunate things until one of the players is stumped.

·········

FREE ASSOCIATION

Psychoanalysis on the road. AKA Word Association

PLAYERS
2+

OBJECT
To continue the train of free association without hesitating.

PLAY

One player says a word. The second player has to *immediately* say the first word that comes into her head—either a word that's associated with the word, or a word that rhymes with it. Working from the second word, the third player has to come up with an instant association or rhyme for the second word, and so on. For example, *Plumber—Pipe—Smoke—Fire—Wire—Telegram—Send.*

Any player who hesitates is out. Play continues until only one player is left—the winner.

·········

FROM A TO Z

If you're trying to tone down the sibling rivalry, this game can be played cooperatively, without pencil and paper: Whoever sees the first "A" calls the word out, then it's on to "B," etc.

EQUIPMENT

• Pencils

• Paper

PLAYERS

2+

OBJECT

To find the most words that begin with the letters of the alphabet, in order.

SETUP

Players write the alphabet in a column down the left-hand side of a piece of paper.

PLAY

When all the players are ready, they start looking for a word that begins with the letter "A" on a sign, a truck, or a building. When they've found it, they say the word out loud and write it down next to the A. Next, they have to find a word that begins with "B," and so on.

The first player to get to the letter "Z" is the winner.

VARIATIONS

In a version for smaller kids, players have to find words that *contain* each of the letters of the alphabet.

·········

THE LAST WORD

Meant more for grown-up music fans, it can be played anywhere.

PLAYERS

2+

OBJECT

To continue a string of song lyrics.

PLAY

One player begins by singing a line from a song. The singer can stop anywhere in the song: The last word he sings is the word the next player has to start singing with. The words don't have to be the first or last words in a lyric.

Here's an example:

First player: "How dry I am, how dry I am, nobody knows how dry I am . . ."

Second player: "Am I blue? Am I blue? Ain't these tears . . ."

Third player: "Tears on my pillow, pain in my heart . . ."

Next player: ". . . heart in San Francisco, high on a hill it calls to me . . ." And so on.

If a player can't think of a song to pick up from the last word, he can challenge the previous singer, who, if she didn't have a particular song in mind that would pick up her last word, has to redo her turn with a different song.

·········

LICENSE PLATE GAME

A free-for-all game that's best played among people who have similar vo-cabularies. For those who live in, or are visiting, a state whose license plates have three letters.

PLAYERS
2+

OBJECT
To think of the shortest word that uses three letters on a license plate.

SETUP
A player spots a license plate and calls out the three letters on it.

PLAY
The players try to come up with the shortest word that's spelled with those letters in sequence. If two or more players come up with a word that's the same length, the word that comes first in the alphabet wins.

Let's say the letters are CLT. One player says CLOSET, but another player beats that by one letter when he says CLOUT. Either of those players, or any other, can take the lead with COLT. Another player says CLOT, which comes before COLT in the alphabet—and wins the round.

Here are some examples from a recent real-life game:

BLH: BLUSH . . . BRASH comes to mind, too, but BLUSH comes before it in the alphabet. How about BLAH? The winner!

TBA: TUBA

NKH: PINKISH? ANKH. Another winner.

VNH: VANISH

JFL: JOYFUL

HLF: HALF

BLG: BUILDING . . . BILLING . . . BILGE looks like a winner . . . no, wait! . . . BLOG!

NRJ: Still working on it . . .

Try it yourself the next time you're stuck in traffic.

. . . .

TRAVELING SCAVENGER HUNT

A calming activity for those times when the backseat natives are restless.

EQUIPMENT

• A list of items to be found

• A pencil for each player

OBJECT

To find all the items on the scavenger hunt list.

SETUP

Make a list of things you might see on a trip, and give each player a copy.

PLAY

Players look out the car window for the items and mark them off as they see them.

The first player to complete her list is the winner.

VARIATIONS

If you'd rather not encourage sibling rivalry, the hunt can be played cooperatively, with one list. Or have the kids write their own lists before the trip begins.

SUGGESTIONS
City Driving

Flashing red light

Bus with the number 2 on it somewhere

Fire hydrant

Construction site

Bookstore

Sign in a foreign language

Policewoman

License plate that starts with "Q"

Manhole cover

Person talking on a cell phone

Garbage truck

Child wearing tennis shoes

Taxi with three people in it

Church

Suburban Driving

Grown-up on a bike

Black-and-white pickup truck

Cemetery

Dog in the front seat of a car

Golf course

School bus with driver only

Swing set

Person on a front porch

Swimming pool

Shopping mall

Christmas lights on a house

Rural Driving

Silo

Railroad tracks

Fruit stand

Post office

Pond or lake

Dirt road

White horse

Wire fence

Yellow tractor

Hawk

Scarecrow

Mailbox with the flag up

The Game Can Be Played on a Plane Trip, Too

Green backpack

Can of tomato juice

Coffeepot

Red suitcase

Snowcapped mountains

Lake

Umbrella

Woman with red nail polish

Man wearing sandals

Pillow

Glass of white wine

Raincoat

Oxygen mask

Crossword puzzle

SPORTY GAMES

BADMINTON

BASEBALL
Softball
Wiffle Ball
Quickball

BASKETBALL
Horse
Around the World
Foul Shooting
Twenty-one
3-2-1
Greedy

BOCCE
Boules
Lawn Bowls

BOWLING

CROQUET
One-Ball Croquet
Poison
Miniature Croquet

DARTS
Round the World
Shanghai

Flat Earth
Baseball
Hound and Hare

DODGEBALL
Team Dodgeball
Prisoner Dodgeball
Firing Squad
Dr. Dodgeball
Army Dodgeball

FRISBEE GOLF
Disc Golf

HORSESHOES

PING-PONG

TETHERBALL
Tenniball

TOUCH FOOTBALL
Flag Football

TUG-OF-WAR

ULTIMATE FRISBEE

VOLLEYBALL
Beach Volleyball

·········

BADMINTON

The play is similar to tennis, but without the bounce. Here's a casual version of the game.

An official badminton court looks like a smaller version of a tennis court; its dimensions are are 44 × 20 feet for doubles play and 44 × 17 feet for singles. For a casual game, any big grassy area or driveway will do.

EQUIPMENT

- Badminton court
- A net hung five feet high in the center
- A shuttlecock (aka shuttle or birdie)
- A racquet for each player

PLAYERS

2 (singles play) or 4 (doubles play)

OBJECT

To hit the shuttlecock over the net and within bounds so that the opposing player or team can't hit it back before it hits the ground.

SETUP

To decide who'll serve first, players can toss a coin or spin a racquet—when the racquet lands, the person standing nearest the handle gets to choose which side of the court to start on and whether to serve first or not.

Players agree on a final point count, either 15 or 21.

Boundaries are marked off; anything outside the playing area is out of bounds. "Short service lines" are marked off from five to nine feet back

from the net on both sides; for doubles play, a "long service line" is
needed, marked off at two and a half feet from the back boundary. All
serves will have to land past the short service line; in doubles games,
serves cannot go past the long service line at the back of the court.

PLAY

The server stands on the right side of the court and serves the birdie by
dropping it and hitting it underhand when it's at or just below waist
height. The serve has to land diagonally in the other player's right-hand
court to be good.

If the serve arrives on the other side inbounds, the other player tries to
keep it in play. If the other player fails to return it, the serving side scores
1 point and keeps the serve. If the server fails to return the other player's
hit, she loses the serve, but the other player doesn't score a point. Only the
serving player or team can score points.

Servers and receivers move to the other side of the court, alternating
right and left, with each new serve.

After a serve, players can hit the birdie from any spot on their side of
the court. Players are not allowed to touch the birdie more than once in
succession. If the birdie hits the net, it's still in play as long as it goes over
and stays within bounds. If it lands on a line, it's considered inbounds.

The birdie is declared out of play if it fails to cross the net or lands out
of bounds. A rally is also lost if a player commits a fault by touching the
net during play with either his body or racquet, hitting the birdie before it
comes across the net, or being hit by the birdie.

SCORING

Only the serving side scores—1 point for every good hit that the opponent
doesn't return. The first player/team to reach the agreed-upon point total
(and wins by at least 2 points) wins the game. Matches can be played, the
winner being the first to win two out of three games, or three out of five.

HISTORY

Playing with a feathered ball goes back to ancient days. Someone added
the racquet along the way, but it was a group of British soldiers in India
who thought of using a net. These sporty types called their game Poona,
after the village where they were stationed. While home on leave in 1873,
some of them introduced the game to the residents of Badminton Hall in
the Cotswolds, hence the name Badminton.

Trivia

- Badminton made its Olympic debut at the 1992 Summer Olympics in Barcelona, Spain.

- The official shuttlecock is topped by sixteen feathers taken from the same goose, usually from the left wing, which is considered stronger. Olympic shuttles travel at speeds in excess of 150 mph (240 kph)—much faster than the other Olympic net sports.

· · · · · · · · ·

BASEBALL

The great American pastime, as played in the great American backyard.

EQUIPMENT

- A local baseball diamond, big grassy field, or vacant lot

- Any kind of hittable ball

- A bat

PLAYERS

10–18

OBJECT

For the batting team, to score as many runs as possible. For the fielding team, to keep the other team from scoring.

SETUP

If you're laying out your own field you can use virtually anything as bases: pillows, rocks, old tires . . .

Players divide up into two teams and decide among themselves who'll play each position, which team will bat first, and how many innings (rounds of play) the game will last. Each team establishes a batting order—who'll bat first, second, and so on. One team takes their positions on the field while the other bats.

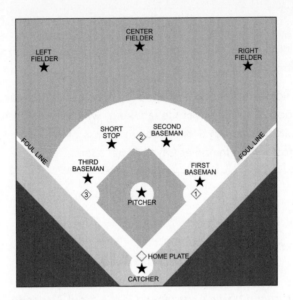

PLAY

Each team will have a chance to bat in each inning. The first batter stands at home plate and tries to hit a pitched ball as far as possible past the fielders, or at least in a way that will make it difficult for them to catch.

With nine players to a team, the fielders position themselves as shown in the diagram. With fewer players, the second-base player can double as right fielder, the shortstop can double as left fielder, and so on. If the number of players is very tight, the batting team can supply its own catcher and the pitcher can cover home plate on a throw home.

Strikes

A batter will have a strike called against him if he:

- misses a good pitch (a throw that comes in over the plate and between the batter's knees and underarms)

- swings at and misses a bad pitch—or a good pitch, for that matter

- hits a foul ball (a ball that's hit or caught outside the foul lines). The first two foul balls count as strikes, but a foul can't count as a third strike to make an out—unless it's caught in the air. In that case, the batter is out.

Batters are allowed three strikes before they're called "out."

Walks

If a batter is thrown a pitch that's too high, too low, or not over the plate and doesn't swing at it, it counts as a "ball." Four pitches like that and the batter scores a "walk"—he can walk to first base.

Hits

When a batter hits the ball, he drops the bat and runs to first base while the other team tries to catch the ball. If it's caught in the air, it's a "fly ball" and the batter is out. Any runners already on base have to tag the base they're occupying after the ball is caught before advancing to the next base.

If the ball is caught after it hits the ground, the fielder closest to it tries to catch it and throw it to the first-base player before the batter reaches first base. The batter doesn't have to be tagged when going for first base— if the ball gets there before he does, he's out.

If a batter's hit is strong enough, he might decide that he has a chance to get to second or third base—or even home plate for a home run— before being tagged out.

After the first batter has finished his turn at bat, the second player in the batting order is up, and play continues. If the second batter gets a hit, he runs to first base. If there's a player at first base, he runs to second while the other team tries to get the batter out at first base and/or tag the player who's running toward second.

Stealing Bases

Once a player is on base, he can try to advance to the next base during another batter's turn at bat. But he can't begin to steal a base until the ball has left the pitcher's hand.

When a team makes three outs, its side is "retired," and the teams change positions: The batting teams takes to the field and the fielders come up to bat. Once the second team has had its chance at bat, the inning is complete.

Play continues until the agreed-upon number of innings are finished.

SCORING

The team that has scored the most runs after the agreed-upon number of innings wins.

VARIATIONS

Official **Softball** games are played to seven innings, the pitch is underhand, and stealing bases is not allowed.

The basic rules of baseball apply to **Wiffle Ball**, but there's no base running. Example: If a player hits a single, his team has a man (an imaginary runner) on first base. If the next player hits a single, the team now has a man on first and second. If the third batter hits a home run, three runs score! (The imaginary runners on first and second, plus the home run.)

The minimum number of players is two—pitcher and batter. The maximum number of players is ten—five players to a side: catcher, pitcher, double-area fielder, triple-area fielder, and home run–area fielder.

Wiffle balls are lightweight (which makes them excellent for playing indoors), with cutouts that make them curve very easily. The Wiffle Ball website (www.wiffleball.com) has some neat diagrams of how the ball should be held for curving and control—as well as a diagram of the suggested playing area.

Quickball, the creation of a former minor-league pitcher, is now being promoted as Ripken Quickball. The plastic ball is a half-inch smaller in diameter than a Wiffle Ball, but twice as thick, and the elongated holes that made the Wiffle Ball unpredictable have been arranged more symmetrically for balanced air flow. The game is fast-paced, played with four-person teams on a field one-fourth the size of a regulation baseball diamond. It's played at more than 100 college campuses. Find out more at www.quickball.com.

See **Stickball** on page 195.

HISTORY

It may sound like heresy, but Abner Doubleday didn't invent baseball—and he didn't invent it in Cooperstown, New York, either, the home of the Baseball Hall of Fame. The name "baseball" had been used as early as the eighteenth century to describe the English game of Rounders (an offshoot of Cricket), the game that seems to be the closest antecedent of American baseball.

Historians give the credit for "inventing" American baseball to a New Yorker named Alexander Joy Cartwright (1820–1892), who established the modern baseball field in 1845. He wrote up the Knickerbocker Rules that formed the basis of modern-day rules. It was still a while before "plugging" (hitting the runner with the ball to get the out) was outlawed. Other early rules included: a ball fielded on one bounce was an out; pitching was underhand; and the game was won by the first team to score 21 "aces" (runs), in however many "hands" (innings) it took.

Cartwright's team, the New York Knickerbockers, participated in the first game played under these rules on June 19, 1846. The Knicks lost 23-1.

Trivia

- The average major league team makes about 150 attempts to steal bases per season, about 85 percent of which are steals of second base. Experts think the positive effects (distracting the pitcher, forcing errors, and opening up the right side of the diamond) can sometimes outweigh the cost of being caught stealing.

- The longest softball game was played at St Mary's Rugby Football Club, Templeogue, Dublin, Ireland, on April 30–May 2, 2004. The game lasted 55 hours and 11 minutes; the total number of innings played was 225.

BASKETBALL

The following half-court games are meant for two players, though most can be expanded if a few more hoopsters drop by. A third player can act as referee for one game, then play the winner of that game. If a fourth player comes along, you can adapt the rules to include two on a team.

EQUIPMENT

- A basketball court

- A basketball

- A basketball hoop with backboard that's mounted so that the hoop is 10 feet above the ground.

PLAYERS
2+ (must be an even number of players for equal teams)

OBJECT
To score more points than one's opponent.

SETUP
Players decide how many points make a game: 11-point games are common, but so are 7-, 15-, and 21-point games. Players shoot from the top of the key to decide who goes first.

A half court can be made in a driveway or playground, with an area of about 20 × 20 feet in front of the basket. Six feet on either side of the center of the basket and fifteen feet back from it is the twelve-foot-long foul line. The inbounds line is about five to ten feet back from the foul line, or where the driveway ends if shorter.

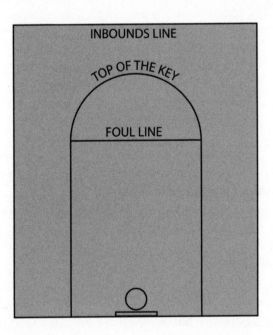

RULES

All baskets are worth 1 point each.

The last scorer gets possession after a basket.

A player who rebounds (catches a missed shot) has to "clear the ball" (go out beyond a certain area) before taking his shot.

PLAY

The first player takes the ball outside the court. To put it in play, he has to bounce the ball at least once inbounds. He can then shoot from that spot or move within the court while dribbling the ball. His opponent tries to prevent him from scoring without fouling or committing a violation. The first player to reach the agreed-upon final point count wins.

Dribbling

Dribbling is the only legal way to move with the ball. Players may not "travel," that is, carry the ball while moving—nor can they "double dribble," start dribbling after they've already dribbled and come to a stop. A player can pivot on one foot without dribbling, but if he lifts the pivot foot he has to dribble, pass, or shoot before he puts that foot down again.

Fouls

A player who's fouled gets to take the ball out again. The offensive player calls his own fouls.

- Blocking: Impeding the progress of an opponent by extending one or both arms horizontally or getting in the path of a moving player.

- Charging: Running into a stationary player while you are moving with the ball.

- Hacking: Hitting the arm or hand of the player holding the ball.

- Holding: Holding a player whether he has the ball or not.

Violations

Violations result in a change of possession; the player who didn't commit the violation takes the ball out at the top of the key or beyond that at an inbounds line.

- Traveling: Taking too many steps without dribbling, or dragging or moving the pivot foot, or taking too many steps after having ended a dribble series by allowing the ball to rest in one or both hands or by losing control of the ball.

- Double dribble: Dribbling the ball with both hands at the same time or stopping a dribble series and starting again.

VARIATIONS

HORSE

OBJECT
To duplicate the shots the first player makes.

PLAY
The first shooter takes a shot from anywhere on the court. If it goes in, the second player has to duplicate it—hook shot, layup, whatever.

If the second player doesn't make it, he's assigned an H. If the second shooter makes the shot, the first tries a different shot.

If the first shooter misses a shot, the second player gets to make a shot that the first has to duplicate.

The right of first shot passes back and forth between the players. Every time they miss a second shot, successive letters in HORSE are assigned to them.

The first player to accumulate all the letters in HORSE loses.

AROUND THE WORLD

OBJECT
To sink baskets from seven spots in a semicircle around the hoop.

PLAY
The first shooter takes a shot from the first position. If he makes the shot, he continues shooting from the following consecutive positions until he misses. If he misses, he'll take up the same position when it's his turn again; in the meantime, the second shooter starts the same sequence.

The first player to make shots 1 through 7—and the reverse of them, 7 through 1—is the winner.

VARIATION

Players get two chances to make a shot—but if they miss the second, they have to start all over from the first position.

FOUL SHOOTING

OBJECT

To sink the most foul shots.

PLAY

Each shooter takes 21 consecutive shots from the foul line. The player who sinks the most shots wins.

TWENTY-ONE

OBJECT

To reach exactly 21 points by completing more foul shots and rebounds than the opponent.

PLAY

One player stands at the foul line, the other under the basket. The foul-line player shoots. If the ball goes in, he scores 2 points and gets to go again. If he misses the shot, the player under the basket attempts a rebound; if his layup goes in, he gets 1 point and the players switch positions. If he misses the shot, the ball goes back to the foul-line shooter, who gets to go again.

The first player to reach *exactly* 21 wins the game. In other words, a player at the foul line who has 20 points should deliberately miss his shot, so that he can try to score one point on a rebound after his opponent has missed a foul shot.

3-2-1

OBJECT

To be the first player to accumulate 21 points.

PLAY

The first player shoots from the foul line. If the shot is good, the shooter wins 5 points and the ball goes to another player.

If the foul shot misses, the shooter rebounds it and has to shoot from where he caught the ball. If he makes this shot, he earns 3 points, and the ball goes to another player.

If the 3-point shot is missed, the shooter has one more chance to make a rebound shot, worth 1 point. After all three shots have been taken, the next player has a turn.

If a player has built up a point total and then misses all three shots in his turn, he loses *all his points* and has to start from zero again.

The first player to score 21 or over wins the game.

GREEDY

EQUIPMENT
- 2 basketballs

OBJECT
To be the first player to score 10 baskets.

PLAY
Each player has his own basketball, and can only shoot with his own basketball.

The players start shooting simultaneously. If a player shoots with the wrong ball, he's an automatic loser.

The first player to score ten baskets is the winner.

HISTORY
The all-American sport of basketball was the brainchild of Canadian-born phys ed teacher James Naismith. Equipment for those first games in 1892: a soccer ball and two half-bushel peach baskets nailed to either end of the gym at the International YMCA Training School in Springfield, Massachusetts.

·········

BOCCE

It's not your grandfather's game anymore.

EQUIPMENT

• A set of bocce balls: 8 large bocce balls (4 of one color or pattern, 4 of another) and a smaller ball called a "pallino"

• A tape measure or other measuring device

PLAYERS

2, 4, or 8 (two even teams)

One-player team: Each player throws all four balls

Two-player team: Each player throws two balls

Four-player team: Each player throws one ball. The teams split up: two players from each team play on opposite sides of the court.

OBJECT

For one team to get as many of their balls closer to the pallino than the opposing team's closest ball.

SETUP

A coin toss determines which team will start. The starting team chooses either to set the pallino or to pick the color balls they want to play with. The other team gets the remaining choice.

PLAY

Playing Surface: The playing surface should be reasonably level, covered with packed sand, clay, dirt, fine gravel, oyster shells, short grass, or a manufactured surface.

Regulation bocce courts are 91×13 feet with or without sideboards and backboards, but a backyard setup can be 60×10 or 60×12 feet, with a center court line and two foot fault lines ten feet from each end. Side-

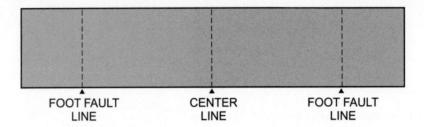

FOOT FAULT
LINE

CENTER
LINE

FOOT FAULT
LINE

boards and backboards make for more interesting play because shots can be banked or rebounded off the walls.

Standing behind the foot-fault line and throwing underhand, the first player rolls the pallino, which has to come to rest somewhere beyond the center line of the court. To be a legal throw, it can't hit the back wall or bounce out of the court. If the first throw isn't successful—or if the player steps over the fault line while throwing—the other team gets a chance to throw the pallino.

Once the pallino is placed properly, the original starting player or team rolls the first bocce ball.

The first player rolls *one* ball as close to the pallino as possible. Then it's up to the opposing player/team to roll a ball (as many as it takes) closer to the pallino than the starting ball—or to hit the pallino and/or any ball on the court to get them closer to the pallino.

RULES

If the opposing team uses all four balls and fails to get closer to the pallino than the starting ball, the starting team rolls its remaining balls, trying to place them closer than the opponents' closest ball. Each one that's closer scores 1 point.

If the opposing team succeeds in placing one of their balls closer to the pallino, they stop rolling and the starting team rolls to try to get closer. If the starting team succeeds, the turn reverts to the second team, and so on.

If a bocce ball hits the backboard, that ball is out of play.

The frame/inning is over when all the balls have been played.

SCORING

Only one team will score, the team whose ball is closest to the pallino: 1 point is awarded for each of its balls that are closer to the pallino than the closest opposing team's ball. A team can score from 1 to 4 points a frame.

No points are awarded if the closest ball of each team is equal in distance from the pallino.

The team that scores in a frame starts the next frame by throwing out the pallino and playing their first ball. Play continues until a team wins by reaching a score of 12 points.

Scoring Variations

There are many more ways to score: Games can be played to 10 or 20 points, bonus points can be awarded for the win, and so on.

VARIATIONS

You may find yourself playing on a bocce court that has pallino fault lines four feet from each back wall. If so, your pallino throw has to come to rest past the center line and *before* the pallino fault line to be legal.

Bocce is nearly identical to the French game of **Boules** or Petanque.

Lawn Bowls is Bocce's British cousin. The game is similar, but it's played with bowls (balls) that are not perfectly spherical, so that they always curve toward the flat side as they slow down. The target ball is called a "jack." The general rules of Lawn Bowls vary from region to region.

Trivia

Bocce fans include sports celebs like John Madden, Bill Walsh and . . . last but not least . . . the late Pope John Paul II.

See them in action at www.ibocce.com/boccepictures

HISTORY

As early as 5000 B.C. the Egyptians played a form of Bocce with polished rocks. The early Romans were among the first to play the game by the modern rules. The Roman soldiers played between battles, using either coconuts brought back from Africa or balls carved out of olive wood. The game spread with their conquests—and with the immigration of Italians in more recent times.

Lawn Bowls began as the Italian game, but the British Isles claimed their own version early on. When it made its way to the American colonies, its spread was kept in check for nearly a century because of strong anti-British sentiments following the American Revolution. Today, both Lawn Bowls and Bocce are played throughout the United States.

·········

BOWLING

The sport of Everyguy and Everygal.

EQUIPMENT

- A bowling ball

- Bowling shoes

OBJECT

To knock down as many pins as possible in a turn.

PLAY

Playing Field: A bowling alley, also known as a lane, is approximately 78 feet long and 41–42 inches wide. Gutters line either side of the alley; if the ball goes off the edge of the alley, it will drop into the gutter and be carried past the pins.

The approach, where the bowler sets up his throw, is fifteen feet long and ends at the foul line. From there, the headpin (the #1 pin) is sixty feet away down the alley.

In each turn the player rolls the ball twice. If she knocks down all the pins with the first roll, it's a strike; if not, she rolls again, trying to knock down the pins still standing. If all the pins are knocked down with two balls, it's a spare; if any pins are left standing, it's called an "open frame."

If a player steps over the foul line during delivery of the ball, it's a foul. The roll counts as a shot and any pins knocked down are respotted (put back in place). Pins knocked down by a ball that has entered the gutter or by a ball bouncing off the rear cushion don't count and are also respotted.

SCORING

Scores are recorded in frames.

1	2	3	4	5	6	7	8	9	10
8 0	3 /	7 2	X	6 /					
8	25	34	54						

1	2	3	4	5	6	7	8	9	10

Frame 1: The 8 in the upper left means that the bowler knocked down eight pins on his first ball. The zero in the small box records that he knocked down none on his second. The 8 at the bottom of the frame records the bowler's entire score for that frame.

Frame 2: The 3 in the upper left means the bowler knocked down three balls on his first try. The slash in the small box indicates a spare—the bowler knocked down the rest of the pins with his second ball. Because of the spare, the total score at the bottom is left empty until the player bowls his first ball in Frame 3.

Frame 3: The bowler knocked down 7 pins on his first ball, so the scorekeeper would add 10 to the 7, and add 17 to the 8 in Frame 1 for a total of 25 points in Frame 2. The 2 in the Frame 3 box means our bowler knocked down two pins on his second ball in the third frame. Adding the 7 and 2 to the 25 in Frame 2 gives our bowler a total of 34 points in Frame 3.

Frame 4: The x in the box means that the player has bowled a strike. That means that both balls in Frame 5 will be added to 10 and scored in Frame 4.

Frame 5: The bowler rolls another spare. The 6 and 4 are added to 10 bonus points, which are added to the total from Frame 3 and recorded in Frame 4.

Frame 6: The number of pins (plus 10) the bowler knocks down on his first roll will be added to the total and recorded at the bottom of Frame 5. If he knocks down all ten pins on his first try, he'll score another strike.

THE PERFECT GAME

Bowling's perfect score, a 300 game, represents twelve strikes in a row—a total of 120 pins knocked down. It's twelve strikes instead of ten because any strike in the last frame earns two more rolls—the score for that frame can't be recorded before rolling twice more. Similarly, if a bowler rolls a spare in the last frame, one more roll is required before the final score can be tallied.

Bowling Specs

The Ball: A regulation bowling ball has a circumference of no more than twenty-seven inches, and weighs ten to sixteen pounds. It can have two or three-finger holes; most bowlers use the three-holed ball, inserting the two middle fingers and the thumb into the holes.

Most bowling alley balls are made of polyester. A lot of privately owned balls are made of urethane, but the Cadillac of bowling balls is made of reactive resin. Its main characteristic is "tackiness"—it grips the lane, adding hook potential and greater hitting power.

The Pins: Regulation pins are made of hard maple; they're 15 inches high with a diameter of 2¼ inches at the base and a circumference of 15 inches at their widest point. They weigh between 2 pounds, 14 ounces, and 3 pounds, 10 ounces.

The ten pins are arranged in four rows, with one pin in the first row, two in the second, three in the third, and four in the fourth. The pins themselves don't carry specific numbers, but the spots on which they're placed do. You don't need to know this, but you'll understand it pretty well the first time you bowl a 7-10 split.

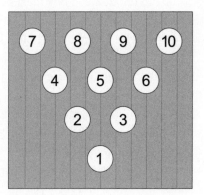

The Shoes: Regulation bowling shoes are an unmatched pair. A right-handed bowler wears a left shoe with a relatively slippery sole, usually of hard leather or vinyl, and a right shoe with a rubber sole that will help "brake." Lefties wear shoes that are vice versa.

· · · · · · · · ·

CROQUET

You may think it's quaint, but Croquet was banned in Boston in the nine-teenth century as "immoral." An anonymous critic of the time wrote, "The ingenuity of man has never conceived anything better calculated to bring out all the evil passions of humanity than the so-called game of croquet."

EQUIPMENT

- A croquet set: 2 stakes, 9 wickets, and a color-matched mallet and ball for each player

PLAYERS

2–6

Two players, four balls: One player plays Blue and Black; the other Yellow and Red.

Two players, six balls: One player plays Blue, Black, and Green; the other plays Yellow, Red, and Orange.

Four players: Each player plays one of the colors: Blue and Black form one team, Red and Yellow the other.

Six players: All six colors are played, the teams divided up into the "cool colors" (Blue, Black, and Green) and the "hot" colors (Red, Yellow, and Orange).

The number of players can expand or contract as need be. With three or five players, a team can alternate turns and can play any one of their own balls in a turn.

OBJECT

To pass the ball through wickets #1 to #7, hit the turning stake, go through wickets #8 to #14, and then go out after hitting the starting stake at the end.

SETUP

Set the stakes so that they're eighteen inches above the ground; the wickets should be ten inches high and four inches wide.

After laying out the course, set the boundaries, which can be as official as tape or string or as casual as a row of hedges or the invisible line between two trees.

Color determines the order of play, based on the top-to-bottom colors on the stakes: Blue, Red, Black, and Yellow. If six balls are being played, the two other colors, Orange and Green, follow.

To choose sides, either decide how players will best team up beforehand, or have all the players hit their balls to the starting stake; the balls nearest the stake and farthest away will be partners. The middle balls can team up.

The ball that lands nearest the stake has the choice of playing first or second.

PLAYING FIELD

The ideal is an open field 100 × 50 feet on relatively even ground. But feel free to stretch it wider or longer, or shrink it to fit into a backyard, park area, or vacant lot.

LAYOUT

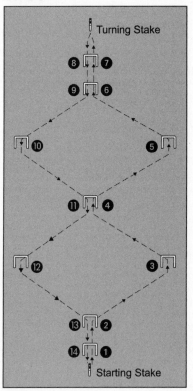

The standard layout for a croquet course.

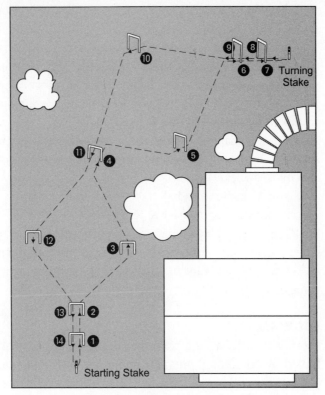

Some home enthusiasts prefer areas with all sorts of hollows and hills, and have been known to lay out a dog-legged course that swings around the corner of a house or across some pretty bumpy terrain. If a tree or bush is in the way, they play around it.

RULES

A mallet cannot strike another's ball.

There's no penalty for a ball played out of turn. It's just returned to its previous position.

If a player hits another player's ball through a wicket or causes it to hit a stake, the wicket or stake is scored, but the other player isn't awarded any bonus strokes for it.

If a player hits two other balls with one stroke and his ball bounces or rolls back and touches the first of the two hit, his turn is over.

A ball that passes through a wicket but rolls back has *not* scored the wicket.

PLAY

A player is allowed one stroke at the beginning of a turn. The first player (Blue) places his ball midway between the stake and the first wicket and tries to pass it through wickets #1 and #2.

If he passes through wicket #1 only, he wins a bonus stroke, also known as a "continuation shot."

If he passes through both wickets, he wins *two* bonus strokes—he gets to go again twice in this turn. This is the only time in the game that a player gets two consecutive bonus strokes in a turn.

If a player makes two wickets in one stroke, he's only entitled to one stroke for the last wicket he went through.

If a player makes a wicket and his ball hits another ball with the same stroke, he's entitled to two strokes for hitting the ball (not three because he also made a wicket).

If a ball hits another ball and then goes through its target wicket, the player is entitled to one stroke for the wicket.

When all the players have had a first turn—Blue through Yellow or Green—each side is allowed to play any of its balls in any given turn.

The first player/team to come back to hit the starting stake wins. The game continues until everyone has finished the course.

SCORING

Scoring is optional. If a game has a time limit, the winner can be determined by counting points: 16 points for each ball (one for each wicket and stake).

Using the Mallet

The ball has to be hit with the end (or "face") of the mallet.

The ball must be *hit*—not shoved.

You can use one or two hands to swing the mallet, but two is best: either swing the mallet forward between your legs, forward along your side, or standing sideways as in golf.

Roqueting

Hitting another ball with the ball that's in play is called "roqueting," which awards the player two bonus strokes that give him four options: He can take two bonus strokes from wherever his ball lands; he can place his own ball a single mallet head's length away from the ball he just hit—in any direction he chooses—and take his two bonus strokes from there; he can put his ball next to the ball hit, then hit his own ball so that it moves both balls in a desired direction (which leaves him one more bonus shot); or he can place his own ball next to and touching the hit ball, then—placing his foot on his own ball—strike it with his mallet so that his own ball doesn't move, but the other ball does. (This also leaves him one more bonus stroke.)

Once a player roquets a ball, he's "dead" on it, that is, he can't strike it again until he goes through a wicket or hits the turning stake (not by accident, but as part of his turn).

Balls sent out of bounds should be placed one mallet length (about 36 inches) from the boundary back within the playing field at approximately the point it went out of bounds. In tournament play, balls that fall within a mallet of the boundary at the end of a turn are moved back from the boundary by the length of one mallet.

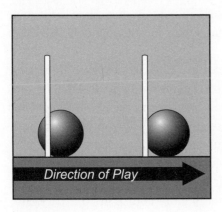

Direction of Play

A ball scores a wicket only if it comes to rest clear of the playing side of the wicket. Its placement can be checked by moving the mallet directly down along the wicket. If the ball moves, it didn't pass completely through. The ball on the left didn't quite make it; the ball on the right did.

STRATEGY

It's not necessarily an advantage to go first, but if you'd prefer to, get on your way quickly, so the player behind you doesn't have the opportunity to hit you.

Don't waste strokes trying to get directly in front of a wicket—plenty of good shots can be made at an angle. If the wickets are set correctly, they can be entered at any angle up to ninety degrees.

Don't hesitate to hit your partner's ball if it's for the good of the team.

Sometimes roqueting a ball out of bounds is the best strategy, even if you're dead on it and will have to end your turn there. It might be more of an advantage to you and your team to get that ball out of a bad position.

Always try to keep a ball or balls in front of yours and in such a position that you can use them to the best advantage.

Partners can help each other by keeping together or by one sending the other a ball he can use.

Trivia

On Sunday, June 28, 1900, two French croquet players became the first female competitors in the modern Olympics; the game made its first and last Olympics appearance that year. A journalist noted that the only paying spectator was an English gentleman who had traveled up from Nice to see the first few games.

VARIATIONS

One-Ball Croquet (aka Cutthroat Croquet) is played as a singles game, one ball per player. The winner is the player who advances her ball around the court first. All the other basic rules apply, including the layout of the course and the bonus strokes earned for hitting opponent balls and scoring wickets.

Poison is usually played as a singles game. When a player completes the course, instead of leaving the game (by hitting the final stake) he can stay in and become "poison." A poison ball doesn't earn bonus shots for hitting other balls, *but* it can eliminate any other ball from the game just by hitting it. A poison ball can be eliminated, too, if an opponent ball hits it, or if it fully passes through any wicket in any direction. When all the players are eliminated, the final player left on the field is the winner.

In **Miniature Croquet**, you set up a random course in your backyard with makeshift ramps, chutes, and bridges and play the game like miniature golf. Then invite all the neighborhood kids over for a game.

. . . .

DARTS

The average speed of a dart hitting a board is around 40 mph (64 kph). So stay out of the way!

EQUIPMENT

• A dartboard

• 2 sets of 3 darts (a set for each player or team)

PLAYERS
2–6

OBJECT
To be the first player to reduce his score to zero.

SETUP
The 20 on the board should be centered at the top. The bull's-eye should measure 5 feet, 8 inches (173 cm) from the floor. A toe line should be marked (in tape or chalk) six to nine feet from the bull's-eye.

A throw determines which player or team goes first; the closest to the bull's-eye takes the first turn. Each player or team gets three darts.

RULES
If a player's foot crosses over the toe line as he throws his dart, the throw counts for no points and may not be rethrown.

Darts have to stay on the board for at least five seconds after a player's final throw to count.

A throw doesn't score if it sticks into another dart or if it falls off the board.

PLAY

Standing behind the toe line, the first player or team throws three darts, leaving them on the board, and records the resulting score. The opponent does the same. At the end of this first leg, all the darts are removed from the board. The second leg begins, the first team going first again and throughout the game.

To win the game, a player/team has to throw a dart that puts their score at *exactly* zero—and that throw has to be a double (a hit to the double ring). For example, with 40 points left, a player needs to hit a double 20. If she hits a single 20 on the first dart, she now has 20 left and needs to hit a double 10 to win.

SCORING

Darts are scored as follows:

- A wedge: the amount posted on the outer ring.

- The double ring (the outer narrow ring): twice the number hit.

- The triple ring (the inner narrow ring): three times the number hit.

- Bull's-eye (outer circle): 25 points.

- Double bull's-eye (inner circle): 50 points.

In the most basic game, both players/teams start with a score of 501. After each throw, they reduce their score by the number of points they hit.

Variations

Playing to 301, 601, or 1001 points are all fairly common. In some versions of the game (notably 301 and 601), a player has to hit a double to start scoring at all; anything hit before the "double-in" doesn't count.

STRATEGY

If you want to play it safe, aim for the left-hand side of the board; there are more high numbers there (e.g., 16, 8, 11, 14, 9, and 12). The scores you rack up might not be huge, but at least you'll never hit a 5 or a 1.

VARIATIONS

Round the World (aka Round the Clock) is simple to play and a great way to practice. Singles and doubles don't count. The object is to hit the numbers 1 to 20 in order, then the outer bull's-eye, followed by the inner bull's-eye.

In **Shanghai**, players start by throwing at the number 1 on the board. The object is to hit a single, double, or triple (in any order). The first player to hit all three in one turn wins. If no player achieves this on number 1, the play moves to number 2, and so on until someone wins. In some versions of Shanghai, a player is out of the game if he doesn't get at least a single on the number in question.

Flat Earth can only be played with a board that isn't permanently attached to the wall. The board is rotated after each game; the first rotation pointing the "20" east, then south, and finally west. Another version of *Flat Earth* is played outside. The board is laid flat on the ground and the players throw their darts downward instead.

Baseball is played in nine innings. Players try to hit the number on the dartboard that corresponds to the current inning. For example, in the first inning players have to hit the 1 to score points. A single is one run, a double is two runs, and a triple is three. At the end of nine innings, the player with the most runs wins. In case of a tie, extra innings are played using the bull's-eye as a target; the player who hits the bull's-eye first wins.

Tip

Hang a scoreboard near the dartboard for keeping score.

FYI

The toe line a player stands behind to throw his darts is called an "oche" (pronounced *ock*). Officially, it should be 7 feet, 9½ inches measured from the face of the board—not the wall behind it. The oche can also be a raised bar, officially one-and-a-half inches high and two feet long, but any temporary line marked on the floor will suffice: think masking tape or chalk.

No one knows for sure where the word *oche* came from. Some theorize that it's from the Old Flemish, meaning "notch" or "nick." But the word "hockey" was used for decades in official competition rules, so others think it derives from hockey—not the sport, but the name of a brewer's case that would have been used to establish the distance between the board and the toe line. Then there's the "hocken" crowd, who think the old English word, which means "to spit," is closer to the truth: that the distance from the dartboard was determined by the length that a given player could spit.

Hound and Hare usually begins with a coin toss to decide who'll be the hare and who'll be the hound. The hare has to travel clockwise around the board starting at 20 and wins the game by returning to 20 before the hound catches up with him. The hound usually starts from either the 12 or 5. The hound wins by overtaking the hare.

HISTORY

The connection between darts and pubs goes way back. Historians think that archery teachers in medieval England shortened some arrows and had their students throw them at the bottom of an empty wine barrel to practice. Their soldier-students supposedly took the short arrows with them to local drinking establishments.

Eventually, someone started using a cross section of a tree to serve as a board; its rings—and eventual cracks—created natural segments that evolved into the classic design of today.

Trivia

The seemingly random numbering on a dartboard was actually the well-plotted design of an English carpenter named Brian Gamlin. First introduced in 1896, Gamlin's design cuts down the incidence of lucky shots and reduces the element of chance. The placing of small numbers on either side of large numbers—for example, the 1 and 5 that flank the 20—penalizes inaccuracy, so if you shoot for the 20, the penalty for faulty aim or lack of concentration—poor you!—is to hit either a 1 or a 5.

·········

DODGEBALL

A favorite of sadistic phys ed teachers everywhere, the game can actually be fun for all, as long as everyone gets to choose whether they want to play or not.

EQUIPMENT
• A large, soft ball

PLAYERS
10+

OBJECT
For the throwing team, to hit the players on the other team with the ball. For the other team, to avoid being hit.

SETUP
Players divide into two teams and decide which one will be the throwing team. The throwing team makes a circle around the other team.

PLAY
The team on the outside throws the ball and tries to hit the players in the middle. If a player is hit, he's out of the game.

Play continues until all the players are out. The teams then trade places, and play again.

VARIATIONS
Team Dodgeball evens up the game. Instead of a circle, the playing area is divided into two halves divided by a center line or central boundary area. The teams throw the ball back and forth, trying to get all the members of the other team out.

If a targeted player catches the ball, the thrower is out of the game, and the player who caught the ball throws it back across the center line, trying to hit someone on the other team. The first team to eliminate all its opponents wins.

A player who steps over the center line or steps out of bounds trying to dodge the ball is out.

In **Prison Dodgeball**, a player who's out waits his turn on the sidelines to be called back into the game. Then, when a player catches a ball, not only is the thrower out, but one of the catcher's teammates (in the sequence they had to leave the game) can rejoin the team.

Firing Squad is Team Dodgeball played against a wall. Two teams face each other: One team stands a few feet in front of the wall, two to three feet apart; the other team—the firing squad—lines up ten to twenty paces from the wall, facing it. The firing squad takes turns throwing the ball. The team with the last player wins. The team against the wall can catch and throw the ball back, trying to hit the firing squad.

Dr. Dodgeball calls for one player on each team to play "Dr. Dodgeball." When other players are hit, they fall on the ground and wait for Dr. Dodgeball to come and save them. When Dr. Dodgeball tags the fallen players, they can get up and play again. The game ends when Dr. Dodgeball is hit.

Army Dodgeball is a little gruesome: Players who are hit in the arm or leg lose the use of that limb for the rest of the game. Players who are hit in the head or torso are "dead," and out of the game. The team with the last surviving member wins.

FYI

Critics of Dodgeball—and there are lots of them—argue that the game provides bullies with the excuse to abuse unathletic and unpopular students. It's been banned from more than one state school system for promoting violence, but it's still played in other places, albeit now usually with a soft foam ball.

· · · · · · · · ·

FRISBEE GOLF

You may never have heard of it, but you can find a disc golf course in every state of the United States, all across Europe, and into the far, far corners of the world. Here's the casual version.

EQUIPMENT

- One or more Frisbees

- Pencil and paper for scorekeeping

PLAYERS

2+

OBJECT

To complete the course with the fewest "strokes."

SETUP

Decide how many "holes" will be played.

PLAY

The first player chooses the first "hole" (a tree, a bench, a telephone pole, etc.) and aims the Frisbee at it. All the players throw the Frisbee at this hole in turn.

Just as in regular golf, if a player doesn't make a hole in one, he walks to where the Frisbee landed on the first throw and aims again from there. Play continues, with players counting the number of "strokes" (throws) it takes to hit the first hole.

After each hole, the players review their scores and (optionally) write them down.

Another player selects the next "hole" (holes should be about 100 to 200 paces apart) and play commences again. The player who completes the course in the least number of throws is the winner.

Tip

Depending on time and space, Frisbee Golf can be played like traditional golf with eighteen holes. Feel free to add hazards to the course: going over bushes, through a tunnel, or across a playground.

VARIATIONS

If you can't get enough Frisbee Golf, you can move up the Frisbee food chain to **Disc Golf**, which is played on actual nine-or eighteen-hole courses. The game uses three different sizes of flying discs that are similar to the Frisbee, but usually smaller and heavier.

Disc Golf courses are usually laid out in wooded areas with diverse terrain and obstacles that add to the challenge. The "holes" are wire baskets hung from poles by chain links.

The Professional Disc Golf Association is the governing body for the sport, and sanctions competitive events for men and women of every skill level from novice to professional. Visit them at www.pdga.com.

· · · · · · · · ·

HORSESHOES

A game from the olden days, when folks in pre–Big Five Sports America played games with whatever was lying around.

EQUIPMENT
• 2 horseshoes for each player

PLAYERS
2 or 4 (for doubles play)

OBJECT
To earn points by throwing more ringers than your opponent.

PLAYING FIELD
A horseshoe "pitch" measures forty feet from stake to stake. At either end of the pitch are two pits, four feet long and three feet across. In the center

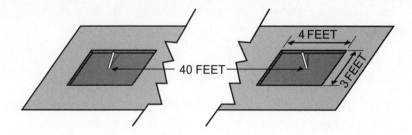

of each pit is a metal stake. The two three-foot-long stakes are driven into the ground until only fourteen inches extend above ground; they lean toward each other at a three-inch angle. The pit is filled with sand, clay, or dirt and defined by 2×6s driven into the ground on edge.

PLAY

Standing either next to or behind one of the stakes, the first player throws first one, then the other of his horseshoes at the opposite stake. The second player does the same thing.

The players walk to the opposite pit, calculate their scores, and begin another round, throwing at the other stake.

Doubles Play: The partners stay at opposite ends of the pitch, and simply return their partner's horseshoes.

Players can take turns pitching first in a round or the winner of one round can go first in the next.

SCORING

A horseshoe that completely surrounds the stake is called a "ringer." If there's any doubt as to whether or not a throw qualifies as a ringer, a straightedge can be placed against the open end of the horseshoe; if the straightedge doesn't touch the stake, it's a ringer. A "leaner" is just that: a horseshoe that ends up leaning against the stake.

Home scoring is easy. Every ringer is worth 3 points; every leaner scores 1 point. If no ringers or leaners are made in a round, only the player whose horseshoe or horseshoes are closest to the stake wins the round, scoring 1 point for every horseshoe that's closer than the opponent's, 2 points if both are closer.

Official scoring is more complicated. For one thing, leaners don't count. Ringers are scored (and sometimes cancelled out) thusly:

If no ringers are thrown, the nearest horseshoe to the stake scores 1 point.

If both players throw a single ringer each, the ringers are cancelled out and the nearest of their other two horseshoes scores 1 point.

If a player gets a single ringer, 3 points are scored—plus an extra point if his other horseshoe is the closest of the remaining three.

If a player gets two ringers and the other player manages none, the two ringers score 6 points.

If a player gets two ringers and the other player gets one ringer, the two ringers score 3 points.

If both players score two ringers each, they cancel each other out and no points are scored.

The first player to reach 21 points wins the game.

HISTORY

The game was adapted from the British game of Quoits, which evolved from the ancient Greek discus throw, which itself was based on the sporty use of quoit-like objects as ancient weapons.

Regulation Play

In official league competitions, a horseshoe should weigh around 2 pounds, 8 ounces, be 7⅝ inches long and 7 inches wide, and the gap should be 3½ inches wide.

Trivia

One master horseshoe pitcher tossed more than 7 tons of steel and walked more than 25 miles in one Florida tournament.

The game was nicknamed "Barnyard Golf" until President Warren Harding made it a respectable pastime in the 1920s.

FYI

The specs of the pitch call for a distance of 30 feet for women, 20 feet for children, but women and kids can play on a full court by simply standing that much closer to the stake.

Roman soldiers were the first to use old horseshoes bent into crude rings, but like the discus, they were thrown for distance, not accuracy. Quoits was born when someone thought of throwing the ring at a stake. The Romans spread the game to the cultures they conquered, including Britain, where the game became so popular that centuries later, in 1361, King Edward III outlawed it, thinking his subjects were spending too much time at it and not enough on honing their skills of war.

Despite it all, the game continued to be played. The early English settlers brought their quoits with them to America, but supplies were scarce out on the prairie, so game enthusiasts started using cast-off horseshoes.

· · · · · · · · ·

PING-PONG

Of course, it's called "table tennis" in official play, but if you're just going down to the basement for a few rounds, you can call it Ping-Pong.

EQUIPMENT
- A Ping-Pong table

- Ball

- A paddle for each player

PLAYERS
2 or 4

SETUP
A coin toss can determine which player serves first, or players can volley for serve. The winner of the coin toss or volley serves first. Players agree on a final point count, usually 11 or 21 points.

PLAY
Without leaning over the table, the server tosses the ball into the air and hits it so that it bounces on his own side of the table, then on the opponent's side. The opponent has to hit the ball back so that it goes over the net without bouncing on his side, and so that it bounces on the server's half of the table. The server returns the volley in the same way.

The players hit the ball back and forth until one of the players hits the ball so that it bounces first on his own side or goes into the net; hits the ball beyond the table on the opponent's side; hits a received ball before it bounces on his side; or fails to hit a received ball after it's bounced once on his side.

If any of these things happen, the other player gets 1 point. Each player serves for 2 points, regardless of who wins the points.

A "let" is called when the ball hits the net on a serve and keeps going over onto the other side of the net. There are no limits to lets in a game; the serve is redone.

Play continues until one player reaches the agreed-upon point count.

SCORING

Games have to be won by at least a two-point difference. In other words, if Player A had 20 points and Player B had 19, Player A could win the game by winning the next point. But Player B would have to score 22 to win, provided he could keep his opponent at 20.

Doubles Play

In doubles play, the serve is always from the right side of the table, delivered crosswise to the opponent's right side of the table. The serve has to land inside that half of the receiving side to be good.

If Players A and B are playing opposite Players C and D, Player A serves twice to Player C. Then Player C serves twice to Player B, after which Player B serves to Player D, then D serves to A, and so on.

If the game reaches deuce (e.g., when the score is 10-10 in an 11-point game), the order of serve changes after every point.

OFFICIAL EQUIPMENT

The ball is a high-bouncing hollow celluloid ball that weighs about 0.1 ounce (2.7 grams) and is about 1.5 inches (40 millimeters) in diameter.

The table is 9 feet (2.74 meters) long, 5 feet (1.525 meters) wide, and 30 inches (76 centimeters) high, made from a Masonite or similarly manufactured timber, coated with a low-friction smooth coating, divided into two halves by a 6-inch (15.25 centimeter) high net.

The rackets (also called bats or paddles) are wooden and covered with rubber. One side is black, the other side is red.

ORIGINS

Both "ping" and "pong" come from the sound of the ball hitting the paddle. Wordsmiths date the origin of the combination, "ping-pong," from 1900, when the word was trademarked by those savvy Parker Brothers.

Today the rights to the name Ping-Pong (and the equipment that's sold under the name) belong to Indian Industries, Inc.

Trivia

- The first commercially successful video game—Pong—was inspired by Ping-Pong.

- Table tennis has been an Olympic sport since 1988.

- "Ping pong ball" is the official name for the sport in China.

- The longest table tennis/Ping-Pong rally took place on November 5, 1977. It lasted five hours, two minutes, and 18.5 seconds. The participants were John Duffy and Kevin Schick of New Zealand.

VARIATION

You can alternate serves every five points, which is the way it was played officially before 2001.

·········

TETHERBALL

If you can't find a tetherball court, you can make your own, but you'll have to weigh down the pole with something like a concrete-filled tire. AKA Swingball

EQUIPMENT

An 8- to 10-foot stationary metal pole with a rope attached at the top and a volleyball-sized ball attached to the bottom of the rope (when not in play, the ball should hang about two feet off the ground).

PLAYERS

2

OBJECT

To wind the rope and the ball all the way around the pole.

SETUP

The players stand on opposite sides of the pole behind a line that divides the area around the pole into two distinct sides.

PLAY

One player serves the ball by holding it in one hand and hitting it with the other (either with the fist or open hand), or by throwing it up and hitting it.

The opposing player then tries to return the serve by hitting it back in the opposite direction.

The game ends when one player hits the ball all the way around the pole in her own direction, so that the ball hits the pole.

RULES

There are four ways a player can commit a violation: stepping over the boundary into her opponent's territory; catching and throwing (known as "carrying") the ball; hitting the rope instead of the ball; and hitting the ball twice before it's either circled the pole or been returned by the opponent.

If a violation occurs, the game pauses and the ball is returned to the position it was in before the violation, with the same number of wraps around the pole. The player who didn't commit the violation then serves the ball.

SCORING

A match can consist of one, three, five, or more games. If playing more than one game, the loser of a game gets to serve the next game.

STRATEGY

Don't stand in the same spot! Move forward and backward in your territory so your opponent can't set you up. And it'll be easier to steal the ball if you suddenly rush to a position—forward or back—that's closer to him.

VARIATIONS

The server has to wait until the receiver hits the ball or the ball wraps four times before she can hit it again. This evens out the advantage of serving, and even works to some servers' disadvantage.

Tenniball uses a smaller ball that's hit with rackets. A homemade version would use an old tennis ball and Ping-Pong or racketball rackets.

The best serve is hit at a sharp angle so that the arc of the ball tilts closer to vertical than horizontal. You may only get one wrap out of it, but it should easily prevent your opponent from getting a clean first hit.

Sometimes you'll need to make a "sacrifice wrap." If a ball is too high or awkwardly angled for you to hit back past him easily, try hitting the ball once in his direction, thereby setting yourself up for an easy hit in your own direction.

FYI

The originators used a volleyball, but today sporting goods manufacturers make tetherballs specifically for the game: The ball is about the size and weight of a volleyball, but firmer, and usually has a recessed bar that the rope is tied to.

· · · · · · · · ·

TOUCH FOOTBALL

The game became a household word when the young Kennedys were ris-ing to political power. Their heirs are still playing, from what we hear.

PLAYERS
4–18

OBJECT
When a team is playing offense, to carry and pass the ball over the oppos-ing team's goal line into their endzone. When playing defense, to keep the other team from scoring.

SETUP
Players divide into two teams and choose a quarterback for each. By flip-ping a coin, players decide which team will be the first to play offense (the team that will have possession of the ball and try to move it downfield to the other team's endzone) or defense (the team that will try to stop the other team from reaching their endzone). They also decide how long the game will last—or if the game will end after a certain amount of points are scored.

Boundaries are decided; anything outside the playing area is out of bounds. The ball is placed midfield, at what would be the 50-yard line on a regulation field, and the teams each form a line on either side of the ball, parallel to the end zones and facing each other, the offensive team close to the ball, the defense a few feet away from it.

The quarterback stands behind the "center," his teammate in the center of the line.

PLAYING FIELD
A regulation NFL football field is a total of 120 yards long—100 yards of playing field with ten-yard-long endzones at either end—and 53 ⅓ yards wide. But any big grassy field, quiet street, empty parking lot, or vacant lot will do for a game of touch football. The field should be rectangular, with goal lines at either of the long ends and ten feet or so beyond them for end

zones. If playing in the street, the curbs can be the sidelines; trees, cars, or streetlights can mark the goal lines.

PLAY

The quarterback calls "Hike!" to signal the start of the play. The center snaps the ball to the quarterback between his legs or hands it to him sideways. The quarterback hands off the ball to a runner or passes the ball to a receiver, who then runs with the ball toward the opponent's endzone while defensive players try to tag him with one hand anywhere on his body. Meanwhile, the other offensive players try to keep the defense from tagging the ball carrier by getting in their way or even bumping them lightly.

The play ends when the runner is tagged, drops the ball, or runs out of bounds—or if a pass is "incomplete" (not caught) or goes out of bounds. This completes a "down."

The offensive team now has three more tries, or "downs," to move the ball to their opponents' goal line and score a touchdown. Players "huddle" to decide on their next play, then line up again at the line of scrimmage, where the last team member was tagged.

If, after three more downs, the offensive team hasn't made it to the endzone, they give up possession of the ball to the other team: the defensive team is now the offense, and vice versa. The game recommences at the point where the ball was last in play. The new offense gets four attempts to move the ball toward the opposite end zone.

If the defense intercepts a pass, the defensive team immediately takes possession of the ball—the player who caught the ball can run with it toward the opponent's goal line or pass it to another team member. If the offense drops the ball, the play is dead at the spot where the ball was dropped and teams switch possession.

Possession is also switched when a point is scored. Play begins again by setting the ball in the middle of the field and lining the teams up as before.

Play continues until the point limit or time limit is reached.

SCORING

Each touchdown scores 6 points.

VARIATIONS

The number of downs can vary according to field size: fewer downs on smaller fields and more downs on larger fields.

Each time a team gets possession of the ball, they can choose a new quarterback.

With an odd number of players, one person can be designated quarterback for both teams.

In some games, the defense has to wait five seconds before rushing in to tag the quarterback. But the defense has the option of surprising the offense by "blitzing" (running in without counting) once every set of downs.

If you're lucky enough to have a couple of good kickers on your teams, you can start the game with a kickoff and add field goals and points after the touchdown.

Flag Football is played by the same rules, except that a flag or bandanna is stuffed into each player's pocket. Instead of tagging an opponent, a defensive player has to pull the ball carrier's flag out of his pocket to end the play.

·········

TUG-OF-WAR

The perfect game for a crowd-size picnic.

EQUIPMENT
- 100+ feet of strong rope

- Bright-colored masking or electrical tape

PLAYERS
10+

OBJECT
To pull the opposing team across the center line.

SETUP
A center line is either drawn on the ground or chosen from a natural straight line like a stream or (better) a large mud puddle.

The rope should be marked with tape in five places: the center of the rope, 15 feet back from the center on either side, and two feet back from the 15-foot marks.

The two teams align themselves along the ends of the rope, behind the 17-foot marks. At each end is an "anchor" (usually the biggest, strongest person on the team) who secures the rope by putting it under his arm and over his shoulder, or around his waist.

When the teams are in place, the rope is pulled taut and a "referee" makes sure that the center mark on the rope is exactly over the center line.

PLAY

The ref calls the start of the "pull" and each team tries to pull the other team so that their 15-foot mark goes past the center line. The team that pulls the other past its mark wins.

If you thought it was only a game played at company picnics, you'll be surprised to learn that there are tug-of-war clubs all over the world—and both men and women participate.

There's an actual TWIF (Tug-of-War International Federation) and they've got some serious rules. Pages and pages of them. Here are some excerpts:

Status: Players must be amateurs.

Age Range: To tug as a Junior you must be between the ages of 15 and 18; Seniors (men), 18 and up; and women must be at least 16 years old.

Teams: Eight tuggers to a team, one substitute allowed, but he/she and the player being replaced must report in full "pulling" outfit (shirts, shorts, stockings, and footwear) to the Chief Judge. The sub must be of equal weight or less than the player he/she is replacing. Only one substitution is allowed per game.

Weight: Team totals have to fit into one of nine weight categories— from Ultra Featherweight (480 kilos, or 1056 pounds) to Catchweight (no weight limit).

The Rope: The all-important rope must be between 10 and 12.5 centimeters (3.94 to 4.92 inches) in circumference. The minimum length of the rope is 33.5 meters (109.9 feet).

Scoring: Each game within a round is called a "pull." Two pulls to nil (zero) scores 3 points; teams winning one pull each round score 1 point apiece. Then it's on to Pull-Offs, Semifinals, and finally, Finals.

To learn more about the serious sport of Tug-of-War, including those "stockings" they're supposed to wear, visit www.tugofwar-twif.org/rules.

·········

ULTIMATE FRISBEE

"Ultimate" is distinguished from other sports and games by having an actual philosophy behind it. Players call it the "Spirit of the Game," the principles of fair play, sportsmanship, and the joy of play. Imagine that. AKA Ultimate

EQUIPMENT

- A big grassy field (an area about 70 × 40 yards, with goal lines at either of the long ends and extra room beyond them for endzones)

- Frisbee

PLAYERS

6–14 (two teams of 3 to 7 players)

OBJECT

To throw the Frisbee downfield and eventually to score by passing it to a teammate in the end zone.

SETUP

After deciding which side will "receive," the teams line up behind their goal lines.

PLAY

The throwing team tosses the Frisbee to the receiving team, who can either catch it and move it downfield by passing it or pick it up where it landed. When a player takes possession of the disc, he has ten seconds to pass it to another member of his team, but without moving from that spot. A player is never allowed to run—only to pivot on one foot. If a player takes a step, there's a turnover—the other team gets possession.

Play continues following these additional rules:

No physical contact is allowed between players. When one player touches another, it's a foul.

Players call their own fouls and line violations. If a call is disputed, the play can be redone. But the idea is to play within the sprit of the game—an honor system that discourages cheating.

If a pass is not completed for any reason (if it's intercepted, goes out-of-bounds, or a player drops it), the other team gets possession.

SCORING

A team scores 1 point for every completed pass into the defense's end-zone.

VARIATION

Some games are played with referees, called "observers," who have the power to make calls and who can resolve disputes if the players involved ask for a judgment.

HISTORY

The first Frisbee (c. 1940) was an empty tin pie plate from the Frisbie Pie Company in New Haven, Connecticut, that some Yale students realized was good for something other than holding pies.

Ultimate Frisbee evolved from Frisbee Football. The first Ultimate game was played in the parking lot of Columbia High School in Maplewood, New Jersey, in the spring of 1968. The first players were the school's non-jocks.

Four years later, the first intercollegiate Ultimate competition took place on the Rutgers New Brunswick campus in 1972 (Rutgers vs. Princeton).

For more information on the rules and strategy of Ultimate visit www.ultimatehandbook.com/uh

---

When a ball dreams, it dreams it's a Frisbee.—Bumper sticker

·········

VOLLEYBALL

The game's inventor fashioned the game for businessmen who were a little too old to play basketball; he styled his game to be a blend of basketball, baseball, tennis, and handball.

EQUIPMENT

- A volleyball court (or an area about 30–60 feet long and 15–20 feet wide)

- A volleyball

- A regulation volleyball net (3×32 feet long, hung eight feet high for men, seven feet six inches for women, seven feet for children), or a rope hung with a blanket, or even a fence that's about the right height.

PLAYERS

Two teams of 2–9 players each

OBJECT

To score the most points by preventing the other team from hitting the ball back across the net.

SETUP

Players divide up into teams, decide which team will go first, and spread out on the court. Six players on a team should have three in the first row, three behind; nine players should have three rows of three across.

Boundaries are decided on; anything outside the playing area is out of bounds.

PLAY

The server for the first team stands in the rear right-hand corner of her side of the court, and either tosses the ball up in the air and hits it with an open palm or fist, or holds the ball in one hand and swings the other arm to hit the ball underhand.

If the ball hits the net and/or fails to go over, or goes out of bounds, the serve goes to the other team.

If the ball hits the net and goes over, the server serves again.

If the serve lands within the boundaries of the other side, the receiving team can take as many as three hits to return the ball, hitting the ball underhand, overhead, or with any of these hits:

Bump: Placing the forearms together stretched out in front, then getting under the ball and "bumping" it up into the air.

Set: Hitting the ball with both hands to place it near the net so another teammate can hit it over.

Spike: Jumping up and hitting the ball with fist or palm, aiming it at the ground on the opponent's side.

If a ball is hit into the net it remains in play as long as it doesn't touch the ground. The teams volley back and forth until one team fails to return the ball; the ball goes out of bounds or touches the ground; or a player makes an error, such as touching the ball twice in succession; holding or carrying the ball; or touching the net.

SCORING

If the receiving team fails to return the ball or errs, the serving team scores a point. The serving team keeps the service until they make an error or fail to return the ball, at which time the service is given to the other team. A team can only score when it's serving.

If the serving team wins the volley, it earns 1 point and serves again. If the receiving team wins the volley, it's a "sideout"—no points are awarded, but the serve passes to their team.

When a team gets the serve, positions are rotated one space clockwise; the last server moves to the left, the player farthest left at the net moves to the center (or to the right, depending on the number of players), and so on.

The first team to score 21 points by a margin of 2 points wins.

Variation

In rally point scoring, the team that wins the rally scores the point. If the serving team wins the point, it keeps the serve; if the receiving team wins the point, it also wins the right to serve.

VARIATION

Beach Volleyball is played on sand, two players to a team, with sideout scoring. It was first played in Santa Monica, California, in the 1920s. The sport started appearing in Europe a decade later.

HISTORY

The first volleyball game was played in 1895 at the Holyoke, Massachusetts, YMCA where its inventor, William G. Morgan (1870–1942), was a phys ed instructor. Morgan had named his new game "Mintonette"—what *was* he thinking?—but an acquaintance suggested "volleyball" . . . and the rest is history.

That first volleyball net was a tennis net hung six feet six inches (1.98 meters) high. The height was raised a foot higher in 1900.

Trivia

Volleyball became an Olympic sport in 1964. Beach volleyball was added in 1996. Brazil won the gold and silver women's beach volleyball medals that first year, the first time that any Brazilian women had ever won an Olympic medal.

Wilson, the volleyball that was Tom Hanks' best friend in the movie *Cast Away*, sold for $18,400 at an online auction in 2001.

CARD GAMES

GENERAL RULES

GAMES FOR GROWN-UPS

BEGGAR MY NEIGHBOR

BLACKJACK

BRIDGE
Double Dummy
Single Dummy
Honeymoon Bridge
Bridge for Three

CASINO
Three-Handed Casino
Four-Handed Casino
Royal Casino
Draw Casino
Spade Casino
Royal Spade Casino

CRIBBAGE
Three-Hand Cribbage
Four-Hand Cribbage
Five-Card Cribbage
Seven-Card Cribbage
Low-ball

EUCHRE

HEARTS
Omnibus Hearts
Pink Lady
Cancellation Hearts
Spot Hearts
Domino Hearts
Heartsette
Draw Hearts
Sweepstake Hearts
Joker Hearts

OH HELL
Looney Gooney

PINOCHLE
Partnership Pinochle

POKER

FIVE-CARD DRAW
Jackpot
Pass the Garbage
Lowball

SEVEN-CARD STUD
Five-Card Stud
Mexican Stud
Chicago
Baseball
Football

TEXAS HOLD'EM
Omaha Hold'em
Cincinnati
Criss-Cross

MISCELLANEOUS POKER GAMES
Indian Poker
Two-Card Poker
Three-Card Poker

RUMMY

BASIC RUMMY
Queen City Rummy
Boathouse Rum

KNOCK RUMMY

GIN RUMMY
Round-the-Corner Gin
Oklahoma Gin

500 RUM
Fast 500
Partnership 500 Rum
Persian Rummy
Michigan Rum

CANASTA

WHIST

GAMES FOR KIDS

CONCENTRATION

CRAZY EIGHTS

GO FISH

I DOUBT IT

OLD MAID

PIG

SLAPJACK

SPIT

SUIT OF ARMOR

WAR

SOLITAIRE GAMES

ACCORDION

CLOCK SOLITAIRE

IDIOT'S DELIGHT

KLONDIKE
Gargantua
Yukon

PYRAMID

SPIDER
Scorpion
Double Scorpion
Black Widow
Black Spider

EXTRA

BUILD A HOUSE OF CARDS

·········

GENERAL RULES

Given the wide variety of card games, there are a surprising number of general rules that players can apply to most all of them. You and your cardmates, of course, can make up your own rules as you go along. But in the interest of order and goodwill, when playing the games in this section, *unless otherwise noted*, the rules are as follows.

The Dealer: The dealer is chosen by draw. The cards are either fanned out facedown and each player selects a card, or the players cut the cards.

In a friendly game, the dealer can be the shuffler, too.

After the shuffle the dealer offers the shuffled deck to the player on his right, who cuts the deck by lifting a portion (at least four cards) off the top and placing it nearer the dealer than the bottom portion. The dealer completes the cut by placing what was the bottom part on the top part.

The cards are dealt one at a time, beginning on the dealer's left, clockwise and facedown. (Remember, this is *unless otherwise noted*. Some games, as you'll see, are dealt two or three at a time.)

After each hand, the deal moves clockwise, to the player to the left of the first dealer.

The Lead: The player to the dealer's left leads the first card of the game. Play proceeds clockwise around the table.

Aces: Unless otherwise noted, aces are high.

Two Decks: Players of Bridge and Whist (and a few other games) use two decks: While the dealer is dealing, the dealer's partner shuffles the other deck. When finished, he places it at his right, next to the player who'll be the next dealer. It isn't necessary, but it speeds up the process and gets the next game going more quickly.

When the next deal begins, the new dealer can shuffle the pack once more, and move the shuffled pack to his right. The player on his right cuts the deck.

Misdeal: When the dealer makes a mistake of some kind—either flipping over a card by accident or dealing out of order—a misdeal can be called before the first round of play is completed; otherwise the deal stands. If a misdeal is called in time, the cards are thrown in and redealt by the next dealer.

Play out of turn: There's no penalty for a lead, or play out of turn, but any other player can ask that it—and any other cards played to it—be retracted. If no one asks for a retraction, the out-of-turn play stands. The player who made the out-of-turn play supposedly can't retract it unless it's demanded by another player.

GAMES FOR GROWN-UPS

·········

BEGGAR MY NEIGHBOR

A game of chance more than skill.

EQUIPMENT
• A 52-card deck

PLAYERS
2–6

OBJECT
To win all the cards.

SETUP
All the cards are dealt out facedown into piles for each player as far as they'll go. (Some players will have more cards than others.)

PLAY
The player to the left of the dealer turns over the top card on his pile and places it faceup in the middle of the playing surface. If the card isn't a face card or an ace the next player turns over one of his cards.

Play continues to the left until a face card or an ace is turned up. When this happens the *next* player has to "pay" the player who turned over the face card or the ace one card for a jack; two cards for a queen; three cards for a king; four cards for an ace

The player paying the penalty turns over one card at a time. If none of them is a face card or an ace, the first player gets to keep them all. But if one of them is a face card or an ace, the original debt is erased and the first player has to pay the second player the corresponding number of cards.

Let's say, for example, that Player A turns over a queen. That means that Player B has to pay two cards. But if the first card that Player B turns over is a jack, Player A now has to pay Player B one card.

Players continue paying debts back and forth until no more face cards or aces are turned up. When this happens, the player who played the last ace or face card wins the central pile, and adds it facedown at the bottom of his stack. The game then continues with the next player.

Play continues until one player—the winner—has all the cards.

·········

BLACKJACK

How close can you get to 21 without going over? The at-home game is usually called Blackjack, but gaming houses call it Twenty-one. In France it's Vingt-et-un (French for "twenty-one").

EQUIPMENT

• A 52-card deck

• Chips (optional)

PLAYERS

2–12

OBJECT

To get a higher point total than the dealer up to, but not over, 21.

SETUP

The first card is dealt facedown. Players bet only against the dealer. If playing for money (or chips or whatever), players can bet based on this first card. Aces are worth either 1 or 11; face cards are worth 10; other cards are worth their pip value.

PLAY

Players are dealt the second card faceup and add the value of the two cards together. Starting with the player on the dealer's left, a player can either "stand" (stick with the cards he has) or call, "Hit me" (ask the dealer for an additional card, dealt faceup). A player who asks to be hit can continue to receive more cards until he signals that he's done or says, "I stand."

If any additional card puts the player's count over 21, he's "busted," and has to show his cards. The dealer collects that player's bet.

Once every player has either stood or gone over 21, the dealer turns over his facedown card and decides whether he wants any additional cards himself. If the dealer goes over 21, he pays every player who has 21 or less. If he stands on 21 or less, he collects from each player who had the same or a lower total, and pays each player who had a higher total.

Payouts

If a player is dealt a "natural," an ace with a facecard or 10, the payout is 2 to 1 in most social games. So if the bet was $1, the player gets $2 back.

If a player is dealt 21 or less in five cards, the payout is 2 to 1; in six cards, 3 to 1.

If a player makes 21 with three sevens, the payout is 3 to 1; a 21 composed of 8-7-6 has a payout of 2 to 1.

If a player ties with the dealer (e.g., both stand with 18), the dealer wins.

If the dealer is dealt a natural, the dealer collects double from the other players.

After the bets have been settled, it's the custom in home games for a player who was dealt a natural to become the dealer in the next game. If two or more players have naturals, the deal goes to the one nearest the dealer's left. If the dealer also has a natural he keeps the deal.

VARIATIONS

Splitting Pairs is an option in which, if a player's first two cards are a pair, he can separate them and use them as the basis for two separate hands. When his turn comes, he turns both face-up and places the amount of his original bet on each. The dealer gives him one card down to each; the player can ask for a hit or stand on either hand.

Doubling Down is when a player turns up both cards and doubles his bet. But he can only be dealt one card. (Some games limit this option to players who have 10 or 11 only.)

·········

BRIDGE

Despite all the exacting rules about bidding, bridge can be played by the seat of one's pants—ask anyone who learned it in college. If you decide you like the game, there are myriad rules and bidding conventions awaiting you.

EQUIPMENT
• A 52-card deck

PLAYERS
4

OBJECT
To win the number of tricks bid; to win a hand or series of hands to make game; to win a series of games to make rubber.

SETUP
Players draw for partners. The two highest cards make a partnership against the other two and sit facing each other. The highest card determines who'll be the first dealer. If two or more players pull the same number or face card, the highest suit wins. The suits are ranked from lowest to highest (conveniently, in alphabetical order): clubs, diamonds, hearts, spades. Clubs and diamonds are the minor suits; hearts and spades are the major suits. So spades beats hearts beats diamonds beats clubs.

All fifty-two cards are dealt. Most players sort their hands, alternating red and black suits from left to right, and from highest to lowest within each suit.

Bidding
In bidding, players try to communicate to their partners what kind of hand they've drawn so they can arrive at the best contract for their partnership.

The bidding proceeds like an auction: Each bid has to be higher than the previous bids, either higher in number of tricks or at the same level in a higher suit. A bid of No Trump is higher than the four suits; e.g., after a bid of three no trump, there can be no more bids at the three level; subsequent bids have to begin at the 4 level at least.

The player to the left of dealer starts by either passing or opening the bidding. The player to her left then has the same option. If all four players pass, the hands are thrown in and the player to the dealer's left deals a new hand.

A trick consists of the four cards played in any given round of play. The number in a bid always refers to the number of tricks that have to be won in excess of the first six. A bid of three spades, for example, means that the bidder has a contract to take nine of the total thirteen tricks with spades as trumps. A bid of five No Trump means that a side will take eleven of the thirteen tricks with no trump suit—unless, of course, someone else makes a bid after that.

To win a game, a team needs a minimum of 100 points. Bids of clubs or diamonds are worth 20 points per trick; hearts or spades are worth 30 points; a bid of No Trump scores 40 points for the first trick and 30 for each additional trick. To win a game in one hand (and thereby receive a game-scoring bonus), players have to bid up to a level of:

- Five or more in clubs or diamonds: 100 points (20 points × 5)

- Four or more in hearts or spades: 120 points (30 points × 4)

- Three or more in No Trump: 100 points (40 for the first trick, 30 for each of the next two)

Double and Redouble

During the bidding, an opponent can "double" a bid and a bidder can "redouble" the double. Doubling and redoubling increase the score for the bid contract if won and the penalties if lost. If a bid of one heart was doubled by an opponent, and the bidder succeeded in making that bid, it would be worth 60 points (30 × 2). If the original bidder redoubled, the one-heart bid would be worth 120 points (30 × 4)—which, by the way, would win the game.

If someone bids higher than a doubled/redoubled bid, the double and redouble are cancelled. The last double or redouble before three passes stands.

Evaluating a Hand for Opening

There are countless bridge bidding systems, but most of them incorporate this point-count system created by Charles H. Goren:

Ace—4 points

King—3 points

Queen—2 points

Jack—1 point

Void (no cards in a suit)—3 points

Singleton (one card in a suit)—2 points

Doubleton (two cards in a suit)—1 point

After evaluating their hands, players can proceed according to the following general rules.

To open the bidding 13 points are necessary. A player with 14 or more points *has to* open. If the first two bidders don't open, the next bidder can open with 11 high-card points and a good suit.

All openings should contain two quick tricks (two high cards that are likely to take a trick in an early round of a suit).

Beyond that, a player should:

Bid the longest suit first. If two suits contain the same number of cards, the one that has the highest high-card points takes priority.

Bid clubs with four clubs and four diamonds (the minor suits), leaving room for partner or self to bid diamonds without raising the level.

Bid a major suit (hearts or spades) if it's five cards in length.

Bid the major suit if he's holding a major and a minor, each five cards in length.

Bid one spade if he's he's holding two five-card major suits.

Bid two of a major suit with 22 or more points if the suit is at least five cards in length.

Bid at the three level if the point count is less than 13 and the hand is long in one suit, but with few high-card points. This is a preemptive bid, intended to discourage the opposition from bidding.

Bid one No Trump if the point count is 16 to 18 and the hand is balanced (no more than one doubleton).

Responding to an Opening Bid

Once one partner has opened the bidding the responding partner adds up points again, with this difference: a void is worth 5 points and a singleton is worth 3 points (a doubleton is still worth 1 point). The player can also now add 1 point for a face card in the suit that his partner bid, and deduct 1 point if he has three cards or less in his partner's suit. So:

0–4 points and no support for partner's suit: Pass.

4–6 points and support for partner's suit: Raise partner's bid by 1.

8–10 points and no support for partner's suit: Bid strongest suit (with 10 points bid at the two level).

8–10 points and support for partner's suit: Bid strongest suit if it's different from partner's suit and support partner's suit at the *next* round of bidding.

12 points or more: Try to take the team to game.

Tip

If you're just learning how to evaluate and bid, don't be afraid to use your common sense to improvise—as long as your partner *knows* you're improvising.

Slams

A team should have at least 33 points between them to bid a small slam (12 tricks), and 37 points between them to bid a grand slam (13 tricks).

The bidding ends when three players pass in succession. The player who mentioned the trump suit (or No Trump) first is the "declarer."

PLAY

The player to the declarer's left plays a card by putting it faceup in the middle of the table. Play continues clockwise around the table, players following the suit of the first card led in a trick. If a player has no cards in that suit, she can play a trump card or sluff off (discard) a card from another suit.

The next player (declarer's partner) lays his entire hand faceup on the table; he and his hand are called the "dummy." The declarer will play the dummy's cards as well as his own. The dummy hand is arranged as follows: The cards of each suit are set in columns sorted from highest to lowest toward the center of the table. The trump suit, if there is one, is on the player's right, declarer's left.

After the first card is led, declarer plays a card from the dummy hand. Then the third player (declarer's right-hand opponent) plays a card, and finally declarer plays a card from his hand. Those four cards, one from each hand, make up a "trick." The trick is won by the highest of the four cards. If no trump cards have been played, the high card of the suit wins. Otherwise, the highest trump wins.

All the tricks won by the same side are collected by one player of each partnership. Each is kept in its own pile and overlapped with other tricks so that players can see at a glance the tricks that have been played and won. The winner of a trick (including the dummy) leads the next hand.

Play continues until all thirteen tricks have been played.

SCORING

The first side to score 100 trick points wins the game.

If the contract was undoubled, players score the following:

20 points for each club or diamond trick

30 points for each hearts or spades trick

40 points for the first and 30 for each additional trick in an NT contract

If the contract was doubled, players score twice the undoubled values.

If the contract was redoubled players score four times the undoubled values.

One player keeps score on a piece of paper marked WE and THEY. The WE column records points made by the scorer's partnership; the THEY column for the other team. The trick score (the value of tricks bid for and made by declarer's side) is written "below the (double) line" and any premium points for overtricks, slam bonuses, or honors go "above the line."

If declarer bids four diamonds and takes only nine tricks (the six tricks that make up a book, and three other tricks), he scores nothing below the line, and the other team scores 50 points above the line for the one "undertrick."

WE	THEY
	500^F
50^C	100^E
20^A	100^D
80^A	120^B
160^C	
	150^E
330^F	970^F

A. In the first hand, WE bid four diamonds (worth 80 points) and took eleven tricks, that is, made five in the first game. The trick score below the double line records the four that WE bid (80 points), and the extra "overtrick" (20 points) goes above the line. (If WE had bid *five* diamonds, all 100 points would have been scored below the line and WE would have won the game.)

B. In the second hand, THEY bid four spades and took the required ten tricks for a score of 120 points below the line. THEY win the game, so a line is drawn under their 120 to show the end of the game. No overtricks were scored in this hand.

When the next hand begins, both teams will be at zero, but THEY are now "vulnerable" because they won a game, which means that game bonuses and penalties will be increased.

C. In the first hand of the second game, WE bid four clubs and the bid was doubled. WE win the ten required tricks and receive *forty* points for each (because the bid was doubled) for a total of 160 points below the line, and a bonus of 50 points above the line for fulfilling a doubled contract. Now, because both teams have won a game, both are vulnerable.

D. In the first hand of the third game, WE bid two NT (no trump) and win seven tricks, one short of the contract. WE receive no points, but THEY score 100 points for the undertrick because WE were vulnerable.

E. In the next hand, THEY win a bid of five hearts and make five hearts exactly. THEY score 150 below the line and 100 above the line for possession of the four honor cards: ace of hearts, king of hearts, queen of hearts, and jack of hearts.

F. THEY have won two games and therefore, the rubber, which earns them a bonus 500 points. Both columns are added up and WE's 330 points are subtracted from THEY's 970. The result is 640, which is rounded down to 600: THEY have won a 6-point rubber. If the difference had been 650 or more, the score would have been rounded up, and THEY would have won a 7-point rubber.

The first side to win two games wins the "rubber."

Overtricks

If the declaring side made more tricks than it contracted for, if the contract was undoubled that side gets 20 points for each overtrick in diamonds or clubs; or 30 points each for each overtrick in hearts, spades, and NT above the line.

If the contract was doubled, that side gets 100 points for each overtrick if the declaring side was not vulnerable, or 200 points for each overtrick if the declaring side was vulnerable.

If the contract was redoubled, the numbers are twice what they would be if doubled.

Undertricks

If the contract falls short by a certain number of tricks, the declaring side gets nothing below the line. The defending side gets above the line 50 points for each undertrick if the declaring side was not vulnerable or 100 points for each undertrick if the declaring side was vulnerable if the contract was undoubled.

If the contract was doubled (not redoubled), and if the declaring side was not vulnerable, that side receives 100 points for the first undertrick and 200 points each for each trick beyond the first.

If the declaring side *was* vulnerable, it receives 200 points for the first undertrick and 300 points each beyond the first undertrick.

If the contract was redoubled, the numbers are twice what they would be if only doubled.

Honor Cards

Honors are scored above the line and are only awarded to cards that were in *one* player's hand, whether the contract was made or not. The amounts aren't affected by doubles or redoubles.

If a suit was trump, the declarer's side scores 150 points for all five honors (A, K, Q, J, 10) of the trump suit; 100 points for any four of the trump suit; or, if the hand was played at NT, 150 for all four aces.

Premium for a Doubled Contract

For making a doubled, but not redoubled, contract, the declarer's side gets 50 points above the line. For making a redoubled contract, the declarer's side gets 100 points above the line.

Slam Bonuses

If the contract was for twelve tricks (a six bid) and was fulfilled, with or without an overtrick, the declarer's side has made a "small slam." If the contract was for all thirteen tricks (a seven bid), it's a "grand slam." Slam bonuses aren't affected by doubles and redoubles.

For a small slam, the declarer's side gets above the line 500 points if declarer's side was not vulnerable or 750 points if declarer's side was vulnerable.

For a grand slam, the declarer's side gets above the line 1,000 points if declarer's side was not vulnerable or 1,500 points if declarer's side was vulnerable.

Rubber Bonuses

If a side wins a rubber in only two games (two to none) it scores 700 above the line; if it wins the rubber in three games (two to one) the bonus is 500.

VARIATIONS

Double Dummy is for two players. They sit in adjoining seats and four hands are dealt so that each player has a dummy hand opposite. Without looking at their dummies, they bid as in Contract Bridge. When the bid is settled, the players expose their dummies and the player to the left of declarer leads the first card.

Single Dummy is played like Double Dummy except that one dummy is turned faceup before the bidding starts. When each player bids, he has to specify if he's bidding "with" or "without" the faceup dummy. "Without" means that he'll be playing with the facedown dummy if he wins the bid. Players can switch, bidding "with" in one round, "without" in another. When the bidding ends, each player's dummy goes opposite him and the facedown dummy is turned faceup.

Honeymoon Bridge is played just like Double Dummy, but the dummies are not exposed; instead they're set into a rack of some kind (be innovative!) so that a player can see his own dummy but his opponent can't.

Bridge for Three is easier to explain using the conventional compass locations: Players sit in positions South, North, and East. South and North are partners against East and the dummy. After the deal, the full dummy is spread in the West position; all the players see it throughout bidding and play.

South bids first. East can bid twice: for dummy and his own hand, in their proper turns. Any player can become declarer. The hand at declarer's left makes the opening lead, but the original dummy hand is the only one that is exposed.

At the end of the rubber, players rotate positions: South becomes East and has the dummy for the next rubber; North becomes South, and East becomes North.

Trivia

Actor Omar Sharif (*Dr. Zhivago, Funny Girl*) is probably the best known Contract Bridge player in the world. He's written quite a few books on the subject and lends his name to a Bridge computer game.

· · · · · · · · ·

CASINO

Easy to learn, Casino is a great game for families. See the variations.

EQUIPMENT
- A 52-card deck

PLAYERS
2

OBJECT

To be the first player to score 21 points by capturing the most cards (and the most valuable cards).

SETUP

The dealer deals the other player two cards, lays two cards faceup on the table, deals himself two cards, then repeats the process so that each player has four cards and there are four cards faceup on the table between them.

PLAY

Each player in his turn takes one of the cards in his hand and uses it to "capture" the cards on the table by using any of the following plays.

Pairing

Taking one or more cards from the table that match in rank. If there are three jacks on the table, a player can pick them all up with a single jack in his hand. Pairing is the only way to pick up a face card.

Combining

Taking two or more of the cards on the table that add up to a card in a player's hand, e.g., taking a 2 and a 7 with a 9. And if there's another combination that adds up to 9—e.g., a 4 and a 5—a player can take that, too, in the same turn. The rule includes combinations of three cards as well, e.g., an ace, 6, and 2. A card from the hand can capture by pairing and combining at the same time: an 8 can take an 8 and a 5 and 3.

Building

Reserving a play for the next round. For example, with two 4s in his hand and a 4 on the table, a player can put one of his 4s on the table 4 and call, "Building fours." That means that he intends to take the two fours on the table with another 4 at his next turn. *Unless*, that is, the other player has a 4 and takes the two 4s before the caller has a chance to.

Players can also call combinations they intend to pick up on their next turn. If, for example, there was an ace and a 3 on the table, a player could put them together, lay one of his 4s on top, call, "Building fours," and pick up all three cards on his next turn.

A player with a 3 and a 9 in his hand can build on a 6 on the table by laying his 3 on the 6 and saying, "Building 9s." And if the other player doesn't pick up the cards in the meantime, on his next turn the builder picks up the 3 and 6 with his 9. Both players have the option of adding to the pile that's being built and making it a higher number. If, for instance, either player added an ace to the previous pile, and said, "Building 10s," he could pick it up on his next turn.

If a player can't capture any of the cards on the table in a turn, he has to "trail," that is, discard one card by laying it faceup on the table with the other cards.

When a player captures cards, he puts them in a pile facedown nearby to be tallied at the end of the game. If a player picks up all four cards in one turn, called a "sweep," the player earns an extra point. Players keep track of sweeps by putting one of the four cards faceup on their captured piles.

When both players have played all four cards in their hands, the dealer deals out four more to each, but doesn't add any more cards to the center of the table—they're replaced by players discarding.

Play continues until all the cards have been dealt and no one has any cards left. The player who made the last capture wins all the cards left on the table. (But this doesn't count as a sweep.)

SCORING

The player with the highest score wins the hand. More hands are played until one player reaches 21.

Scoresheet

The most cards—3 points

The most spades—1 point

Big Casino (ten diamonds)—2 points

Little Casino (two spades)—1 point

Each ace—1 point

Each sweep—1 point

VARIATIONS

In **Three-Handed Casino** the dealer deals four cards to each player and four cards to the table. There will be four deals. The player to the left of the dealer plays first, and the deal passes to the left.

Four-Handed Casino is a partnership game. Four cards are dealt to each player and four cards to the table. There are only three deals. One partner collects all the cards for the partnership.

Kids seem to prefer **Royal Casino**, in which the face cards have assigned values—jacks are worth 11 points, queens 12, and kings 13, and aces are worth 1 or 14 points. So, for example, if you have a queen in your hand and there's an 8 and a 4 on the table, you can take them with the queen.

Draw Casino is for two players, and based on either basic casino or Royal Casino. The first deal is the only deal; after playing a card, the player draws from the stock, thus keeping his hand at four cards until the stock is depleted.

In **Spade Casino**, all the spades score points. The jack of spades and Little Casino score 2 points, all the other spades score 1 point each. Game is to 61 points. A cribbage board, if you have one, is perfect for scoring.

Royal Spade Casino combines the rules of Spade Casino and Royal Casino: All the face cards have their assigned values and all the spades score 1 points each.

· · · · · · · · ·

CRIBBAGE

Six-Card Cribbage is the standard game. It's meant for two players, but easily adapts for three, or four in partnerships. The game is named after the dealer's advantage—the cards that make up the "crib."

EQUIPMENT
- A 52-card deck

- A cribbage board (or pencil and paper for making one)

PLAYERS
2 (but some variations allow for 3 or 4)

OBJECT
To form combinations of cards and to be the first to score 61 (or 121) points.

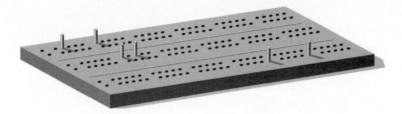

One of the many varieties of cribbage boards, this one is set up for three players. The player closest to us is already in the final leg and heading for home. If he "pegs out" before the others reach their final legs, he'll have "skunked" them.

Cribbage boards come in a wide variety of shapes with any number of tracks. A double-track board (sixty playing holes on each side) can be used to play to 61 or 121 points, but can only be used when two or four are playing. On a double-track board the pegs make their first advance along the outer rows, mirroring each other.

There are two pegs for each player so that if a player loses track of the count, one peg still marks the previous score. The holes are divided into groups of five.

SETUP

After each player sets one peg in the starting hole—the left of the two "game holes" at the bottom of the board—the players cut for the deal; high card wins. The nondealer shuffles. Players will "peg" points as they accumulate them.

Aces are low, worth only 1 point; face cards are worth 10 points; the numbered cards are worth their pip value.

Each player is dealt six cards. After looking at their cards, players each put two aside, facedown, to form the "crib," an extra hand that belongs to the dealer and that will be included in her score at the end of the hand.

The nondealer cuts the remaining cards. The dealer turns over the top card of the lower half and, when the deck is put back together, places it faceup on top of the deck. This top card is called the "starter." If the starter is a jack, the dealer pegs 2 points for it, that is, moves one of his pegs from the starting area forward two holes.

Do-It-Yourself Cribbage Board

You can make a homemade cribbage board with pencil and paper: Sketch out two rows of "dots" for each player, each row consisting of six groups of five dots each (because groups of five are easier to count). At the top of each row draw a single dot for starting the game and finishing the game.

Each time a player scores he marks off the appropriate number of dots.

PLAY

The nondealer leads any card faceup, putting it directly in front of herself, and announces its value (e.g., "two" if it's a deuce, "ten" if it's a ten or a face card). Then the dealer puts a card down and announces the total of the two cards (e.g., "fourteen" if he's played a four after a face card).

Note: The two players' cards don't mix as in other card games—players need to keep their own cards in front of them for scoring purposes at the end of the hand.

Players continue adding cards in turn until one of them is unable to throw down any more without going over 31. Which brings us to the "go."

The Go

If, say, the total is 27, and the player whose turn it is doesn't have anything lower than a five, she calls, "Go." If her opponent can't lay down a card within the 31 limit, he also calls, "Go," and the first player pegs a 1-point bonus. But if the second player is holding a card that will keep the score under 31, he has to play that card. If 31 is still not reached and he has another card that will play under 31, he has to play it. When he can't play another card and the sum total is still less than 31, he can peg 1 point. If he brings the total to *exactly* 31, he pegs 2 points.

When 31 is reached—or neither player can reach it without going over—the count resets to zero, and the player who said "Go" leads the next card.

Anytime a player has no cards left, he misses his turn.

SCORING

The "show" takes place after all the cards have been played. The nondealer scores his hand first. If he counts out enough points to "peg the game" (get to the total of 61 or 121 or more), he wins, even though the dealer may have scored an equal or higher total score.

If the nondealer doesn't score enough to win, the dealer scores his hand (including the starter) and then the crib.

The deal alternates with each hand. Play continues until one player "pegs out" (reaches or exceeds 61 or 121 points).

During Play

If the starter is a jack, the dealer earns 2 points.

Calling the Go if the opponent can't lay down a card within the 31-point limit earns 1 point.

Playing the last card under 31 earns 1 point.

Playing a card that brings the total to 31 exactly earns 2 points.

Bringing the total of two or more consecutive cards to 15 earns 2 points. For example, Player A lays down a ten and says, "ten." Player B lays down a 5 says "fifteen for two," and pegs 2 points immediately. If Player B had played a four, he would have said, "fourteen." Then if the next player had an ace he could have played an ace and said, "fifteen for two," scoring 2 points immediately.

Completing a pair is worth 2 points. If Player A lays down a 7 and Player B plays a 7, he'll say, "Fourteen and a pair for 2." Player B pegs the 2 points immediately.

Playing a third consecutive card of the same value is worth 6 points. Continuing the above example, if the next player plays a 7, he would say, "Twenty-one for 6," pegging the 6 points immediately.

Playing a fourth consecutive card of the same value is worth 12 points. If the next player has a 7 he would say, "Twenty-eight for 12," and peg 12 points immediately.

Completing a run of three cards earns 3 points. If Player A plays a 3, Player B plays a 5, and the next player plays a 4, that player would say, "Twelve and a run of 3 for 3."

Completing a run of four cards earns 4 points.

Completing a run of five, six, or seven cards scores the corresponding 5, 6, or 7 points. All runs are regardless of the order of play, so if the cards played are 4-2-6-5-3, the player who plays the three will score 5.

The last card played in a hand scores 1 point.

End of Game

Any combination of cards that totals fifteen (7+8, J+5,9+6, A+5+9) = 2 points

One pair = 2 points

Three of a kind = 6 points

Four of a kind = 12 points

A run of three or more = point per card

A four-card flush (four cards of the same suit in sequence) = 4 points

A five-card flush = 5 points

A flush that's the same suit as the starter = 1 point

A double run of three (5,6,7,7) = 8 points

A double run of four (4,5,6,7,7)* = 10 points

A triple run (4,5,6,7,7,7) = 15 points

A quadruple run (4,4,5,6,6) = 16 points

A jack that's the same suit as the starter = 1 point

*It can be tricky learning how to score all the possible combinations. As an example, here's how the cards 4-5-6-7-7 should be scored. It's a run of four, worth 4 points, and the other 7 is another 4 points (another run of four). You also get 2 points for the pair of 7s, *and* 4,5, and 6 total fifteen for another 2 points. The total for this hand is 12 points: 10 points for a double run of four (including the 2 points for the pair) and 2 points for the fifteen (4,5,6).

STRATEGY
The Crib
If you're the nondealer, try to keep these cards in your hand:

5s: Four out of every thirteen cards are worth 10 points, so there's a good chance that a 5 in the crib will help make 15s.

7s and 8s: They not only total 15, but have a chance of ending up next to a 6 or 9 to complete a run.

3s, 6s, and 9s: They're likely to combine to 15 (6-9, 3-6-6, 3-3-9, and so on).

If you're the dealer: Try to keep any good combinations together, either in your hand or in the crib: pairs, runs, and combinations totaling 15 are good.

The Play
Don't lead a five; chances are good that your opponent has a ten or face card.

Play a card from a pair; if your opponent completes the pair for 2, you can complete a triple for 6 (as long as the total isn't fast approaching 31).

Try to hold on to small cards. This will make it more likely that you'll play the last card for 1 point or even reach 31 for 2 points. On the other hand, when you go first, leading a card lower than five could likely prevent the next player from immediately scoring a 15.

VARIATIONS

In **Three-Hand Cribbage**, five cards are dealt to each player and one card is dealt to the crib. Players put one card in the crib. When a player calls "Go," the others play in turn for as long as they can until 31 is reached. The point for Go is pegged by the last to play. In scoring, player to dealer's left scores his hand first, then player at *his* left, then dealer's hand, and finally dealer's crib.

Four-Hand Cribbage is played in two partnerships. Five cards are dealt to the players, who each put one in the crib. When a player calls Go, the others play in turn for as long as they can until 31 is reached, and the point for Go is pegged by the last partnership to play. Precedence in showing is: player and partner to dealer's left first, then dealer and partner, and finally dealer's crib.

Five-Card Cribbage for two players is the original version, and is sometimes called "the old game." Five cards are dealt to the players, who each put two in the crib. The first nondealer is given a 3-point start; play is to 61.

For four players, five cards are dealt to each player; each places one card in the crib, after which play is as in Six-Card. If playing in partnerships, partners sit opposite each other and the scores are combined.

Seven-Card Cribbage is for experts only—it can get complicated. Seven cards are dealt to the players, who each put two in the crib. The play and the show are conducted with five cards each. Play is to 181 points or three times around the board.

FYI

The highest Six-Card Cribbage score for any five cards is 29, which can be reached only when holding J-5-5-5-5 when the starter is a five of the same suit as the jack. The four 5s total 12 points (for four of a kind); the eight ways of forming 15 are worth 16 points (2 points for each 15); and 1 point for the jack (what the experts call "His Nobs," a jack that's the same suit as the starter).

Low-Ball is a variation of Six-Card, in which the first person to score 121 points *loses*.

Buying a Cribbage Board
If you're in the market for a cribbage board, note that some of the newer boards that have three or four rows totaling 120 holes with a pegging-out hole at the end are obviously only suitable for games played to 121.

HISTORY

Cribbage was the brainchild of seventeenth-century British poet and soldier, Sir John Suckling, who adapted it from an older card game called Noddy. Suckling inherited his father's fortune when he was only eighteen. Besides being rich and handsome, he was also—so they say—the best card player in Britain.

In 1641 he led a conspiracy to rescue a friend who was being held in the Tower of London. When the plot was discovered, Sir John fled to France. A year later—pining away for England—he killed himself with poison.

·········

EUCHRE

Pronounced "yoo-ker," it's a fast trick-taking card game with no time to recover from mistakes. So don't forget which jacks are high.

EQUIPMENT
- 32 playing cards (deuces to 6s are left out)

- Ace is high in all suits—**but** . . .

- The **highest card** in the deck is the jack of trump.

- The **second highest** is the jack in the suit of the same color, and is considered a trump card.

- The **third highest** is the ace of trump, followed by K, Q, 10, 9, 8, 7. In a nontrump suit, cards are ranked A, K, Q, J, 10, 9, 8, 7.

PLAYERS

4 (two teams of 2)

OBJECT

To take three tricks out of a possible five.

SETUP

The total score for a win is decided on—either 5 or 7 or 10 points. Partners sit across from each other. A common method of choosing the first dealer is to deal the cards around until a black jack appears.

Each player is dealt five cards—not one at a time, but three to each player, then two to each player. After the deal, the next card in the stock—the rest of the deck—is turned faceup.

The player who decides the trump suit is called the "maker."

The first player has two options: If she wants to make the suit of the faceup card trump, she says, "I order it up"; or she can pass. If she accepts, the suit will be trump.

If she passes, the player to her left (dealer's partner), goes next. That player also has two options: She can accept the trump by saying, "I assist"; or she can pass. If the second player says, "I assist," the suit will be trump.

If she passes, the third player has the same two options as her partner. She can accept the trump by saying, "I order it up," or she can pass.

If the third player accepts, the suit will be trump. If she passes, the dealer can say, "I take it up," accept the suit or not or signify her acceptance of the suit as trump by discarding one of the cards in her hand facedown on the table. By custom, she'll leave the upcard on the table until she decides to play it. Or she can decline the proposed trump by turning the card over.

If the dealer turns the card down, there's one more round in which the players have another chance to either pass or declare a different suit as trump. Once another suit has been named, it becomes trump; no one else can name another suit. If all the players pass again, the deal is thrown in and the next dealer deals a new hand.

The "maker," the player who accepted or named the suit, has the option of playing alone. She signifies this by saying, "I play alone," at which point her partner discards her hand and doesn't participate in the hand. When the maker plays alone, the nonmaker team has the same option: Either player can declare, "I defend alone," at which the lone defender's partner stays out of the game.

PLAY

If the maker is playing alone, the player to her left leads the first card. Otherwise, the lead belongs to the player to the dealer's left, no matter who the maker is.

Any card can be led. Players must follow suit if they can. If they can't follow suit, they can play any card. The trick goes to the highest trump, or, if it contains no trump cards, to the highest card of the suit led. The winner of a trick leads the next.

The hand ends when all five tricks have been played.

SCORING

Only the team that wins three or more tricks scores. Winning all five tricks is called "march." If the maker's team fails to win at least three tricks, it's "euchred."

If the maker's team wins, they score 1 point for winning three or four tricks, 2 points for march. If the maker played alone, her partnership scores 1 point for winning three or four tricks, 4 points for march. If the making side is euchred, the other side scores 2 points. A lone defender scores 1 point for taking three or four tricks, 4 points for march.

The first side to reach the agreed-upon totals wins.

STRATEGY

If you have two fairly sure tricks with perhaps the chance of a third, it's usually a good idea to accept the upcard as trump and count on your partner's hand for a trick. If you hold the trump jack and the jack of the same color, you should accept the upcard as trump even without another good card.

If the Stick-the-Dealer variation is being played (see below), a dealer without a good alternative suit should accept the upcard as trump with a weaker hand than usual, rather than risk having to name a new trump suit.

With four fairly sure tricks, it's usually a good decision to go alone.

VARIATIONS

In **Stick-the-Dealer**, if all players pass during the second round, the dealer is "stuck," and *has to* choose a trump suit. The game continues with no redeal.

In one scoring variation, if the making teams takes no tricks (called a "super Euchre"), the defending team scores 4 points.

Railroading is a variation in which, if your partner is going to play alone, you can pass her your best card facedown. Without looking at it, your partner has to decide whether or not to pick it up and discard a card from her hand.

Euchre is widely played in the southwestern counties of England, where pubs have their own teams and take part in competitive league matches. UK Style is played with a twenty-five-card deck consisting of the ace, king, queen, jack, ten, and nine only of each suit, with an extra card called the "Benny"—either a joker or the deuce of spades—which is the highest trump no matter which suit is called. If the dealer turns the Benny over at the start of a game, he has to decide which suit to call trump before looking at his own hand. The bidding then continues as normal.

HISTORY
Euchre originated among the Pennsylvania Dutch sometime before 1864. The game is still popular in Pennsylvania and the Midwest, and has a wide following in Canada, Britain, and Australia, too.

The joker was first added to the standard American deck around the time that Euchre first appeared in the United States, strictly for use in a Euchre deck. The word "joker" itself is derived from "Euchre" or "Jucker," a similar game from the French-German area of Alsatia.

·········

HEARTS

They call it "Hearts," but most aficionados—whether they know it or not—are playing this version, called "Black Lady." Aka Slippery Anne, Calamity Jane, Black Maria

EQUIPMENT
• A 52-card deck

PLAYERS
• 3–7 (but 4 is ideal)

OBJECT
To avoid winning tricks that contain hearts or the queen of spades. Or to "shoot the moon": to try to win all the hearts and the queen.

SETUP

If the number of players isn't four, certain cards have to be removed so that each player will have the same number of cards.

Three Players: Remove the two of clubs.

Five Players: Remove the two of clubs and the two of diamonds.

Six Players: Remove the two of clubs, two of diamonds, three of clubs, and two of spades.

Seven Players: Remove the two of clubs, two of diamonds, and the three of clubs.

After all the cards are dealt out, but before the first card is led, players pick three cards from their hands and pass them to the player on the left—without looking at the cards they're receiving from an opponent.

PLAY

The player to the left of dealer leads the first card, with this restriction: Hearts can't be led until hearts have been broken (i.e., a heart has been discarded on a previous trick). Of course, if a player *only* has hearts in his hand, he can lead a heart even if they haven't been broken. Note: In one variation, whoever has the lowest club leads it.

After the first card is led, the other players follow suit if they can; if not, they can play any card. The highest card in the suit that was led wins the trick. The winner of the trick leads next.

Play continues until all the tricks have been played.

SCORING

Each heart counts for one penalty point; the queen of spades is worth 13 penalty points. The exception is if a player shoots the moon, that is, manages to win all thirteen hearts and the queen. In that case, she *subtracts* 26 from her point total.

Most often, the game is played in rounds, to a total of 50 points. Once one player has reached 50, the player with the lowest score wins.

FYI

Taking all tricks in the deal is called "shooting the sun."

STRATEGY

When choosing which three cards to pass to another player, pass the ace of spades, king of spades, and queen of spades if you have fewer than four spades in your hand. Otherwise, you might be forced to take the queen of spades if spades are led. Also, pass diamonds or clubs if you have fewer than four in either suit. That way, you can get rid of your hearts when hearts are led.

In general, the player who has the fewest points (and is thus leading) is the one to try to give the queen to. Just be careful about giving it to a player who'll use it to shoot the moon. Always be on the lookout for another player trying to shoot the moon.

VARIATIONS

Omnibus Hearts adds more strategy to Black Lady. The ten of diamonds (in some games the jack of diamonds) is worth negative 10 points to the player who takes it in a trick. If a player wins all thirteen hearts, the queen of spades, and the ten of diamonds, she scores 26 points.

Pink Lady (aka Bloody Mary) doubles the fun of Black Lady: The queen of hearts also counts 13 points. The game is played to 100 points.

Cancellation Hearts is a variation of Black Lady for six or more players. Shuffle two standard decks together and deal them out as far as they will go evenly. The extra cards go facedown on the table to be picked up by the winner of the first trick.

When identical cards fall on the same trick, they cancel each other out so that neither can win the trick. It's possible, in fact, for all the cards in a trick to be canceled out in this way, making the trick unwinnable. If this is the case, the trick is put aside and goes to the winner of the next trick. If the last trick of the deal is cancelled out, the cards are dead and not scored.

In Basic Hearts (the original game) the queen of spades does not carry any penalty or bonus points. Hearts count for one penalty point apiece and shooting the moon subtracts 13 points.

Spot Hearts differs from basic hearts only in scoring: Each heart card counts as many penalty points as its face value. The suit counts for 14, the king of hearts for 13, queen of hearts for 12, jack of hearts for 11, and so on, down to deuce.

If you're playing Spot Hearts with the queen of spades variation, the queen of spades counts for 25 points. Because of the higher point value of the cards, the game can be played to 500 points.

Domino Hearts is played with these additional rules: Six cards are dealt to each player, with the leftover cards placed facedown in the center to form the stock. If a player can't follow suit, he has to draw cards from the top of the stock until he can. When all the cards have been drawn from the stock, play reverts back to that of basic hearts.

Each player drops out when he has played all the cards in his hand; if he wins a trick with his last card, the lead passes to the first active player to his left.

When only one player has any cards left, he adds them to his tricks, scoring penalty points for any hearts in his hand as well as his tricks.

The winner is the player with the lowest score when another player reaches 31 points.

In **Heartsette**, all fifty-two cards are played, no matter the number of players. Cards left over after the deal (called the "widow") are set aside and go to the winner of the first trick.

Draw Hearts (aka Hearts for Two) is a game for two players. Each player is dealt thirteen cards; the remainder forms the stock. The play is the same, but the winner of a trick picks the top card from the stock and the loser picks the next, so hands stay at thirteen cards until the stock is exhausted, after which cards are played out.

Sweepstake Hearts is basic hearts played with chips. When it's time for scoring, players have to put one chip in the pot for every one of their hearts. Then, any players who are "clear" (didn't win any hearts) divide up the pot, leaving any odd chip for the next round. If all the players are "painted" (won at least one heart), the pot remains for the next round, and is now called the "jackpot." A player who shoots the moon wins the pot.

Joker Hearts works well in three-handed play. By adding the joker to the deck, each of three players will get 17 cards. The joker ranks between the jack of hearts and the ten of hearts. It's the only trump card and wins any trick it's played on, unless the trick contains one of the four higher hearts that can beat it (in which case the higher heart takes the trick).

The joker, which counts 5 penalty points in most games, is worth 20 points in Spot Hearts.

·········

OH HELL

But you can call it "Oh Heck." AKA Oh Heck, Oh Pshaw, Blackout, Up and Down the River, Elevator

EQUIPMENT

- A 52-card deck

- Paper and pencil for keeping score

PLAYERS

3–7

OBJECT

To win exactly the number of tricks bid.

SETUP

One player is chosen to be scorekeeper. In the first deal of a game, players get one card each; in the second deal, two cards; and so on. The remaining cards go facedown on the table. The top card is turned faceup: This will be the trump suit for the hand. With three players there are fifteen deals, four players, thirteen; five players, ten; six players, eight; seven players, seven. In the last deal of a game, no remaining card (if there is one) is turned up. The hand is played out at no-trump.

Bidding

Based on the trump suit, each player "bids" on how many tricks she thinks she can take. The scorekeeper keeps track of the bids on a piece of paper.

PLAY

The player to the dealer's left leads. The other players put down their cards in turn, going clockwise. The winner of that trick leads the next hand.

The deal rotates in subsequent hands. From now on, as one more card is dealt in each round, the players have to follow suit if they can. If a player has no cards in the suit that was led, she can throw down any card—including a trump, which will take the trick if a higher trump card isn't played after it.

Special Rule for Four Players

In the thirteenth round, when the four players are dealt thirteen cards apiece, the round is played without a trump suit.

SCORING

The scores are totaled after each hand. Players who made their bids *exactly* score 10 plus the number of tricks they bid. Players who don't make their bids don't score at all. For example, if a player bid three and took exactly three tricks, her score would be 13. If she bid three and took four, her score would be 0.

After the hand is scored, the deal passes to the left and this time, each player gets *one less card*. This continues until the last hand—in which each player gets only one card.

The player with the most points wins.

VARIATION

Looney Gooney is Oh Hell in reverse: In the first round, players are dealt an equal number of cards as far as the deck will go. The top card of the remaining stock is trump. (If there are four players, it's a no-trump hand.) In subsequent hands, players are dealt *one less card*, until the last round, when they get one card apiece.

·········

PINOCHLE

If you like both meld-making and trick-taking games, Pinochle's the game for you. Beginners: Don't forget that ten is the second highest card in all suits. This classic two-handed version of the game is almost identical with the French game Bezique.

EQUIPMENT
- A 48-card pinochle deck (made up of eight aces, kings, queens, jacks, 10s, and 9s)

PLAYERS
2

OBJECT
To build high-scoring groups of cards called *melds* and to take high-scoring cards in tricks.

SETUP
Players cut for the deal; lowest card deals first. Each player is dealt twelve cards, three at a time. The dealer turns up the next card—this suit will be trump—and places it partly under the rest of the stock. If the trump card is the dix (pronounced "deece")—the 9—the dealer scores 10 points.

Tip
After the deal, it's a good idea to arrange your cards A-10-K-Q-J-9 to help you remember that 10 is the second highest card in a suit.

PLAY
Nondealer leads any card; the second player to a trick can either follow suit, play a trump, or discard an unimportant card. The highest card wins the trick; if a trump or trumps are played, the highest trump card wins. The winner of a trick leads the next.

   The player who wins the trick can lay down one meld if possible, then draw a card from the top of the stock. The loser draws the next card, so that the hands are maintained at twelve cards until the stock is depleted. Melds can only be made immediately after a trick is taken and only by the trick-taker.

The Dix
After the first trick is taken—but before the draw—the dealer, if he's holding the nine of trumps, can exchange it for the turned-up trump card. By putting the dix faceup in the trump card's place, the dealer thus not only

gets a higher trump card, but also chalks up 10 points for the dix. This move can be made in the same turn as a meld. When the second dix turns up, it can be laid down in a turn with any other meld, at which time the player scores 10 points.

Melding

There are three classes of melds.

Sequences

A-10-K-Q-J of trump (flush) = 150 points
K-Q of trump (royal marriage) = 40 points
K-Q of nontrump suit (marriage) = 20 points

Groups

A♠-A♥-A♣-A♦ (called "100 aces") = 100 points
K♠-K♥-K♣-K♦ ("80 kings") = 80 points
Q♠-Q♥-Q♣-Q♦ ("60 queens") = 60 points
J♠-J♥-J♣-J♦ ("40 jacks") = 40 points

Pinochle

Q♠-J♦ (pinochle) = 40 points
9 of trump (dix) = 10 points

A card can be used in more than one meld, as long as the melds are of different classes. For example, the Q♠ can be used both for a marriage, a pinochle, and 60 queens, but a K-Q combination in a flush can't be used as a marriage as well.

Endgame

The winner of the twelfth trick draws the last facedown card in the stock and shows it to the other player, who draws the faceup trump card (which may be the dix exchanged earlier). This signals the beginning of the endgame, which is played out differently.

The players pick up their melds, add them to the cards in their hands, and play out these twelve cards in tricks. Now players must follow suit if able, and if void in the suit led play a trump card if able. If trump is led, the player who is led to must trump if able. No further melding is allowed during this part of the game.

Play continues until all the cards have been played.

SCORING

Melds are scored during play. After the trick-taking phase of the game, players add up their scores accordingly:

Ace   = 11 points

Ten   = 10 points

King   = 4 points

Queen = 3 points

Jack   = 2 points

The winner of the last trick scores an extra 10 points. Players add their scores from melding and trick-taking to get their final score for this hand.

The nondealer of this hand deals the next. The first player to reach 1,000 points wins the game. However, at any time during the game a player can claim that he's reached 1,000 points. Play ends and the cards are examined. If the claim is correct, that player wins, even if the other player has a higher point count. If the claimant is wrong, he loses.

If there's no claim and both players pass 1,000 points on the same deal, the game continues to 1,250, then 1,500, and so on, if necessary.

VARIATIONS

In some games, a marriage in each suit (called a "roundhouse" or a "roundtable") is worth 240 total points and a double pinochle is worth 300 points.

And some seasoned players extend the list of melds to include double runs and double groups, which increase a player's score exponentially.

Partnership Pinochle is for four players. Partners sit opposite each other. The deal is the same: twelve cards to each player, three at a time.

·········

POKER

The game of poker came to the Americas from a long line of European card games. An Englishman described the game as played in New Orleans in 1829: Four players used a twenty-card deck and bet on which player's hand was the most valuable. From New Orleans, the game spread throughout the United States via Mississippi riverboat.

During the Civil War—after the full fifty-two-card deck had made its debut—games like Draw Poker and Five-Card Stud were added. Wild cards were introduced around 1875, and community card poker games surfaced around 1925. Today, the game's popularity spans the globe—probably largely due to the travels of the U.S. armed forces.

There are three main poker variants:

Draw Poker: Players have the option of drawing new cards during a game, e.g., Five-Card Draw

Stud Poker: Players are dealt both facedown and faceup cards, e.g., Five-Card and Seven-Card Stud

Community Card Poker: Players are dealt facedown cards and make their final hands with some or all of a shared series of cards that are dealt to the middle of the table, e.g., Texas Hold'em.

Then there are the miscellaneous games (sometimes called "freak games") that don't fit into any category, but still manage to fall under the "Poker" umbrella.

PLAYERS
As many as fourteen people can play some versions of poker but five to eight is considered the best number. And according to Hoyle, Stud Poker is the only game that will accommodate more than eight.

THE DEAL
In a casino, a "house" dealer handles the cards for every hand, but in a home game, the deal typically rotates around the table clockwise. One

way of choosing the first dealer is to have players cut the deck or turn over a card each. The first jack deals.

Most home games are "dealer's choice"—the dealer chooses the game and what, if any, cards are going to be wild. If his choice is a game in which the cards are thrown in if no one opens, that dealer can deal again until a game is played and completed.

BETTING

After the deal, the first of what may be several betting rounds begins. Between rounds, the players' hands develop in some way, either by being dealt additional cards or replacing cards previously dealt. During a round of betting, there will always be a *current bet amount*, which is the amount of money bet by the player who bet last in a round.

Betting Limit

Players decide on a betting limit before a game—or long evening of games—begins, the highest amount that anyone can bet at any one time. They generally "ante up" before the deal by putting one chip in the pot (the middle of the table).

The amount depends on the people at the table and the rules they subscribe to. Games between friends should have low limits on the ante, on the amount a player can raise, and even on the top amount the pot could grow to.

Depending on the strength of his hand, the player to the dealer's left has the first chance to open—he can bet or pass. If he passes (also known as "checking"), it means he's still in the game but isn't ready to bet yet, and the chance to open the betting goes to the player on his left. If all the players check, the cards are thrown in, and a new hand is dealt.

The player who opens the betting declares the amount of his bet and puts the corresponding chips in front of him (which makes it easier to keep track of individual bets).

Once a player has bet, the players who follow him in the round can either fold (drop out of the current round), "call" or "see" the original bet (put down the same number of chips—the current betting amount), or raise the original bet (put down the original number of chips plus a number of chips beyond that). This means that the current betting amount has changed by the amount of the raise and that subsequent players have to either see or reraise this amount to stay in the game. Most house rules limit raises to three per round.

A round is over when either everyone has checked or everyone has answered any bets (folded, called, or raised).

The Showdown
All the players who haven't folded place their cards on the table faceup. The player with the best hand wins the pot.

RANK OF POKER HANDS
Unless otherwise specified in the rules of the variation being played, hands are evaluated using the traditional set of five-card hands. Ace is high, but also ranks low in the sequence 5-4-3-2-A. In some games, the joker is used as a wild card. In wild-card games, five of a kind (for example, 7-7-7-7-wild card) is possible, and beats all. But in most games the hands rank this way, from best to worst

Royal flush: The highest cards (**A-K-Q-J-10**) of a single suit.

Straight flush: Five cards in sequence in the same suit. If two players have a straight flush the highest wins (e.g., **Q-10-9-8-7** beats **10-9-8-7-6**).

Four of a kind: Any four cards of the same rank (e.g., **J-J-J-J-7**). Higher ranking four of a kind wins.

Full house: Three of a kind and two pair (e.g., **J-J-J-2-2**). Highest three of a kind wins.

Flush: Five cards of the same suit (e.g. **J-8-6-5-3** of hearts). The hand with the highest card wins. If the cards tie, the next-highest ranking card wins, and so on.

Straight: Any five cards in sequence but not all of the same suit (e.g., **8-7-6-5-4**). The hand with the highest ranking card wins; if a tie, the next highest ranking card decides, and so on.

Three of a kind: Three cards of the same rank (e.g., **3-3-3-Q-9**).

Two pair: Two cards of any one rank and two cards of any other rank (e.g., **Q-Q-9-9-2**). If a tie, the highest ranking pair wins. If both hands hold the same pair, the highest of the second pair wins. If they're the same, the remaining unmatched card decides it.

One pair: Any two cards of the same rank (e.g., **8-8-J-9-2**). If a tie, the highest ranking pair wins. If both hands hold the same pair, the highest of the other three cards determines the winner. If those two cards are the same, the next highest wins, and so on.

High card: A hand with no matching cards (e.g., **K-Q-9-6-2**). The highest ranking card wins.

HIGH-LOW GAMES

Just about any poker game can be played high-low, but the option is used most often in Stud Poker and the miscellaneous games.

The strict definition of the lowest hand is the hand that wouldn't in a regular game win from any other hand in the showdown, according to the ranking shown above. The lowest possible five-card hand would be 7-5-4-3-2 made up of more than one suit.

In a high-low game the players have to declare, before the showdown, whether they're trying for the highest hand, the lowest hand, or both.

A player who declares for both has to win both, otherwise he loses both. A player who wins both takes the whole pot. If all players try for high or all try for low, the winner takes the whole pot. Otherwise, the pot is split evenly between the highest hand and the lowest hand, with anything extra going to the high-hand player.

Unless it's stipulated in the rules of a game, even when going for low, aces are high. If deuces are wild in a high-low game, they're only wild when a player is trying to make a high hand. Otherwise a deuce is just a deuce.

CHIPS

You don't need regulation chips to play—you can use coins, matchsticks, Monopoly money, or whatever else you can find around the house. But if you'd like to play at being a pro, the most basic set of chips—in red, white, and blue—are valued as follows:

White = 1 (or $1 or 1 cent)

Red   = 5 (or $5 or 5 cents)

Blue   = 10 (or $10 or 10 cents)

THE ODDS

No discussion of poker would be complete without a peek at the odds. Here are your chances of getting a particular hand in five cards

Royal flush	1 in 649,740
Straight flush	1 in 72,193.33
Four of a kind	1 in 4,165
Full house	1 in 694.16
Flush	1 in 508.80
Straight	1 in 254.80
Three of a kind	1 in 254.80
Two pair	1 in 21.03
One Pair	1 in 2.36

·········

FIVE-CARD DRAW

Five-Card Draw is the basic poker game—often the first poker variation a player learns.

EQUIPMENT

- A 52-card deck

- Ace is high or low

- Poker chips (or coins or matchsticks or beans, etc.)

PLAYERS

2–8

OBJECT

To build a winning hand by, if necessary, discarding and replacing cards in one's hand.

SETUP

Players decide on a betting limit, the highest amount that anyone can bet at any one time. They "ante up" before the deal by putting one chip in the pot (the middle of the table). Each player is dealt five cards, all facedown.

PLAY

Depending on the strength of his hand, the player to the dealer's left has the first chance to open—he can bet or pass. If he passes (also known as "checking") it means he's still in the game but isn't ready to bet yet, and the chance to "open" goes to the player on his left. If all the players check, the cards are thrown in, and a new hand is dealt.

The player who opens the betting declares the amount of his bet and puts the corresponding chips in front of him (which makes it easier to keep track of individual bets).

Once a player has bet, the players who follow him in the round can either fold (drop out of the current round); "call" or "see" the original bet (put down the same number of chips—the current betting amount); or raise the original bet (put down the original number of chips plus a number of chips beyond that). This means that the current betting amount has changed by the amount of the raise and that subsequent players have to either see or reraise this amount to stay in the game. Most house rules limit raises to three per round.

A round is over when either everyone has checked or everyone has answered any bets (folded, called, or raised).

If only one player remains at the end of the first betting round, he takes whatever is in the pot and the hand is over. If more than one player remains, the next round—the "draw"—begins.

The Draw

Going around the table again, players who are still in the game can discard some of their cards and ask the dealer to deal them the same amount of new cards as replacements. A common house rule is that a player can't replace more than three cards, but Hoyle doesn't put any limit on the draw; theoretically, a player can replace an entire hand. A player who doesn't want any new cards can signal it by knocking on the table or otherwise signifying that he's "standing pat."

Once all the players have had the chance to replace their cards, the second betting round begins.

The player who opened in the first round goes first; he can bet, check, or fold. If he checks or folds, the next active player to his left can do the same or bet. Once a bet is made, all the other active players in turn have to either fold, call, or raise, until the bets are equalized.

The player with the best hand wins the pot.

VARIATIONS

Jackpot is a variation on Five-Card Draw in which a player needs a pair of jacks or a higher hand ("jacks or better") to open the betting. If no one can open, there's a new deal and everyone antes again into the same pot. Jackpot is also played with an option that in the second hand, a player would need queens or better to open. And if no one opened that hand, the next would require kings or better, and so on.

In **Pass the Garbage**, players get seven cards. After the first round of betting, each player selects the three worst cards in his hand and passes them to the player to the left. Players then discard the two worst cards in their hands and bet on their remaining five cards.

Lowball is the flip side of Five-Card Draw; the idea is that the *worst* hand wins.

·········

SEVEN-CARD STUD

Five-Card Stud was the first of the stud family, but Seven-Card is the most often played. AKA Down the River, Seven-Toed Pete, Peek Poker

EQUIPMENT
• A 52-card deck

PLAYERS
2–10

OBJECT
To make the best five-card poker hand out of seven cards.

SETUP
Players are dealt two rounds of facedown cards and then one card faceup.

PLAY

The dealer announces which player will bet first, naming the player with the highest exposed holding at that point (e.g., "King high bets"). The first player bets, and each player who wants to stay in the game has to match the first player's bet. Any player can raise the bet when it's his turn. If a player raises, any player who wants to stay in the game has to match the additional amount so that each player has the same number of chips in the pot.

After bets have been placed, three more rounds of faceup cards are dealt, followed by the betting rounds in which the dealer announces any player's combination that, when combined with his hole card, could produce a flush or a straight (e.g. "possible flush," "possible straight").

Finally, each player is dealt one more card facedown, followed by another betting round. Players use their best five cards from the seven to make a hand.

The highest exposed holdings are ranked from highest to lowest as follows:

Four of a kind

Three of a kind

Two pair

One pair

High card

If more than one player has the same combination, the higher combination bets first. If two players have the same high-ranking two pair, the player with the higher-ranking second pair bets. If two players have the same one pair, the highest unmatched card bets; if the second cards are the same, the player with the next highest card bets first. If players tie for highest high card, the next highest card determines the first bettor, and so on.

If two players hold identical hands, the player nearest the dealer's left bets first.

Play continues until either all players have been dealt a total of seven cards—three facedown and four faceup—or any player makes a bet that no other player calls, in which case the bettor wins the pot and the next dealer deals a new hand.

At the end of the final betting round the active players turn up their hole cards and the highest-ranking hand wins the pot.

VARIATIONS

Five-Card Stud is played with a maximum of ten players. Players are dealt one card facedown the second card faceup. The betting intervals are the same after each new faceup card for a total of four faceup cards. Play continues until all players have been dealt a total of five cards.

Mexican Stud is played like Five-Card Stud except that all cards are dealt facedown and after each card is dealt, a player can choose one card to turn faceup and one card to leave facedown as his hole card.

Chicago is played exactly like Seven-Card Stud, except that the winner has to split the pot with the high spade in the hole—the highest spade among all the cards that were dealt facedown.

Baseball is Seven-Card Stud with all nines and threes in the hole wild. The first player to be dealt a three faceup has to either fold or "buy the pot"—add to the pot so that its total is doubled. If someone buys the pot *all* threes are wild for that hand. Also, if a player is dealt a four faceup, he can either keep it or discard it and be dealt another card to replace it. In both cases, the player has to make a decision before another card is dealt.

Football is the same as Baseball except that sixes and fours are wild, a four dealt faceup means that the player has to fold or buy the pot, and a two dealt faceup immediately entitles the player to a free hole card.

FYI

To stay in on the first round you should have a pair; three cards in sequence; three cards of the same suit; or two cards as high or higher than the highest card showing.

The average winning hand in Seven-Card Stud is a medium-ranked three of a kind, eights or nines of a suit.

·········

TEXAS HOLD'EM

The most popular of the community card games, it's the one that's played on the TV versions of the game.

EQUIPMENT
- A 52-card deck

- Ace is high or low

- Poker chips (or coins or matchsticks or beans, etc.)

PLAYERS
2–8

OBJECT
To make the best five-card poker hand out of seven cards—two personal cards and three community cards available to all players.

SETUP
Players decide on a betting limit, the highest amount that anyone can bet at any one time. They "ante up" before the deal by putting one chip in the pot. Each player is dealt two hole cards, facedown.

PLAY
The player to the dealer's left has the first chance to open—he can bet or pass. If he passes (also known as "checking") it means he's still in the game but isn't ready to bet yet, and the chance to "open" goes to the player on his left. If all the players check, the cards are thrown in, and a new hand is dealt.

The player who opens the betting declares the amount of his bet and puts the corresponding chips in front of him (which makes it easier to keep track of individual bets).

After the first round of betting, three community cards, called the "flop," are laid faceup in the middle of the table. This is followed by another round of betting. On this and each succeeding round, players can check if no one has bet.

Then a fourth community card, called the "turn," is exposed, followed by another round of betting. The last community card, known as the "river," is turned up, followed by the last round of betting.

The winning hand is the best five-card poker hand using any combination of the player's two cards and the five community cards. A player can use both of his own two cards, only one, or none at all to form the final five-card hand. If the best five-card hand he can make is to play the five community cards, he is said to be "playing the board," and splits the pot with others playing the board if no one has a better hand.

VARIATIONS

In casino play, the two players to the left of the dealer put a predetermined amount of money or chips in the pot before the deal. This is called "posting the blind." Also, the dealer discards or "burns" the top card before he turns over the first three community cards, and again before he turns over the fourth.

In **Omaha Hold'em**, each player is dealt four hole cards instead of two at the start. To make a hand, a player has to use only two of his hole cards and only three of the five community cards. The betting is the same as in Texas Hold'em. At the showdown, the entire four-card hand has to be shown. The best possible five-card poker hand wins the pot.

In **Cincinnati**, the first betting round takes place after the players are dealt five hole cards and the dealer places five cards facedown in the center of the table. The dealer turns up the center cards one by one, each turn-up followed by a betting round, after which there's a showdown in which each player selects any five cards from among hole cards and the community cards to be his poker hand.

Criss-Cross is played like Cincinnati, except that the five community cards are laid out in the shape of a cross. The card in the center of the cross is turned up last; this card, and all cards of the same rank, are wild. At the showdown, players select their five-card poker hands from among their hole cards plus either row of three cards in the cross.

Trivia

Phil Gordon, expert poker commentator on *Celebrity Poker Showdown*, is a world-class poker player who won $1,150,000 in poker tournaments in 2002–2003.

· · · · · · · · ·

MISCELLANEOUS POKER GAMES

A small sampler . . .

INDIAN POKER

The object is to bet and win based on the other players' cards. Players ante. Each player is dealt one card. Without looking at it, players place the card, facing out, on their foreheads so that the other players can see it. Players bet or fold based on what cards the others are holding. The highest card wins the pot.

TWO-CARD POKER

Players ante. Players are dealt two cards facedown, each round followed by a betting interval. At the showdown, the winner is the holder of the highest two-card hand: A pair is the highest hand in Two-Card (straights and flushes don't count), followed by high card (with otherwise unmatched cards). This is usually played high-low with the ace high in the high hand and low in the low hand; and with wild cards: either deuces or one-eyes (jack of hearts, jack of spades, king of diamonds). Also known as **Hurricane** when played high-low.

THREE-CARD POKER

Players ante, then are dealt three cards facedown, each round followed by a betting interval. At the showdown, the winner is the holder of the highest three-card hand, ranked from highest to lowest:

Three of a kind

Straight flush

Flush

Straight

Pair

High card (with otherwise unmatched cards)

Also known as **Three-Card Monte**.

·········

BASIC RUMMY

The daddy of all the rummy games is based on a Spanish card game that crossed the border from Mexico in the 1800s. Since then, it has spawned dozens upon dozens of variations.

EQUIPMENT
• A 52-card deck

PLAYERS
2–6

OBJECT
To get rid of all one's cards by melding them into sets and sequences.

SETUP
The cards are dealt thusly:

Two players: ten cards

Three to four players: seven cards

Five or six players: six cards

The rest of the deck, the stock, is placed facedown in the middle of the table. The top card is turned over and placed faceup next to the stock to make a discard pile.

PLAY

The first player has the option of taking the top card of the stock or the top card of the discard pile. After adding the card to his hand, he discards one card. (The discard may be omitted if the player goes out.) If he chose the card on the discard pile, he can't discard that same card in the same turn.

Melding

During the game, players can lay down melds faceup. There are two kinds of melds: Sets, which are three or four of a kind (5-5-5 or K-K-K-K), and sequences, three or four cards of the same suit in order (ace is low, and can only be used in a sequence with a deuce, not with a king).

Also during a turn, a player can "lay off" a card or cards, adding to the melds that are already on the table—his opponent's as well as his own—such as laying off the seven of spades on the meld of four of spades-five of spades-six of spades.

If all the cards in the stock are used before the game is over, the next player can either take the top discard or turn the pile over, without shuffling, and draw the top card of the new stock.

The first player to lay down all his cards, with or without putting one on the discard pile, wins the game.

SCORING

The winner gets points for all the cards that are left in the other players' hands.

Aces   = 1 point

Face cards   = 10 points

Number cards = pip value

A player who "goes rummy" by laying down all his cards in melds in one turn collects double the amount of points from the other players.

When two people play, the winner of each hand deals the next. When more than two play, the deal passes to the player on the left.

STRATEGY

Get rid of high cards (like face cards) as early in the game as you can. That way, if you lose, you won't have to give away too many points.

VARIATIONS

There's an optional rule that if a card that could be laid off on an already existing meld is discarded instead, another player can call "Rummy!" and claim the card. After laying it off, the claimant makes a discard and the turn reverts to the player who would have been next. If two or more players call at the same time, the player closest to the discarder's left gets the card.

In **Queen City Rummy**, all the players get seven cards. Instead of melding throughout the game, players have to put down all their cards in melds in one turn. The player who goes rummy is the winner and gets points for all the cards she lays down. The other players don't get any points at all.

Boathouse Rum is played like basic rummy with these exceptions: Each player in turn can draw two cards from the stock or, before drawing those cards, two cards from the top of the discard pile. Players discard only one card, and have to put down all their cards in one turn. The ace is either high or low in a sequence and a sequence can "go around the corner," as in 2-A-K. In scoring, players pay the winner only for the cards in their hands that don't form matched sets. The ace counts 11 points.

· · · · · · · · ·

KNOCK RUMMY

Hold onto your hats—a game of Knock Rummy can be over almost as quickly as it begins. AKA Poker Rum

EQUIPMENT
• A 52-card deck

PLAYERS
2–6

OBJECT

To knock—end the game—by melding as many cards as possible in one move, holding the least amount of unmelded cards in one's hand.

SETUP

The cards are dealt the same as basic rummy:

Two players: ten cards

Three or four players: seven cards

Five or six players: six cards

The rest of the deck, the stock, is placed facedown in the middle of the table. The top card is turned over and placed faceup next to the stock to make a discard pile. Ace is low, and can only be used in a sequence with a deuce, not with a king.

PLAY

The first player has the option of taking the top card of the stock or the top card of the discard pile. After adding the card to his hand, he discards one card. (The discard may be omitted if the player goes out.) If he chose the card on the discard pile, he can't discard that same card in the same turn.

Players either draw from the stock or take the top card of the discard pile and then discard.

Knocking

Play continues until one player, after drawing a card, "knocks" by laying down ten cards and discarding one card facedown. The knocker separates the ten cards into melds and puts the *deadwood*, the cards not included in any of his melds, to the side, announcing its total count. The other players lay down their cards, separate their own melds from their deadwood, and announce their counts. The custom in some circles is for players to knock on the table to signal knocking.

If the player who draws the last card of the stock discards without knocking, the deal is thrown in and the player to the previous dealer's left deals the next hand.

SCORING

In scoring deadwood, aces are worth 1 point, face cards are worth 10 points, and number cards are worth their face value—a deuce is worth 2 points, a three is worth 3 points, and so on.

The player with the lowest count—knocker or not—wins the difference in counts from each opponent. If any other player ties the knocker for low count, that player wins instead of the knocker. If the knocker doesn't have the lowest count, he's penalized 10 points plus the difference in counts to the player with the lowest count.

If the knocker *goes rum*, that is, melds all his cards with no deadwood, he gets 25 points from each of the other players, even if one of them melded all their cards, too.

With two players, the winner of a hand deals the next hand. If three or more are playing, the deal rotates clockwise.

STRATEGY

If there are two players, try knocking on 50 points or less; three or four players, 35 or less; five or six players, 25 points.

VARIATIONS

The knocker's opponent(s) can lay off their deadwood onto the knocker's melds to lower their own deadwood counts, e.g., the six of spades on a meld of the three other 6s, or a sequence with a seven of spades or a five of spades.

Or, an opponent isn't permitted to lay off deadwood if the knocker doesn't have deadwood.

. . . .

GIN RUMMY

Gin was created to be faster than basic rummy, but without the potential breakneck speed of Knock Rummy.

EQUIPMENT
• A 52-card deck

PLAYERS
2

OBJECT
To knock—end the game—by melding as many cards as possible in one move, holding the least amount of deadwood in one's hand.

SETUP

Each player is dealt ten cards. The rest of the deck, the stock, is placed facedown in the middle of the table. The top card is turned over and placed faceup next to the stock to make a discard pile.

PLAY

The nondealer has the option of taking the faceup card, but if she doesn't want it, the dealer has a chance to take it and so have the first turn. If neither wants it, the nondealer draws the top card from the stock and discards from her hand.

Players either draw from the stock or take the top card of the discard pile and then discard.

Play continues until one player, after drawing a card, goes gin or knocks.

If the player can lay down all ten cards in melds (discarding one facedown) he's gone gin.

If the player has 10 points or less in deadwood—unmelded cards—he can knock by laying down ten cards, discarding one. The knocker separates the ten cards into melds and puts the deadwood to the side, announcing its total count. The other player lays down his cards, arranged in melds, and announces the count of his deadwood. He can also lay off his deadwood on a knocker's melds (add a fourth card to three of a kind, or extend a sequence)—but not on the melds of a player who's gone gin.

The two last cards in the stock are off-limits. If the player who drew the fiftieth card doesn't knock, the game is over. If he discards, his discard cannot be picked up. The hand is declared a draw and the same dealer deals again.

SCORING

The winner gets 25 bonus points for going gin, plus all the points from the other player's deadwood.

Aces	= 1 point each. Ace is low, and can only be used in a sequence with a deuce, not with a king.
Face cards	= 10 points each
Number cards	= pip value

If the game ended by knocking, and the knocker has the smaller number of points, he subtracts his score from the other player's—his score is the difference between the two. But if the other player has a smaller total or ties the knocker, he scores the difference if there is one, as well as a bonus of 25 points.

The winner of a hand deals the next hand. Play continues until one player reaches 100 points. The winner of a game deals the first hand of the next game.

VARIATIONS

After each player is dealt ten cards, the next card isn't turned up—instead it's dealt facedown to the nondealer, who makes the first discard to begin the game.

The nonknocker can lay off his deadwood on the melds of a player who's gone gin.

The deal alternates instead of going to the winner of the previous hand.

In **Round-the-Corner Gin**, the ace is either high or low, so it can be used in the sequence 2-A-K, which can be extended in either direction. If you end up with an ace in your hand after your opponent goes out, the ace is worth 15 points. But you can lay off deadwood on the knocker's melds.

The bonus for going gin is 20 points, but if the nonknocker reduces his own count to zero, he gets a bonus of 20 points, which means that neither player scores for the hand. The game ends when either player reaches 125 points.

Oklahoma Gin's twist is that the points needed to go out are decided by the value of the first card that's turned over. If it's a five, you need 5 points; if it's a face card, 10 points. If it's an ace, there are two ways to play: You can either knock with 1 point, or you have to go gin.

·········

500 RUM

A direct descendant of basic rummy, and an ancestor of Canasta, it was one of the first rummy games to add scoring values to the melds themselves. AKA Pinochle Rummy, Rummy 500, Michigan Rum

EQUIPMENT
• A 52-card deck (two decks when five or more are playing)

PLAYERS
2–8 (but 3–5 players is ideal)

OBJECT
To score points by melding and laying off cards as in regular rummy, in sets and sequences, and to be the first to discard all the cards in one's hand.

SETUP
Players draw for the deal; low card deals first, the ace being the lowest card in the draw. The cards are dealt thusly: Two players get thirteen cards each; three or more players get seven cards each.

The rest of the deck, the stock, is placed facedown in the middle of the table. The top card is turned over and placed faceup next to the stock to make a discard pile.

Melding
During the game, players can lay down melds faceup in sets—three or more of a kind (5-5-5 or K-K-K-K)—or sequences, three or more cards of the same suit in order.

During a turn, a player can lay off a card or cards, adding to the melds that are already on the table—her opponent's as well as her own—such as laying off the seven of spades on the meld of the four, five, and six of spades. When a player lays off a card on an opponent's meld, she keeps it on the table in front of herself, scoring later after announcing which meld she's adding to.

PLAY

The discard pile should be spread to the side, so that the players can easily see all the cards in it. Each player in turn, beginning with the player to the left of the dealer, has the option of drawing either the top card of the stock or *any* card from the discard pile.

If the player draws only the top card from the discard pile, he doesn't have to use it immediately. But if he takes a card that isn't on the top, the player has to take all the cards on top of the selected card and the card has to be used immediately, either by laying it down in a meld or by laying it off on a meld already on the table. The other cards taken with the discard can be melded in the same turn or added to the player's hand.

Each player in turn, after drawing but before discarding, can lay down any meld or lay off any card that matches a meld already on the table—but the player keeps any laid-off cards on the table in front of her. Every turn ends with a discard.

Sequences may not "go round the corner"; thus, A-K-Q or A-2-3 may be melded, but *not* K-A-2.

Play continues until one player discards the last card in her hand, either as part of a meld or on the discard pile.

If no one has gone out by the time the stock is depleted, each player, in turn, can draw from the discard pile until either it is depleted or one player refuses the draw.

SCORING

An ace scores 1 point when melded in the sequence A-2-3; 15 points in all other circumstances. Face cards are 10 points each. Other cards are their pip value.

Scores are calculated as follows: the total value of all cards that a player has showing on the table minus the point value of all cards remaining in her hand. For example, if the cards a player melded total 75 points, and the cards left in her hand total 80 points, 5 points are subtracted from her previous net score.

The first player to reach 500 points wins the game. If two or more players reach 500 on the same hand, the one with the highest score in that particular game is the winner.

VARIATIONS

Instead of playing to 500, seven hands only can be played—the winner being the player who wins the majority of the hands.

In **Fast 500**, an ace counts as 25 points in all situations. Face cards and the ten are worth 10 points. All other cards are worth 5 points.

Partnership 500 Rum is for four players; partners face each other across the table. Each player keeps her melds separate from her partner's, but their scores are added together and kept as one running total.

Persian Rummy is played with 56 cards: the standard 52 cards plus four jokers. The jokers are worth 20 points, but they can't be used in sequences or as wild cards—only as their own rank in groups of three or four jokers.

Any meld of four laid down at the same time counts for double its face value. So four jokers melded together count 160; three at once count 60, and the fourth joker when later added counts only 20 more. Aces rank high, and count 15 points. They can only be used in the sequence A-K-Q, never in 3-2-A.

Any unmelded cards taken from the discard pile are not added to the player's hand but instead are laid faceup in front of the player who took them up. Of course, they belong to that player as part of her hand.

Two deals make a game. The side that has the higher total score after two deals gets a bonus of 50 points and wins the difference between its final score and the opponents' score. If a player gets rid of all his cards, his side scores a bonus of 25.

When there are no more cards left in the stock, play continues. Each player continues to draw from the discard pile in turn, and either lays off a card or forms new melds if possible.

In **Michigan Rum**, melds are scored as they're put on the table. When the first player goes out, the cards left in the hands of the other players aren't subtracted from their scores, but instead their value is added to the winner's total point count.

·········

CANASTA

Rummy with a South American beat. The game saw its heyday in the 1950s, when it edged out bridge as America's favorite card game. It's complicated, frustrating, and can be highly addictive. Here's the four-player partnerships version.

EQUIPMENT
• A canasta deck or two 52-card decks with jokers (108 cards total)

PLAYERS
2–6 (four players in teams of two makes for the best game)

OBJECT
To create melds of cards of the same rank—called "canastas"—and to be the first to discard all the cards in one's hand.

SETUP
Partners sit opposite each other. The cards are dealt as follows: *Two players* get fifteen cards each; *three players* get thirteen cards each; and *four players or more* get eleven cards each.

The dealer places the rest of the deck facedown in the center of the table and turns the top card over to start the discard pile. If this upcard is a red 3 or a wild card (a joker or deuce), another card is turned over and placed on top of it until the upcard is neither a red 3 nor wild. Any player who receives a red three in her initial hand must immediately play it to the table for her team and draw a new card.

PLAY
To begin a game, a player/team has to meet certain initial meld requirements. Players have to meld (lay down three or more cards of the same rank) to open, and at the very beginning of a game, those initial melds have to add up to at least 50 points.

This minimum point score depends on the side's score at the beginning of the current deal, as accumulated from previous deals.

Team Score	Minimum Initial Meld
Less than 0	15
0–1499	50
1500–2999	90
3000 and above	120

So, at the very beginning of a game, when the score is zero all around, to begin play, a player has to create a meld (or melds) that adds up to at least 50 points. And the melds have to be "natural" melds; that is, they have to be made up of at least three cards of the same rank with no wild cards.

Point Values	
Joker	= 50 points
A, 2	= 20 points
8, 9, 10, J, Q, K	= 10 points
Black 3s, 4, 5, 6, 7	= 5 points

Opening natural melds would look something like:

A-A-A (60 points)

J-J-J *and* 8-8-8 (60 points)

9-9-9 *and* 5-5-5-5 (50 points)

To open, a player has to do one of two things:

Draw the top card of the stock, then lay down her meld or melds; or

If she wants to take the upcard—and she has to use it in the meld she's about to make—she has to first lay down the two or more cards from her hand that she'll be using to make the meld, then take the entire up-card pile and add the top card to complete the meld. She adds the rest of the cards to her hand, and discards one card. Only the top card can be used in this initial meld.

Melds and Wild Cards

A meld in canasta is a group of at least three cards of the same value that consists of at least two natural (nonwild) cards. The first meld that a player (when playing individually) or team makes in any game must be completely natural—three or more cards of the same rank.

As melds grow (hopefully into canastas) they can never consist of more

---

Special Cards

Wild Cards

Jokers and deuces are wild.

Wild cards can't be melded on their own.

Wild cards can be used as any rank except for threes.

If a wild card is discarded to the pile, the discard pile is frozen, which means that it can only be picked up by a player who can meld the top card with two natural cards of the same rank in the player's hand.

Red 3s

Red 3s are never melded, but are laid down singly in front of a player for bonus points at the end of the game.

If player is dealt a red 3 in his original hand, on his first turn he has to lay it down and draw another card to replace it.

If a player draws a red 3 from the stock, he lays it down and draws another.

If a player picks up a red 3 when he picks up the discard pile (which is possible only on the first pickup), he has to lay it down, but in this case, he doesn't draw another.

Black 3s

Three or four black 3s can be melded, but only when a player is going out at the end of a hand. No wild cards can be added to a black 3 meld.

Black 3s are called "stop cards": if one is discarded, the discard pile is frozen for the next player's turn.

than three wild cards. For example, 4-4-2 and K-K-K-2-2-Joker are legal melds, but 5-2-2 isn't because it contains only one natural card. Similarly, 8-8-2-2-2-Joker isn't legal because it contains more than three wild cards.

Once a card is laid down in a meld, it cannot be moved.

After a player completes her melds, she discards a card faceup onto the discard pile. This first meld counts as the initial requirement for a player's partner as well. From now on in subsequent turns, both can make melds and canastas using wild cards.

Each team keeps their melds and canastas separate from the other team. During play, they can add to their own or their partners melds, but never to an opponent's meld.

Canastas

A canasta is a meld of at least seven cards, either natural or wild. A natural canasta is made up of seven cards of a kind. A mixed canasta is made up of both natural and wild cards. At the end of a hand, natural canastas will score more points than mixed canastas.

Picking Up the Discard Pile

At at the beginning of a turn, a player must either draw a card from the stock, or pick up the discard pile. The discard pile is an option only if the player can use the top card either in an existing meld or by making a new meld with two other cards from her hand.

If making a new meld, a player first has to lay down the two or more cards from her hand that she'll be using to make it, then take the entire discard pile and add the top card to the meld on the table to complete the meld. She adds the rest of the cards to her hand, and discards one card.

If a team hasn't yet made any melds, the discard pile is frozen for them until one player meets the initial meld requirements.

Play continues until either a player—whose partnership must have formed at least one canasta—goes out by discarding or melding her last card, or the stock is depleted.

Going Out

If a player's team has made one or more canastas, either player can go out by using all the cards in her hand. She can meld all cards in her hand or meld all cards except one, and discard that final card.

Note: If a team hasn't yet made any canastas, neither player can make a

---

Popping the Question: The "Going Out" Controversy

As if canasta wasn't complicated enough, here's a further complication.

Some rulebooks say that a player is entitled to ask her partner "May I go out?" as a way of alerting said partner to put down as many melds as possible at her next turn. Other rulebooks say that a player *has to* ask her partner for permission. Of the latter group, some say that the questioner has to abide by the partner's answer—if the partner refuses permission, the player can't go out on that turn. Also within this group are the experts (including Hoyle) who think of it as more of a formality; the partner must always answer, "No."

---

play that would leave them with no cards in their hand at the end of their turn.

Depleted Stock

If there are no more cards in the stock when a player has to draw a card, the hand ends immediately. This includes a case where a player is required to draw an additional card as a result of drawing a red three. The player cannot meld any cards before the hand ends. If the player can legally pick up the discard pile when there are no cards remaining in the stock, she is required to do so.

SCORING

At the end of a hand, the score for each team is calculated as follows: the total value of all cards melded by that team, including canastas, minus the total value of all cards remaining in the team's hands, plus any bonuses.

If a team has made no melds during a hand, the bonuses for red threes are subtracted from that team's score rather than added.

The game ends when a team's total score reaches 5000 or more.

The player to the left of the dealer deals the next hand.

VARIATIONS

If you can't get up a foursome—or have more than four players—you can play as individuals.

Two Players are dealt fifteen cards each.

Three Players are dealt thirteen cards each.

Five or More Players are dealt eleven cards each.

The play is virtually the same, except that each player has to meet the initial meld requirements to begin a hand.

Bonus Scores

Going out	=	100
Going out concealed*	=	additional 100
Each mixed canasta	=	300
Each natural canasta	=	500
Each red 3, up to three	=	100
The fourth red 3	=	500 (a total of 800 for all four red 3s)

*A player goes out concealed when she makes her team's initial meld and goes out in the same turn.

ORIGINS

Canasta originated in Uruguay. At its peak of popularity, it boasted twenty million American fans.

FYI

Canasta means "basket" in Spanish, so named because a basket is sometimes used in the center of the table to hold the stock and discards.

Tip

If you have four of a kind in your hand, you can meld three of them, and keep the fourth. That way, if you already have, or later get, a wild card or another card of the same rank, you'll be able to pick up the discard pile with them.

·········

WHIST

Whist is the forerunner of bridge, played with no bidding and no dummy.

EQUIPMENT
- A 52-card deck

PLAYERS
4 (two teams of 2)

OBJECT
To win as many tricks as possible.

SETUP
Draw cards to choose partners; the two highest will be partners against the two lowest. If two or more players draw cards of the same rank, the suits decide. Spades is the highest ranked suit, followed by hearts, diamonds, and clubs.

   Partners sit facing each other. The dealer deals all the cards. The last card (which belongs to the dealer) is turned faceup on the table. The suit on that card is the trump suit for the hand. The card stays where it is until it's the dealer's turn to play the first hand or trick of the game.

PLAY
The player to the dealer's left goes first, playing any card. Going clockwise, the other players have to follow suit. If they have no cards in that suit, they can throw down any card, including a trump, which will take the trick if a higher trump card isn't played by a player on the other team.

   When it's the dealer's turn to play the first hand, he picks up the trump card, adds it to his hand, and then plays any card on the trick.

   If no trump cards have been played in a trick, the high card of the suit wins. Otherwise, the highest trump wins.

   The winner of a trick leads the next hand. As tricks are won, each is kept in its own pile and overlapped with other tricks so that players can see at a glance the tricks that have been played and won.

Play continues until all thirteen tricks have been played.

SCORING

In each game, six tricks makes a "book," but only the tricks over six are counted. Seven tricks win 1 point, eight tricks win 2 points, and so on.

When all thirteen tricks have been played, the side that won the most tricks scores 1 point for each trick in excess of six: e.g., seven tricks scores 1 point, eight tricks scores 2 points, and so on.

The first team to reach 7 points wins the game. The team who wins two out of three games wins the rubber.

VARIATIONS

Another way of determining the trump suit is to fix a trump suit before the deal, and then work your way through the suits in each subsequent hand. After you've gone through the four suits, you can play a hand with no trump.

Honor cards (ace, king, queen, jack) in the trump suit also contribute to the score of the winning team. All four cards score 4 points; three of them score 2 points for the winning team. But this makes it more of a game of luck and less a game of skill, so it's frowned on in some whist circles.

Some games are played to 5 or 9 points instead of 7.

GAMES FOR KIDS

·········

CONCENTRATION

A game of memory. In fact, in some game-playing circles, that's exactly what it's called: "Memory."

EQUIPMENT
- A 52-card deck

PLAYERS
2+

OBJECT

To win the most cards by remembering and matching them.

SETUP

Shuffle and lay out the whole deck on a table or the floor, in a roughly rectangular shape.

PLAY

The first player turns over two cards. If they match, she can remove them from play and go again. If not, she turns them facedown, and the next player takes a turn. Play proceeds until all the cards have been removed from the table.

SCORING

The player who makes the most matches wins.

VARIATION

The game can be played solitaire, too—which is also a good way to practice. The more you play, the better you'll get at it.

·········

CRAZY EIGHTS

*It's played all over the world under different names, some of which have little to do with where they're played, like **Mau-Mau** in Germany, and **Swedish Rummy** in Australia. Among the scads of American variations on the basic game are **Crates, Crazy Jacks, Last One, Rockaway, Spoons, Switch,** and last but not least, the game that Mattel markets as **UNO**.*

EQUIPMENT

- A 52-card deck

PLAYERS

2–4 (5 or more can play, but with two decks)

OBJECT

To be the first to get rid of all the cards in one's hand.

SETUP

If two players are playing, each is dealt seven cards. Three or more players get five cards each.

The rest of the deck is placed facedown in the center of the table, and the top card is turned over and placed faceup next to it. If it's an 8, the dealer buries it somewhere in the stack and turns over the next card.

PLAY

Players try to match the rank or suit of the faceup card. If the top card is the jack of spades, any spade or jack can be laid on it. If, say, the first player laid down the two of spades, the next player would have to play another two or a spade.

If a player can't match the top card, he has to draw cards one by one from the stack until he finds one.

Play proceeds clockwise, each player laying down a card that matches the top card in rank or suit—except in the case of those crazy eights. Eights are wild; one can be played no matter what the top card is. After an 8 is laid on top of the pile, the player has to call a change of suit—any suit.

Note: Even if a player can match the faceup card—or even play an eight—he can still draw as many cards as he likes from the stack during his turn.

When the stack is exhausted, players must play from their hands, and pass if they can't lay down a card.

The Win

The first player to get rid of all his cards is the winner. In four-hand partnerships, both players have to get rid of all their cards to win. If the stack is exhausted and no one can play a card, the game ends in a draw.

Scoring is optional. If you want to play with points, the winner can score for cards remaining in the other players' hands, then play a certain number of rounds or to a certain point count, like 100 or even 500.

50 points for an 8

10 points for face cards and 10s

Face value for each of the other cards

1 point for an ace

If the hand ends in a draw, the player or team with the lowest point count wins the difference in points between their hands and the other players'.

STRATEGY

Even though you can incur serious point penalties if you're left with an eight when someone else wins, try to hold on to it for your last or next to last play. It may win the game for you.

Having more cards than your opponent may turn out to be a good thing toward the end of the game. You'll have more options while he goes digging for a card.

On the other hand, once the eights are eliminated, a player with a lot of cards can limit his losses by getting rid of as many high-point cards as possible.

VARIATIONS

When a queen (or some other designated rank) is played, the next player in rotation misses a turn, and the turn passes to the following player.

When an ace (or some other designated rank) is played, the direction of play reverses.

When a two is played, the next player must either draw two cards or play another two. If a certain number of consecutive twos have been played, the next player must either play another two or draw two cards for each two in the sequence.

Some versions require a player to say, "Last cards," when she can make a final play on her next turn. Failure to announce it incurs a draw penalty (usually two cards).

FYI

Theoretically, you can win nine out of ten games by taking the entire stock on your first turn.

....

GO FISH

The children's classic, often the first card game a little kid learns.

EQUIPMENT
• A 52-card deck

PLAYERS
2+

OBJECT
To make "books," sets of four cards of the same rank, by asking the other players for them.

SETUP
The dealer deals five cards to each player (or seven cards apiece if there are only two players). The remaining cards are put in the center in a pile, the stock.

PLAY
The first player looks at her hand. Since she's not allowed to ask for a card that she doesn't already have, she asks another player by name if they have a particular rank of card that will match one of her cards. "Joe," she might say, "do you have any jacks?" If Joe has one or more jacks, he has to give them to the first player, and her turn continues. If Joe doesn't have any, he says, "Go fish." That means that the first player has to pick a card from the stock.

If the card the first player picks isn't a jack, she adds it to her hand and the person to her left goes next. If the picked card is a jack, the player shows the card to the other players and gets another turn. If the jack completes a book, the player shows the four jacks to the rest of the players, places the book facedown, and goes again.

Play continues clockwise until one of the players—the winner—has no more cards, or there are no cards left in the stock, in which case the player who put together the most books wins.

STRATEGY

Once a player has asked for a particular card (a jack, for instance), try to remember this. Then, if you pick up a jack from the stock later in the game, you know who to ask for a jack to match it.

VARIATION

Books can be made up of two cards instead of four, an easier option for beginners.

. . . .

I DOUBT IT

Good training for tomorrow's poker players. AKA B.S., Cheat

EQUIPMENT

- A 52-card deck (one deck for 3–6 players, two decks for 7+ players)

PLAYERS

3+

OBJECT

To be the first player to get rid of his cards.

SETUP

All the cards are dealt facedown. It's okay if some players have more cards than others.

PLAY

The first player puts from one to four cards facedown on the table and announces that he's putting down as many aces as the number of cards. For example, he might put down three cards, saying, "Two aces," whether the cards are aces or not. The second player has to put down from one to four cards while announcing the cards are twos, e.g., "Three twos." The third player will do the same with threes, and so on around the table, all the way up to kings, at which point the next player starts over with aces again.

But whenever a player puts down cards, any other player can say, "I doubt it," in which case the cards have to be turned up.

If the player's statement was true, the doubter has to take those cards into his own hand—as well as any other cards that have been played on the table previously.

If the player's statement was false, he has to take all the cards on the table, including the ones he just put down.

If two or more players doubt it, the one who said "I doubt it" first is the official doubter.

If two players doubt at exactly the same time, the one nearest to the player's left is the official doubter.

The game ends when a player puts his last card on the table and either is not doubted or is shown to have told the truth.

A player is allowed to pass, e.g., saying, "No sevens," even if he has one or more sevens.

When two decks are used, players can lay down any number of cards from one to eight.

SCORING

The winner gets 1 point for each card remaining in the other players' hands.

STRATEGY

Arrange the cards in your hand in the sequence they'll be played in.

If you "doubt" early in the game you can fill empty spaces in your hand.

Try to plan to be "honest" during the final hands.

The ideal hand for going out has every rank represented.

·········

OLD MAID

AKA "The Bachelorette"?

EQUIPMENT

- a 52-card deck with three queens removed, or an Old Maid deck

PLAYERS

2+

OBJECT

To avoid being the player who ends up with the single queen: the "Old Maid."

SETUP

The cards are dealt as far as they'll go.

PLAY

Players look at their cards and discard any pairs they have. If they have three of a kind, they can discard two; if they have four, they can discard them as two pairs.

The player to the left of the dealer fans out his cards and offers them facedown to the player on his left, who selects one card and adds it to her hand. If the selected card makes a pair with one of her original cards, she discards them. Then it's her turn to offer her cards facedown to the person on her left.

Play continues until all the players have managed to pair and discard their cards. There's no winner in this game—only a loser, the player who's left with the odd queen.

VARIATION

To make the game a little more challenging, you can add the rule that cards have to be matched in color, too. For example, the four of diamonds can only be matched to the four of hearts, and so on.

Trivia

In France the game is called *Le Garçon Vieux* (the Old Boy). The jacks of hearts, diamonds, and clubs are removed, and at the end of the game the player holding the jack of spades is the loser.

·········

PIG

One of those charming, but occasionally humiliating, children's games.

EQUIPMENT
- A 52-card deck

PLAYERS
3–13

OBJECT
To get all four cards of the same rank, and not become the Pig.

SETUP
The deck has to be specially prepared. It should have one set of four cards (one of each suit) for each player. So for three players, twelve cards total (e.g., the four aces, the four kings, the four queens); for four players, sixteen cards; for thirteen players, the entire deck.

Players are dealt four cards apiece.

PLAY
If a player has been dealt all four cards of the same rank, she puts her finger on her nose. As soon as they see her, the other players have to do the same. The last player to put her finger on her nose is the Pig. She is "awarded" a P, the first letter in PIG.

If no one gets four of a kind on the deal, the dealer says, "Go," and the players remove one card from their hands and put it facedown to their left. Once all the cards are put down, players pick up the facedown card on their right and add it to their hands. If the new card hasn't helped anyone to get four of a kind, the dealer calls, "Go," again. As soon as a player gets all four cards of the same rank, she puts her finger on her nose. The last to follow gets a letter.

A player who loses three times gets a P-I-G, loses the game, and—according to the rules—has to oink like a pig.

·········

SLAPJACK

Test your reflexes with a game of slapjack.

EQUIPMENT
- A 52-card deck

PLAYERS
2+

OBJECT
To win all the cards.

SETUP
All the cards are dealt, divided as equally as possible among the players, who stack them up in front of themselves without looking.

PLAY
The first player takes the top card of his stack and places it faceup in the middle of the playing surface so that all the players can reach it. If the up-turned card isn't a jack, the next player, going clockwise, does the same, and so on until someone turns over a jack. This is where the "slap" in slap-jack comes in.

As soon as the jack is spotted, players try to be first to slap a hand down on the pile. The first player who covers the stack with his hand takes the whole pile and adds it to the bottom of his stack.

The game continues until one player—the winner—has all the cards.

· · · · · · · · ·

SPIT

A free-for-all game that can be played in under two minutes—once you learn the rules and get to be an expert.

EQUIPMENT
• A 52-card deck

PLAYERS
2

OBJECT
To be the first player to get rid of all one's cards.

SETUP
The entire deck is dealt out equally. Players arrange the cards so that each has a stock facedown in front of them.

PLAY
The players turn over the first four cards, laying them out faceup in front of themselves and making two "spreads." Then they count together, "One, two, three . . . SPIT!"

At the word "spit," each turns over the top card of his stock and lays it down in the middle of the table, making a "spit pile." Then—as quickly as they can, using *only one hand* and moving *only one card at a time*—they put as many of their own stock cards and spread cards as they can onto the spit piles. The cards must be next in sequence up or down—a 6 can go on a 5 or a 7; aces are high/low—they can can go on a 2 or a king. Suit and color don't matter.

When a card from a spread is put on a spit pile, the player replaces it with a card from the stock.

When neither player can add another card to the spit piles, they start all over again.

Play continues until one player has no cards left in his stock or his spread cards. The player who is out of cards takes the smaller spit pile to be his new stock. The other player takes the larger one and adds it to his current stock. Both players shuffle their stocks and start again.

The game ends when one player is completely out of cards.

VARIATION

When one player has no cards at all, or when neither player can put any more cards on the spit piles, each player tries to slap the spit pile she thinks is smaller. The player who slaps it first takes it. The other player has to take the bigger pile.

·········

SUIT OF ARMOR

The easiest of games to learn and play. But be careful: Since all the cards aren't used, you might want to change your suit in the middle of the game. AKA My Ship Sails

EQUIPMENT
• A 52-card deck

PLAYERS
3–7

OBJECT
To be the first player to collect seven cards in the same suit.

SETUP
Players are dealt seven cards each. The rest of the deck won't be used.

PLAY
Players look at their cards and, if they have more cards in one particular suit, try to see if they can collect even more of them.

The dealer starts by putting one card of a suit that he doesn't want face-down to his left. The player to his left puts down a card he doesn't want to *his* left, and picks up the card the dealer put down. The third player puts down an unwanted card, and picks up the second player's discard, and so on around the table. Play continues until one player has all seven cards of the same suit and calls, "Suit of Armor!"

·········

WAR

They say that War was a favorite game of France's King Charles VI, who played a variation where the object was not to win all the cards, but to lose them. Maybe that's why he was also known as Charles the Fool.

EQUIPMENT
- A 52-card deck

PLAYERS
2

OBJECT
To win all the cards.

SETUP
One player deals out the complete deck, so that each player has twenty-six cards. Without looking at their cards, players arrange the cards in a neat pile.

PLAY
Players turn over their top cards at the same time and put them faceup in the center. High card wins. The player who wins takes both cards and puts them at the bottom of his deck.

Play continues until the players turn over the same card, two jacks, for instance. This means War!

The two cards are placed in the center and each player plays three cards facedown and a fourth faceup. The highest card wins. If they've drawn another pair, they repeat the war.

Toward the end of the game, if one player doesn't have enough cards to complete the war, his last card has to serve as his war card. If he loses this round, the game is over.

The winner is the player who ends up with all the cards.

SOLITAIRE GAMES

....

ACCORDION

Some long-time Accordion players (and we're talking decades) confess to never having succeeded at the game—so consider yourself warned.

EQUIPMENT
- A 52-card deck

OBJECT
To get the entire deck into one pile.

SETUP
Deal the whole deck out in one long row (or do it in stages as you go along).

PLAY
The idea is to deal the entire pack faceup into one long row from left to right while putting the cards into piles based on this rule: Whenever a card matches—in either suit or rank—its immediate predecessor or the third card to its left, it can be placed on top of the card it matches.

Say the lineup is three of hearts, nine of spades, three of clubs, four of diamonds, four of spades, six of diamonds. The four of spades can go on top of either the four of diamonds or the nine of spades. If you put the four of spades on the four of diamonds, that ends that particular move. But if you put it on the nine of diamonds, the six of diamonds can move to the left and then on top of the four of diamonds.

The game ends when the entire deck consists of a single pile.

CLOCK SOLITAIRE

You can try playing for points, by giving yourself 52 points if you succeed in completing the number piles before the pile of kings. If you finish the kings before the clock, count the other cards you've turned over so far; that's your score for the game. Play to 100 or 200 points.

EQUIPMENT
- A 52-card deck

OBJECT
To complete a clock face with four of a kind of all the clock numbers in the right place before the four kings are placed in the center.

SETUP
Deal the cards facedown into thirteen piles of four cards apiece, arranging twelve of them in a circle, as though they were the numbers on a clock. The thirteenth pile goes in the center of the circle.

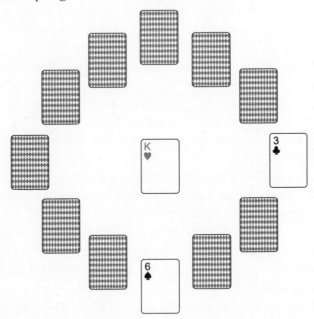

PLAY

Turn over the top card of the center pile. If it's a king, put it on top of the center pile and turn over the bottom card from that pile. If that card isn't a king, put it on top of the pile in its correct position on the clock face: an ace at one o'clock, a jack at eleven o'clock, a queen at twelve o'clock, a 9 at nine o'clock and so on. Every time you put a card on the clock face, take the bottom card from that pile and move it to where it belongs.

If you complete the clock before the center pile of kings, you've won. If the king pile is finished first, you lose.

....

IDIOT'S DELIGHT

It's simple, fun, and should come with a warning: Caution—highly addictive. AKA Aces Up, Aces High

EQUIPMENT
• A 52-card deck

OBJECT

To finish the game with all the cards except the aces discarded.

SETUP

Deal four cards faceup, next to each other. These cards will form the basis of the layout.

PLAY

If one or more of the cards are of the same suit, move the lower-ranked ones into a discard pile.

When you can't make any more moves, deal another set of four cards on, but not completely covering, the previous cards (so that the rank and suit of the previous cards is visible).

Continue to move cards to the discard pile if they match the suit of any higher-ranked available—that is, topmost—card in any of the four piles. If a pile is emptied, it has to be filled with any available card from another pile before the next deal.

Because aces are high they can't be discarded.

The four aces make up the winning layout, after all the other cards have been discarded.

STATISTICS
The chance of winning: 1 in 10 games.

·········

KLONDIKE

The classic game that most people think of as plain old solitaire.

EQUIPMENT
• A 52-card deck

OBJECT
To build up from the four aces so that all the cards are in four piles above the layout.

SETUP
Deal a row of seven cards from left to right, with the first card faceup and the rest facedown. Then deal a row of six cards on top of the six facedown cards, putting the first card faceup and the rest facedown. To complete the layout, deal a row of five cards, followed by four cards, then three cards, then two cards (still beginning with a faceup card), until finally dealing one card faceup on the last pile.

The layout should look like this:

PLAY
Start by building in downward sequence from the layout, putting a red card on a black card and vice versa: a red 4 on a black 5, a black queen on a red king. Turn up the facedown cards as they're exposed.

Any card or sequence of cards in the layout can be moved from one column to another as long as the top card in the sequence being moved belongs under the card or sequence it's being moved to. For example, a black 6, red 5, black 4 sequence can be moved to fit under a red 7.

After removing a faceup card or sequence that leaves the facedown pile exposed, turn the top card over. When all the cards in a column are gone, a king—and only a king—can go in that space.

At the same time, using only the faceup cards in the layout, take any ace that surfaces and place it just above the layout, because you'll be trying to build up from your aces in sequence, matching suits this time: ace, 2, 3, 4, and so on up to king.

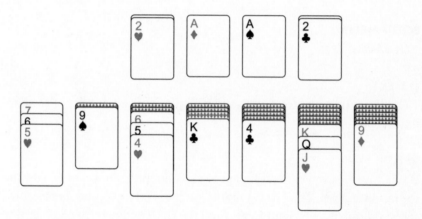

Once you've done all you can with the opening layout, take the undealt cards and turn them over one at a time, adding them to the layout whenever possible. When you've gone through the stock once, start again. The stock can be gone through twice in total.

If you manage to build the entire deck from aces to kings above the layout, you've won the game.

VARIATIONS

Some players prefer to go through the undealt cards three at a time, turning over the top three cards and using the top card if possible (and the card just below it, if the top card is used). If the top card can't be used anywhere, deal another three cards in the same way. Keep dealing three cards in this way, going through the deck again and again until you go through one time without coming across a card you can use.

Other players use the three-card version, but go through the entire deck three times only.

Gargantua is played with two decks. The layout is the same as Klondike, but uses *nine* piles instead of seven, and the row above the layout is available for the *eight* aces.

Yukon has a similar layout but is a little more interesting to play and easier to win. Deal out the seven rows of cards as in Klondike, then take the undealt cards (there'll be 24) and add them to the layout, dealing four apiece faceup on the six piles to the right of the single card. All the cards will be available for building onto the other piles. When you start moving cards from one column to another, say a red 4 to a black 5, you move *all* the cards that are covering that red 4 as well.

FYI

To make things more interesting, make believe you're betting against the house. Put down a fictional $50 every time you start a game. At the end of a game, you win $1 for every card that makes it into the four aces layout. If you're successful in building up the entire deck from the four aces, you win $520 ($10 per card).

· · · · · · · · ·

PYRAMID

First you build the pyramid, then you tear it down.

EQUIPMENT
- A 52-card deck

OBJECT
To remove all the cards in the pyramid.

SETUP
Lay out twenty-eight faceup cards in seven rows: Starting at the top, set down one card. Just below and overlapping it, two cards. Lay down three

cards for the third row, and so on until the seventh row of seven cards. Set aside the rest of the deck facedown as the stock.

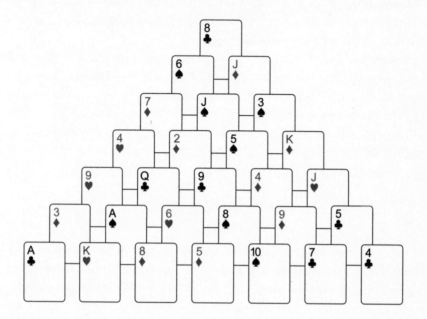

PLAY

Working only with cards that are completely exposed (for now, the bottom row of the pyramid), see if any of them add up to 13, for example, a queen and an ace, or a 4 and a 9. (Aces are worth 1, kings 13, queens 12, jacks 11, and number cards their face value.) If they do, pick them up and discard them. Kings can be discarded by themselves. If their removal has exposed any cards in the sixth row, see if they can be added together to make 13.

When you've done all you can with the pyramid, take the undealt cards and turn over the top card. If it adds up to 13 with one of the available pyramid cards, put them both in the discard pile. If the card can't be used, place it faceup next to the stock of undealt cards, and turn over another. The top faceup card will always be available for matching.

Go through the stock, working back and forth between upturned cards and the pyramid. When all the cards in the stock have been turned over, the cards can be turned facedown again (without shuffling) and the stock can be gone through twice more.

If the pyramid hasn't been cleared entirely by the end of the third go-through, the game is over.

········

SPIDER

President Franklin D. Roosevelt's favorite game.

EQUIPMENT
• Two 52-card decks

OBJECT
To discard all eight suits from the layout by building sequences of kings to aces in each suit.

SETUP
Deal a layout of ten piles: six cards in each of the first four piles, and five cards in the remaining six. Turn the top card of each pile faceup. The rest of the cards are the stock.

PLAY
Start by building in downward sequence, putting a 4 on a 5 or a jack on a queen, regardless of suit. Aces are low. Following suit will come in handy later, but it's more important at first to get as many cards turned up as possible. After removing a faceup card or sequence that leaves the face-down pile exposed, turn the top card over.

When a pile is finished, any card or sequence can be placed in the empty space.

Cards can be moved as a unit, but only if they're of the same suit. For example, the six of hearts, five of hearts, four of hearts sequence can be moved to fit under any seven, but of the six of hearts, five of clubs, four of clubs sequence, only the five of clubs and the four of clubs can be moved together. Unless, of course, there's a card or cards covering them: e.g., if the sequence was six of hearts, five of clubs, four of clubs, three of hearts, the five of clubs, four of clubs can't be moved until the three of hearts is moved.

Once you've done all you can with the opening layout, make sure that all ten spaces are filled, and deal ten cards from the stock faceup, one on each pile.

When a thirteen-card sequence of king to ace in the same suit is built, those thirteen cards can be discarded—though you have the option of breaking up the suit instead, to help you manipulate the layout.

VARIATIONS

Scorpion uses only one deck, dealt into seven piles of seven cards each. The first three piles contain three facedown cards and four faceup cards. The other four piles contain all faceup cards. The last three cards in the deck are the "reserve." Play is the same, but only kings can be moved to a free space. When layout play is stopped, deal the last three cards on the first three piles and continue.

Double Scorpion is Scorpion played with two decks. When layout play is stopped, deal seven new cards on top of the seven piles.

Black Widow is a Spider variation in which any sequence of cards can be moved, whether or not they're of the same suit.

Black Spider is played like Black Widow, but only a king or a sequence topped by a king can be moved to an empty space.

EXTRA

. . . .

BUILD A HOUSE OF CARDS

If you get tired of playing cards, try playing with them.

BUILDING MATERIALS

Don't go out and buy top-of-the-line cards for this: The experts agree that lower quality cards work better.

FOUNDATION

Start out on a nonslip surface—a pool table would be ideal.

And don't hold the cards too tightly between your fingers as you're adding them. Try to "float" each card as you're adding it. That way, if you wobble, the card won't.

BUILDING YOUR HOUSE

First you build a box: The upright cards have to lean against each other a teensy ten to fifteen degrees.

Lean two cards on their long edges to form a T.

Place a third card against the middle of the base of the T to form another T and lean a fourth card against that to produce a box that's made up of half cards by half cards, with a tail extending from each corner for stability.

Place two faceup cards side by side to form a flat roof that covers the whole shebang.

Then add another flat layer of faceup cards, but turned ninety degrees for added support. Face cards have more texture; this will give your structure more stability. Repeat the process until you run out of cards.

The most important rule: Have patience.

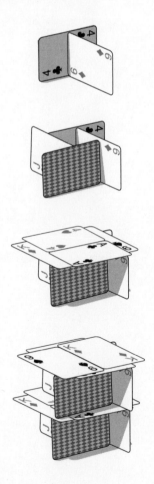

Playing with a Stacked Deck?

If you've tried and tried again—and failed—try this. Cut a snip in the middle of all four edges of the cards. Then join them together by interlocking the notches.